The Laundry Man

The Laundry Man

KEN RIJOCK

VIKING
an imprint of
PENGUIN BOOKS

VIKING

Published by the Penguin Group
Penguin Books Ltd, 80 Strand, London WC2R ORL, England
Penguin Group (USA) Inc., 375 Hudson Street, New York, New York 10014, USA
Penguin Group (Canada), 90 Eglinton Avenue East, Suite 700, Toronto, Ontario, Canada M4P 2Y3
(a division of Pearson Penguin Canada Inc.)
Penguin Ireland, 25 St Stephen's Green, Dublin 2, Ireland (a division of Penguin Books Ltd)
Penguin Group (Australia), 250 Camberwell Road,
Camberwell, Victoria 3124, Australia (a division of Pearson Australia Group Pty Ltd)
Penguin Books India Pvt Ltd, 11 Community Centre,
Panchsheel Park, New Delhi – 110 017, India
Penguin Group (NZ), 67 Apollo Drive, Rosedale, Auckland 0632, New Zealand
(a division of Pearson New Zealand Ltd)
Penguin Books (South Africa) (Pty) Ltd, Block D, Rosebank Office Park, 181 Jan Smuts Avenue,
Parktown North, Gauteng 2193, South Africa

Penguin Books Ltd, Registered Offices: 80 Strand, London WC2R ORL, England

www.penguin.com

First published 2012
001

Set in Garamond MT Std 13.5 /16 pt
Typeset by Palimpsest Book Production Ltd, Falkirk, Stirlingshire
Printed in Great Britain by Clays Ltd, St Ives plc

A CIP catalogue record for this book is available from the British Library

ISBN: 978-0-241-95417-1

www.greenpenguin.co.uk

Penguin Books is committed to a sustainable
future for our business, our readers and our planet.
This book is made from Forest Stewardship
Council™ certified paper.

MIX
Paper from
responsible sources
FSC™ C018179
www.fsc.org

ALWAYS LEARNING   PEARSON

Dedicated to Deputy US Marshal Ken Sands
and Sergeant Bruce Benjamin, who brought me out
of the darkness and back into the light.

Contents

Contents

Acknowledgements

The assistance of Doug Wight in the preparation of my story is gratefully acknowledged.

Author's Note

I recently came upon a faded manila envelope that had been misfiled in some real-estate documents. It was sealed and bore a handwritten note.

It read: 'Last letter sent from his cell in Cuba, before he was executed.'

Accompanying it was a letter from the condemned man's sister, asking him to cooperate and deposit half a million dollars into a bank account. Inside the envelope was a handwritten letter with a passport and banking details.

I took the discovery of the document to be a sign. Rather than let such slices of life fade away, I thought it was time to tell my story.

Only the names have been changed, but not to protect the guilty – they are mostly deceased or disappeared. Their identities are masked to spare their families the pain of revisiting those losses.

Of course there are still those who never felt the hand of justice. Those few are now legitimate and even affluent, but they still fear the knock on the door in the middle of the night.

I have no wish to disturb their troubled sleep, for they may then disturb mine.

Prologue

The tension was palpable. They were taking an age to look over the documents.

I considered explaining it again, but it was all there in black and white.

One of the brothers was fidgeting over the paperwork; his fat, cigar-stained finger danced over the lines of text, like a child learning to read ... well, a kid who'd just sampled too much of the pure, uncut cocaine they had just shipped into the United States.

The other two stood behind him, equally jumpy. One grinned, or was it a grimace? The other flashed a glint of chrome at his waist. He was always posturing.

How had I got myself into this?

At the start it was easy, it was hardly even breaking the law – just helping out a few people who were more friends than clients. They were good guys, not badasses.

These three, however, were human garbage.

The Martinez brothers: Cuban Americans whose parents were exiles from Castro's regime; guys who'd started off in life in Miami without a dime in their pockets and who were now comfortably millionaires, thanks to the cocaine that was flooding through south Florida and into the rest of the US and Canada.

And thanks also to me.

I had assisted them in ensuring that the millions of dollars of dirty cash they got through drug deals could be safely washed, cleaned and folded without any trace.

You see: I was the Laundry Man.

I offered unique services.

Got two million dollars of filthy drug money you don't know what to do with? I'm your man. Need to set up companies to hide your illicit business from law enforcement agencies? Not a problem.

This meeting was in their safe house in suburban Miami. In a matter of weeks they'd have moved on from here, taking all traces with them.

At that moment, however, we had business to attend to. My assistance had been mainly low profile – I'd set up some bogus companies in the Caribbean, registered a couple of boats with fictitious details in the United Kingdom and moved some money into the tax havens to accomplish that. All simple stuff, but priceless to gangs without the know-how.

This was my first encounter with all three brothers together and they didn't yet trust me. How could they know that the smart lawyer before them hadn't just set up a paper maze that enabled me to stash the money in an offshore vault . . . one that only I had the key to?

I glanced at Charlie. He was their partner, exactly why I never knew, and the only person in the room I trusted.

'It's all there,' he piped up. 'Ken's done you a great service, like I said. He's a genius, isn't he?'

The younger brother, Joey, looked up. Of all the siblings he looked the most assimilated to North American ways. Young and athletic, he appeared clean and intelligent and spoke with the clearest south Florida accent.

The older the brothers got, the more stereotypically Cuban they became. Hugo, the middle one, was obese, with a thick mop of black hair and two days' stubble. The eldest, Enrique, was heavy set with an imposing moustache and thick beard and spoke, by choice, in that maddening English-Cuban patois – the worst of both languages.

Joey finally lifted his head from the papers I'd presented him with. He smiled. 'I know. This is beautiful. So simple.'

He turned to the others and nodded.

I breathed out.

Charlie shot me a look that said: 'I told you there'd be no problems.'

Joey signalled to Enrique, the eldest brother. From behind a sofa the big Cuban produced a small holdall.

'Regalito', he grunted as he placed the bag on the floor a foot in front of me.

I turned to Joey.

'A little gift,' he translated, but I knew what it meant.

Gingerly I reached over and slid the gym bag to my feet. I glanced around. All eyes were on me, the brothers' grimaces now widening to expectant grins.

Although I never set a fee and considered it almost impolite to discuss such matters, a cash reward wasn't unexpected. For what I'd done ten thousand dollars wouldn't have been over-charging.

I caressed the side of the bag. Something told me I didn't want to know what was there.

Slowly unzipping the fastener, I peered inside.

My heart stopped.

No cash. Instead there was a clear plastic bag, packed solid with white powder.

I lifted it out and held up my trophy, sparking raucous laughter among the Cubans.

I smiled, hoping it wouldn't convey what I was thinking: What the hell am I expected to do with this?

'Your gift,' Joey smiled.

All I had done was set up a clutch of bogus companies and registered a series of boats that allowed my clients to success-fully ship hundreds of kilos of cocaine into Miami.

Charlie did the explaining. 'Half a kilo. Worth ten thousand dollars on the street.'

Half a kilo? I did the calculations in my head. Just 400 grams is a minimum fifteen-year mandatory sentence. You don't get out of prison before that time is up.

I smiled. It was all I could do. As I placed the block back in the bag and zipped it up, I knew refusal was futile. At best, saying thanks but no thanks would be considered impolite. At worst it could cause real offence.

I smiled. 'You shouldn't have.'

I made hurried goodbyes and fled, my feet hardly touching the steps down the two flights to the car lot.

I walk-ran to the car, glancing round to see if I could detect any signs that the building was being watched, and loaded the bag in the trunk. For all I knew the safe house was under surveillance. If the brothers were willing to hand out this amount of uncut coke free, how much more did they have stashed? The place could have been staked out by Metro-Dade or the Drug Enforcement Administration (DEA) for days.

I drove, but for the first few blocks I was directionless. It was 3 p.m. People were going about their business. Schools were about to let out, meaning a 15 mph speed limit, and plenty of local law. Shit.

Every other second I glanced in the mirror. How long had that car been behind me?

Only then did the location sink in. I was west of Dadeland, in the heart of strictly suburban Kendall, just a few blocks' drive from a mall where Colombian drug gangs had settled their differences with a liquor store bloodbath in broad daylight. That shooting signalled the moment when the underground drug wars spilled on to Main Street USA. Two gunmen had calmly got out of a truck, walked into the store and gunned down two other men, wounding the store clerk.

When their bloodstained bodies were eventually identified, it emerged the victims were one of the biggest traffickers in Miami and his bodyguard. The quarrel was probably a disagreement over an unpaid debt.

Now I was in the middle of a neighbourhood targeted by the cops.

Paranoia took over.

Did I have a faulty tail light, anything that could bring me to the attention of an eagle-eyed traffic cop? If I got stopped my life was over.

I started to sweat, my stomach churning. What would have been a routine thirty-minute drive to the house had become a white-knuckle ride. If I got pulled for speeding I was in big trouble. Try persuading a judge that half a kilo is for personal use.

That got me thinking. The going rate for cocaine had once been fifty-five thousand dollars a kilo but was now only twenty thousand, thanks to the deluge flooding Miami via Colombia. It wasn't ideal but, if Charlie was right, I could make a nice piece of change.

I pulled over to a pay phone, raking through my pockets for a quarter, my eyes scanning the street.

I called Andre, the man who had pulled me into my new career.

No answer.

There was nothing else for it. I'd have to drive carefully over to his house. I pulled up just as he arrived back.

I explained my little problem.

He couldn't shift it now but that might change by tomorrow.

All I had to do was sit on it for twenty-four hours. No big deal. I could take it home and hide it in the house.

The house I shared with a police officer.

1. The Crossroads

I caught sight of my reflection as I went for the fattest line.

The coke shot up my nose, straight to my brain. I surfaced and snorted loudly, taking in so much air it felt my lungs were ten times their size.

I sat back on the sofa, exhaled and gestured to the man sitting next to me that the upturned mirror and three remaining carefully cut lines were his.

I'd only met him five minutes before and already I'd forgotten his name. I only knew he was an investment banker who, strangely, did not drive. My old lawyer instincts had taken over and I suspected most likely there was a driving under the influence charge in his not too distant past.

'Wow,' he smiled, patting me on the shoulder like we were old pals.

Silently I stood up and, running my fingers through my curly hair to feel the tingles of coke rush, went looking for some entertainment.

It was the last day of summer, it was party time, and I'd agreed enthusiastically when my two newfound flatmates had suggested taking the twenty-minute trip to Fort Lauderdale from Miami to check out a show at a gay bar. We'd then attend what was amounting to an all-night coke party.

Carol and Michaela, nightclub waitresses, had taken me in as their new rent-paying room-mate after my marriage collapsed and now they were hell-bent on showing me a good time.

And, boy, were they.

In the villa that backed on to the canal network, cocaine was everywhere. Served up like hors d'oeuvres. I'd taken it before but only occasionally. I'd been a child of the sixties so smoking pot was a rite of passage and I'd tried opium in Vietnam but as a lawyer I'd never been into drugs. Clearly I'd been in the minority.

For the whole of the seventies, south Florida had been in the grip of cocaine madness. Everyone was at it. For lawyers, doctors, accountants, professionals of any kind, it was the drug of choice. The subculture had become the mainstream. By the turn of the decade, America was awash with cocaine and Miami was the hub where it all flooded in. Until then this had largely passed me by.

Now I was getting a crash course.

Nodding my head in time to the music – 'Ain't No Stoppin' Us Now' was blaring from the state-of-the-art stereo – I half-walked-half-boogied from room to room, squeezing past sweaty bodies. Couples cavorted in corners while every other available square of floor space became a makeshift cocaine bar. I caught up with Carol and Michaela on the way to the kitchen.

'Hey there,' Carol exclaimed, her pupils dilated.

'Havin' a good time?' she asked in her slight southern drawl.

I nodded, grinning. The rush was coming on fully now. I was no square, I'd had my share of parties but this rocket-fuelled revelry was heaven after what I'd been through in the last few months.

It wasn't that long ago that I was starting to think things were going well. I'd been working as a bank lawyer in a big city law firm, with a lovely wife and an apartment with views over the bay and ocean.

Yet in the space of a few months my marriage and dreams of settling down to what I'd thought was a normal life were in tatters. My wife Sarah had never recovered from the triple tragedy of losing her parents and sister in relatively quick succession.

It was a situation that would have knocked the strongest person sideways and our marriage sadly collapsed under the strain.

I then realized I wasn't cut out for the ruthless dog-eat-dog world of the big city firm and didn't share the relentless drive of my colleagues to step over other lawyers to get to the top.

In desperation I'd quit and set up on my own as a lawyer practising in low-level litigation and real estate. I was my own boss but my experience with the downtown firm had left me wondering if my heart was still in practising the law. I simply stopped caring about my work after the trauma of my failed marriage.

Now, at thirty-four, I was disillusioned and alone. I was drowning my sorrows one night in Ménage, the nightclub that occupied the basement of my apartment building, when Carol and her room-mate offered me a way out of my troubles.

'Come and live with us,' Michaela had said. 'It'll be fun.'

It was an offer I couldn't refuse.

That had been two weeks ago.

Since then I'd discovered my new room-mates were party girls extraordinaire. I was quickly seduced by their carefree life-style. So far there'd been no suggestion of a romance with either of them. They were on the hunt for someone with access to serious coke and serious cash.

Carol could have made a living as a Cher lookalike, at a time when Cher still looked like herself. Nearly six feet tall and dark, she had a devilish twinkle in her eye, and Michaela was built for fun. Both in their early twenties, they liked having me around because I shared the rent, but the age gap meant that I was a bit old for the fun they had in mind.

They were on a mission – a sexual, drug-fuelled thrill-seeking crusade that was mesmerizing to observe and a world apart from the life I'd been living during my four-year marriage to Sarah.

They lived with energy only cocaine could supply. Forget about food.

I caught up with them only momentarily. They'd attracted the attention of two young dealers who hauled them squealing into an adjacent bedroom.

'Friends of yours?'

I turned. A strawberry blonde was leaning against the opening into the kitchen clutching two glasses of champagne.

'My room-mates.'

'Ah. I see.' She was stunning – tanned, in a skimpy gold dress, with long, wavy hair.

'They're uncontrollable.'

She seemed to nod knowingly.

'You here with anyone?' I asked, keen to keep the conversation going while at the same time establishing if she was available. God, it seemed so long. I was rusty.

'In there,' she gestured with her head towards the door behind which I could hear muffled snorting and laughing from the girls.

'Oh. Right.'

'Friends, likewise. They always do this. Invite me to parties then leave me standing with a spare glass.'

'I can take that for you.'

She smiled and handed me the flute. The regular me would have simply been grateful for the conversation, but stimulated by the coke I started to think this might be an opportunity to get back in the saddle.

We found a quieter place to chat where we weren't being buffeted by revellers shuttling between the drinks coolers and the bathrooms.

Her name was Kimberly. She was a banker, based in Fort Lauderdale. The fact that I'd dabbled in banking law for my previous employer gave us something in common but I wasn't interested in talking shop. I was interested in how I was going to get her out of that little gold dress.

She too wasn't averse to coke, and before long she'd invited me back to her place a few streets away. I interrupted my friends' little session to arm myself with some Colombian marching powder and then we were out into the balmy air.

The sex was fast and frantic. I don't know if it was the coke or the release after the frustration of my failed marriage, but I felt great. All thoughts of Sarah went out of my mind as we got hot and heavy in the sticky heat.

I broke off for some refuelling and, pumped up by two more lines, retreated to the bathroom to catch breath. Splashing my face with cool water, I looked in the mirror.

My hair, not so long ago clipped to regulation standards for the military was now frizzy and in danger of going all curly in the humid air. My skin was flushed from all that coke.

'Hey, what's keeping you?' came the shout from the bedroom.

I paused and smiled at my reflection.

Nothing was keeping me. Nothing at all.

I dived back into the bedroom.

Friday night merged into Saturday blended into Sunday.

From being a dedicated professional I was now burning the candle all ends. Since I'd moved in with the girls life had become one long weekend. My legal practice, my pride and joy when I'd initially branched out, became an irritation. I shuffled into work late but found an excuse to knock off early and hit the bars. My law practice was fast becoming dead last in my priorities.

I'd catch up on any clients tomorrow. Work could be bumped until I found a suitable window.

My newfound freedom made me feel invincible. It didn't matter that I was staying up all night on the white lines because

I'd do the work when I got round to it. Everyone in Miami was the same. Doctors and bankers, other lawyers, it seemed they were all at it.

When the girls went out at night I wanted to join them. Even if they stayed in we chopped up some lines or smoked dope and popped open the drinks. There was always something to celebrate, another day in paradise.

It was a never-ending party and it seemed nearly everyone they knew was a dealer they could call to keep it going.

Of course, after a few weeks of living like this something had to give. Inevitably, it was the day job. Soon clients started taking their business elsewhere.

My response was simple. I went out and got more blitzed. I was living every day as it came.

And I was in that frame of mind when one day the phone rang.

It was Michaela.

She had been away for the weekend. With characteristic recklessness she'd gone to Ohio to take part in a motorcycle race, not as the driver but as the passenger on the back. Neither Carol nor I had heard from her since she'd left.

'Ken, you're not going to believe what happened. I was in a crash on the bike.'

This wasn't as hard to believe as you might think.

She was in hospital with a broken leg, she told me.

'Listen,' she added. 'When I get out of here I'm going to stay with a friend off Coral Way. I'll let you know when. You'll come visit me, yeah?'

My first reaction was disappointment that Michaela was breaking up our little party but I figured it was temporary and she'd be back when her leg was better. It was some two days later when she called again. She'd moved in with the friend and wanted me to see her.

At the time Shenandoah was a lower-middle-class predominantly Cuban community just south from downtown Miami. Most of the people who lived and worked there were blue-collar immigrants. An area distinguished by its ordinariness, neither poor nor affluent, it was a quiet corner of almost-suburbia.

The house Michaela was staying in was an old, traditional Florida house with a white-wood facade, a porch and swing. An old sign for Pan American airlines stood outside. Her friend must have worked in the industry.

The door opened and she stood there, balanced precariously on crutches. She invited me in. The single-storey house was what they called a 'shotgun shack'. If you fired a gun in there you'd hit every room. From a quick glance I could see it comprised a living room, a dining room, a kitchen and two bedrooms, all on the same level. The house was eclectic, with wood floors throughout and a large fireplace in the living room – pretty unusual for south Florida where the temperature rarely dips below 75 °F. The walls were full of drawings and artwork from Colombia and Jamaica and lying around were artefacts like whalebones and other things I'd only seen in museums.

Ceiling fans spun overhead as Michaela and I chatted. After a few minutes there were footsteps on the wood floor and a man appeared.

Handsome, with shaggy hair and a remarkable Pancho Villa moustache, he had a relaxed air about him as he came over towards us.

Michaela turned in his direction and then to me.

'Ken. This is Andre, the guy I've been telling you about.'

'Andre,' she turned back to the man. 'My good friend Ken.'

With that I was introduced to the person who would change my life beyond all recognition.

2. Outside the Mainstream

I could have been looking in the mirror at myself.

No, I wasn't sporting the same impressive facial hair. But in Andre I instantly identified similarities. Not only was he exactly my age, but he had also served in Vietnam and seemed to harbour the same resentment for the system I had on my return.

As soon as we started talking, there was none of the awkwardness that comes with initial introductions. I warmed to his easy-going nature and the more we chatted the more I grew intrigued.

He introduced himself as a teacher of Spanish. In a Spanish-speaking town where more than half the people were Hispanic, I wondered if it was a job that kept him busy.

Initial introductions made, over the next few days I found myself popping around to the house a lot. He lounged around in jeans or shorts and a T-shirt and never seemed to wear a suit or do anything remotely work-related.

There was another thing I noticed. Often, when Michaela, Andre and I were sitting around chatting, there would be a knock at the open-screen door. Andre would usually excuse himself and go off to his own room or the kitchen with his companions, but at other times they would hang out and chat with us. Some of them were Cuban Americans but their grasp of Spanish didn't suggest they needed a refresher course.

Michaela's plan was to stay at Andre's until her leg was on the mend. By the end of the second week since her accident, I dropped by but she was sleeping.

'Come in, Ken,' Andre said. 'Hang for a while.'

We chatted for a long time but the more he revealed about himself the less straight answers I was getting. What I did learn was that he was the son of two missionaries from St Louis. When he was very young his family had moved to Cuba to spread a fundamentalist form of Christianity. They'd settled in Oriente, Cuba's easternmost province and about as far from Havana as you could get. His upbringing in this rural environment had made him not only bilingual but also truly bi-cultural. He spoke fluent Spanish like a native Cuban and knew even the most obscure slang.

For the first time since I'd come back from Vietnam, I found I was able to open up to someone about my own experiences. Here at last was someone who knew and understood the feeling of isolation and loneliness I'd encountered when I returned home. We'd left a country at best ambivalent and at worst vehemently opposed to the military action but generally sympathetic to the troops who marched to war yet returned as outcasts – living reminders of our government's folly in waging an ultimately futile conflict. Nothing prepared me for the attitude Vietnam veterans faced when they came home. Our fathers had returned from World War Two to a hero's welcome. But Vietnam vets were anonymous. Old friends didn't want to know, while dates quickly dropped contact once they knew where I'd been.

I found it hard to take. Unlike many, I hadn't dodged the draft. I'd enlisted voluntarily because I thought it was my duty and I knew they'd be coming for me anyway. Doing it on my terms meant I got the chance to spend a couple of months at home after leaving graduate school. Arriving in Vietnam aged twenty-two, I felt like an old-timer. The rest of the men in my unit were mostly nineteen or twenty, just kids from the ghetto. They had no idea what they'd got themselves into, but they soon found out, to their infinite regret.

Andre said he'd been wounded in the battle of Khe Sanh, a nasty and extended skirmish in the northern part of South Vietnam. I recounted some of my experiences near Saigon and then into Cambodia. It was a relief to speak to someone who had also been there. I felt a bond forming between us.

I liked his style. He looked effortlessly cool with that moustache and thick, black hair, yet his life seemed full of contradictions. He liked smoking dope but was muscular and into fitness, often roller-skating to a nearby gym each morning. A keen traveller, he regaled me with tales from South America, including exploring the Amazon river and west out to the Galapagos Islands. He seemed to have an expert knowledge of Colombia.

He retained a bohemian spirit but embraced modern technology and was happy to have in his enclosed backyard motorbikes and eccentric, ancient convertible automobiles from the UK. If one broke down, he simply stored it at the rear of the house and drove the other. Despite his strong Christian faith, he adopted the same laissez-faire attitude he had to automobiles with women. Frequently I would call in at the house to find the charismatic charmer schmoozing a new girl. Strangely, being replaced in his affections rarely seemed to discourage the girls from coming round. Just being in his circle of friends was enough for some. He showered them with attention, only to move on to some new female challenge soon after. Many of them had to console themselves with being only a small part of his life thereafter, but they were clearly so taken with his company that they did not break ties.

Despite the absence of a full-time job, cash flow never seemed to be an issue. The city was booming, inflation was rocketing and the cost of living soaring, yet Andre seemed to have an endless supply of money. A few weeks after we met, a group of us went out for dinner downtown. He was holding court in the middle of the restaurant, naturally enigmatic and enjoying the attention he was getting from the rest of the group.

'You know, I have enough in my pocket to buy dinner for everybody in this entire place,' he laughed, as he picked up what must have been a sizeable tab for all of us.

From anyone else it would have been rank arrogance, but Andre's easy charm made him hard to dislike. He was friendly, humble and fun-loving. How can you resist?

Like everywhere else, drugs formed a large part of the social scene at his house. While Michaela's leg was on the mend I went round there for parties. We drank beer and rum under the mango trees in his backyard and partied to reggae.

When the sunset came on we smoked spliffs to ease ourselves into the evening.

I was still hoovering cocaine like it was going out of fashion but there was also a lot of experimentation at Andre's house; it had been going on long before I moved in there. Sometimes he was able to acquire something different, like hashish from the Middle East.

The parties could be lively but I noticed his attitude differed from other hosts. At the other parties I'd been to lines of coke were chopped out on the table for everyone to enjoy, like after-dinner mints. At Andre's it was more discreet. Sure, people still got high, but generally they slipped off to the bathroom or a bedroom for their fix. I put it down to nothing more than 'Andre's house, Andre's rules', but for a man who seemed to live outside normal society I found it peculiar he would be so particular about an activity which was rife across the city.

I had replaced the chaos of my divorce and the routine practice of law with sex, drugs and rock 'n' roll. Miami style.

Hanging out there one day, there was a knock at the door. My host returned accompanied by a striking man with a thick head of blond hair and a petite dark-skinned woman. I stood to greet them. They struck me as a slightly odd pairing.

'Ken, this is Ed Becker – ship's captain and blues lover. He might be moving in here.'

'Ed, Ken. He's a lawyer friend of Michaela.'

'Lawyer, eh? Pleased to meet ya,' the newcomer drawled in a soft Californian accent.

He sat down and there was an awkward moment where his companion stood expectantly. Andre, spotting the social faux pas, stepped in.

'And this is Brigida, Ed's wife,' he said with a laugh, indicating he was well used to this mild chauvinism. 'She's from Colombia.'

'It's a pleasure to meet you,' she said, in an accent that suggested she might have spent a large portion of her life in the US.

I said, 'Likewise,' before sitting.

Ed looked decidedly uninterested, as if he couldn't be bothered with social niceties. Brigida, on the other hand, seemed engaging and friendly. She couldn't have been more than five feet tall, while her husband stood at over six feet.

'So, what's the latest with your spare room?' Ed asked.

'I think Michaela'll be out soon, once she's on her feet. Then it'll be all yours.'

Brigida filled in the blanks for me. She needed a place to stay when Ed was delivering cargo in the Caribbean, plying the triangle route between Miami, Cap-Haitien and Grand Turk, as a captain on a tramp steamer.

'Sounds interesting,' I said.

'It's not going to make me rich anytime soon,' he replied.

There was a pause before he was suddenly animated.

'So you're a lawyer, eh? What's your field of expertise?'

'Bit of everything. Banking, real estate, litigation.'

'Accountancy?'

'Not especially. I can recommend someone though.'

This seemed to perk him up.

'Might just take you up on that. I never get time to sort my shit out. I need someone to navigate all this tax shit.'

'I'm sure my friend will help. Just let me know.'

'Will do,' he said. 'Will do.'

Needing to be somewhere else, I made my excuses and went to leave. I shook Brigida's hand and moved to do the same with Ed. For the first time since he'd come into the house he smiled. Either he seemed to have a lot on his mind, or he just had a temperamental nature.

I didn't know it then, but for the next decade our lives would be intertwined – in both crime and punishment.

A few months later, Andre invited me to move in.

'Great idea,' I said when the offer came. 'But won't it be a bit crowded? Your spare room is full.'

'Not for long,' he replied. 'Ed and Brigida have split. They're moving out. Ed's got a new girl now and he's moving into a house in Coral Gables.'

'Fast work.'

'You don't know the half of it.'

'Ed was cheating on her for months. She finally had enough. He was on the boat when she told him. They were talking on the radio so the whole crew could hear when she shouted, "I'm leaving you".'

'That's got to hurt.'

'For most guys. It seems he already had her replacement lined up. A young blonde called Kelly who just joined the crew in place of a cook who got sick. Call it rebound but Ed hooked up with her right away. He's moving her into a place round the corner.'

'Impressive manoeuvring.'

'By all accounts they're a perfect fit – this Kelly and Ed.'

'How so?'

Andre checked himself as if he was saying too much.

'Let's just say they share a passion for getting rich quick.'

What did that mean? I didn't care what the reasons were for Ed and Brigida not wanting the room any more. The simple fact was that Andre had a spare room exactly when I wanted it. It was all the invitation I needed.

Being able to observe Andre up close became an education in itself. He soon confirmed that, despite his seemingly endless amounts of cash, he hardly worked at all, from what I could see. Now I was part of his inner circle, he no longer felt the need to usher his Cuban or North American visitors into another room as soon as they arrived but, although he felt relaxed enough chatting with them in front of me, there always came a point in the conversation where they went off for a private discussion.

He had a small closet in the second bedroom, and once his visitor had departed he'd disappear in there with the door shut. Not long after he emerged from the closet, other visitors would arrive. More often than not these would be people who would also prefer a private chat at some point.

One day I glanced into the room and saw the door ajar. I had to see what was in that room. Andre was out so I walked in and peered into the closet.

It was just a tiny space with no desk or chair. What did he find to do in there?

As time went on I started speaking more to his visitors. Some had travelled from all over America just to be there. I'd always suspected that he had the knack of befriending people from all walks of life, but the array of characters that showed up was astounding.

I soon started to suspect what was going on. Then a gang of Colombians showed up. Rough around the edges, they looked out of place even in quiet Cuban exile suburbia, and might as well have had 'drug traffickers' tattooed on their foreheads.

Once the gang had left I went into the room and knocked on the closet door. Although slightly nervous about how Andre would react to having his little operation rumbled, I felt sure he knew me well enough for it not to be too much of an issue.

He opened the door without a hint of surprise.

'Hey, buddy. What's up?'

Over his shoulder I could see an opened bag of cocaine so big it could have been half a kilo. Next to it, on a little cabinet, was a very serious looking set of scales. Other containers half-filled with more white powder sat on a shelf above.

'Sorry, Ken, I've been working,' he added as if I'd disturbed him doing his end-of-year tax return.

He squeezed his back up against the doorframe and beckoned me to observe with a wide sweep of his hand. With his characteristic nonchalance he confirmed he was the broker, a liaison, a middleman, between Colombian traffickers who were shipping cocaine and marijuana into Miami and the Cubans and Americans who were transporting, distributing and retailing it across the States.

'Sorry, buddy, but you know how it is. Thought it might be better that the less you knew the less you could get into trouble about.'

'No, no. Not a problem,' I smiled, staring open-mouthed at his little empire.

He was a natural link. Because he could speak their language like a native, the South Americans and the Cubans treated him as their own. He'd found a niche in the market. After helping out one friend who came across a stash that he wanted to move on he discovered there were Colombians sitting on a mound of smuggled cocaine they didn't have buyers for.

His job was to take the pure, uncut cocaine from the suppliers, cut it slightly for domestic American consumption, and sell it to his growing network of purchasers in North America.

He cut the coke with Inositol, a naturally occurring nutrient derived from corn, to keep toxic chemicals out of the process and to promote an ethical approach to dealing. The going rate for each kilo bag was fifty-five thousand dollars.

Andre had to be careful. He had a previous conviction from years back for selling a small bag of coke to an undercover officer. On that occasion he got off with probation but he knew the courts wouldn't be so lenient if the cops found out about this little operation. He showed me his arrest form. I noticed his alias was 'Easy Rider'. Well, I thought, he did love riding motorcycles and bore more than a passing resemblance to Dennis Hopper's Billy.

Yet far from being a frustrated hippie who liked the odd doobie, he was the vital connection in the trade. He was what 1980s America was looking for, better living through chemical stimulation.

Confirmation of his business was obviously high risk for me.

If I'd cared more about my career I would have gotten the hell out of there.

For a lawyer to be living in the middle of a trafficking empire was not only career suicide, it was risking a lengthy stretch in jail. Should cops or the DEA raid the house I would be arrested as an accessory staring at a mandatory fifteen-year minimum sentence in Florida.

By staying in that house a moment longer I was risking throwing away everything I'd worked to achieve since coming back from Vietnam and, although I had been neglecting my clients, I was in danger of ruining my professional reputation for ever.

Yes, if I'd had any consideration for my career I should have left that house there and then. Instead I did the opposite.

I resolved that if I was living at the heart of a narcotics operation, maybe I'd better enjoy it.

Instead of thinking like a lawyer, I started to think like I had in the army. I hung camouflage cloth as wallpaper and draped a mosquito net over the slow moving ceiling fan. I had a South Vietnamese flag custom made and hung it from another wall. I laid a camouflage poncho liner on the bed as a comforter. I developed the military theme even further and soon had amassed an arsenal of weaponry. I purchased someone's Vietnam war souvenir, an old-style Chinese rifle, a single-action version of an AK-47 with a screwdriver bayonet, an M-14 rifle, a .45 pistol and a handful of assorted bayonets, as if I was expecting to repel an infantry charge.

Well, I told myself, if I was going to be living in a house full of coke, one day who knows who I might have to defend myself from?

Andre laughed when he saw my room but was as fascinated by the firearms as I was. Arming ourselves with the rifles, we went out to the Everglades for target practice. In my mind I felt I was reverting back to being in the service. With Andre it felt I was living in a place with our rules.

Over the following weeks, I received a crash course in the trade. It wasn't only cocaine he shipped out. He handled marijuana too, sometimes LSD and heroin, although by then in Miami the demand was only for stimulants. He'd fallen into the business after Vietnam almost by accident while a college student. Yet disillusioned by life and society's reaction to people like him, he'd seen a way to justify it to himself. In addition, even though he was rising to a position as one of the more influential players in the trade in the city, Andre was very much a practising Christian and couldn't see any inconsistency. Occasionally, he told me, a supplier or dealer had ripped him off, but his philosophy was never to lose his temper about it nor go seeking for revenge. He shrugged and put it down to experience. Life was too short, and he had obviously seen enough carnage in Vietnam.

Two months after I'd moved in I was in the house on my own when the phone rang. It was a woman for Andre. That wasn't unusual but she was intrigued as to who I was.

'I'm his lawyer, I live here,' I replied.

'What trouble is he into now that he needs his lawyer living with him full time?' she said. There was a hint of the south in her accent. She sounded friendly but being wary not to blow Andre's cover to anyone, I remained coy.

'You can never be too careful these days,' was my non-committal response.

'Tell him Monique called, will you?'

I was vaguely aware of Andre mentioning her. She was an old friend from his days at Bible College and she'd been in his class. Like the many women in his life, she hadn't been discarded as an ex-girlfriend, more like recycled.

Two nights later I came home to find Monique sitting on the sofa.

The girl's eyes widened. 'Ah, the lawyer,' she said with a smile that made my cheeks redden. She was beautiful.

'At your service. What do you do?'

'Oh,' she said, hesitating and shooting a look at Andre, who sat beside her. 'I work for the county.'

'Really? What doing?'

'Ken, stop grilling the poor woman and get yourself a drink.'

I fetched myself a beer from the fridge and joined them on the sofa. As the drink flowed, I found myself becoming attracted to Monique. She was petite and her olive skin gave her an air of the exotic and she was smart and funny. I'd been used to Andre's steady stream of women coming into the house but she was different, far more intelligent, as well as pretty.

I left Andre and Monique still drinking and laughing on the sofa that night but went to bed with my head filled with thoughts about her.

Over the coming days, Monique was a regular visitor to the house but nothing of a romantic nature seemed to be happening between her and Andre so I felt there was no harm in asking her out. To my delight she agreed and the following night we went out alone to the movies. I brought her back to the house and, thrilled that my room-mate wasn't around, took Monique to my bedroom.

The reality of being with her was better than I expected and the fact I was with my friend's former girlfriend never crossed my mind once. Or, if it did it only added to the frisson.

As Monique lay in bed, I got up, pulled on a robe and went to the bathroom. At that moment, Andre came back.

'Hey,' he said. 'Isn't that Monique's car out back?'

'Um, yes,' I stammered, not feeling so bold. But any fears about a reaction were instantly dispelled. He knew what was going on.

'Nice one,' he winked. 'Wish you all the best there. She's a great girl.'

Relieved there were going to be no awkward issues I made to return to my room.

'Ken?' He wasn't quite finished.

'Yeah?'

'You might have your hands full there, buddy. You know she says she works for the county?'

'Yes, what of it?'

'You know what she means by that?'

My blank look gave him my answer.

'She's a cop.'

He walked past me into his room, laughing, leaving me standing agog outside the bathroom, thinking of the small bag of cocaine I'd left lying in my drawer.

3. First Client

If living with one of Miami's most interesting traffickers was hard for a lawyer, you might think that the last thing I needed thrown into the mix was a police officer. But in fact the revelation that Monique was a cop only added to the thrill. By embarking on an affair with a cop – in a house full of drugs – I was risking everything. I was playing with fire.

And, although Monique was a police officer, I realized drugs weren't going to be a problem. She was a friend of Andre's after all.

As a child of the sixties, she had a relaxed attitude that was at odds with the policy of her force at the time. She liked taking cocaine but she had to be careful. Her occupation wasn't something she could broadcast. That's why she always introduced herself as a worker for the county. While strictly true, she knew the last thing people wanted to hear when they were getting high was that the woman they were snorting line after line of cocaine in front of was a police officer.

With Andre she could relax because she'd known him long before she even became a cop.

Things got steamy between us from the beginning. It was intense and passionate, but also relaxed and fun.

As we lay in bed one morning, she flicked her long black hair from her eyes and said, 'Ken. You're a lucky guy. I can tell you now I don't ever want to settle down and get married again. And that's a promise.'

I laughed. It was true that, after the marriage I had just come out of, I was in no way ready to settle down again so soon. I was happy to take things as they came.

And it was clear Monique had been put off the idea of marriage for life.

Coming from a French Canadian family, she had endured a tough childhood, and was raised in an orphanage in Tennessee when her mother couldn't take care of her. Like Andre she saw no contradiction in taking drugs while staying true to her faith; her children still attended their father's congregation in Miami. She'd met and married a roofer but settled down too early and, despite having two children with her husband, their marriage was ill-fated from the start and she longed to be something more than a dutiful wife and mother. Her affair with Andre was the catalyst she needed and soon she was divorced and starting life all over again.

With her children living with their father, Monique enrolled at police academy. Her relationship with Andre had fizzled out as they all did with him but they never lost their closeness and, like many women who'd been under his spell, she found it hard to break the habit of coming round his house.

Within weeks of the revelation that he was a major player in the trade I had met dozens of his clients. I was astounded by how far his network spread.

Smugglers brought the product into the country by a number of methods, usually by sail boat or motor vessel. They would pass the consignments to wholesalers and distributors who deployed similarly inventive ways of transporting the goods across the US and Canada.

Monique knew Andre dealt in drugs but she hadn't fully grasped the magnitude of the transactions going through that little closet. She didn't know he was supplying right across North America.

Andre loved introducing me as a lawyer but I didn't let on

how much I knew. Call it attorney–client privilege, but when a lawyer participates in criminal activity with his client that privilege goes right out the window.

What impressed me was how Andre conducted business in the most low-key manner possible. He seemed to be able to glide along completely under the radar of the authorities. He was nothing like the 'Cocaine Cowboys' who'd brought violence to this formerly sleepy south Florida town in the seventies. He had started at the same time as many other Vietnam vets, angry at a government who abandoned them, who looked to the trade to earn them a crust. They were joined by Cuban Americans, who learned how to covertly operate in a hostile environment during the CIA's secret war against Castro. They now turned their unusual skills towards smuggling and trafficking.

Maybe it was that early bust in 1973 that served as a constant reminder to Andre how fragile his liberty was – while his competitors were punctuating transactions with guns and violence, he offered a much more civilized service.

When that first wave of cowboys arrived in Miami the police, Drug Enforcement Administration (DEA) and Customs didn't know what had hit them. Millions of dollars' worth of coke started flooding into the town. Until then, marijuana had been the preferred drug of the trafficker. But once the demand rocketed the price soared and there was a new game in town. Almost overnight, cocaine was arriving in shipments off boats, smuggled in aircraft or air-dropped from small planes. As quickly as the drugs flooded the streets, money followed it. Such was the haste for the gangs to launder their gains, they pumped millions into real estate and snapped up practically all the auto dealers' stocks of certain luxury cars.

Much of the economic growth in Miami through that time could be attributed to drugs. Huge bay-front condominiums sprang up, giant monuments to affluence that only wealthy

South Americans and drug dealers could afford to live in. But with such a lucrative business came rivalry and violence. The streets of Miami became killing fields as rival gangs settled scores in the bloodiest of fashions. The profits were just too lucrative to share, at least in the mindset of certain individuals from Colombia.

Crime lords like 'the Godmother' Griselda Blanco of the Medellín cartel came down from New York and started a killing spree that resulted in as many as 200 murders in the Dade County area.

Miami had already become linked to violence at the turn of the decade during the Liberty City Riots, when the black community reacted with outrage at the acquittal by an all-white jury in a trial of five white cops who had beaten a black motorist to death. The rioting that ensued resulted in the deaths of eighteen people and millions of dollars' worth of property damage.

As if that wasn't enough, by the time I moved into Andre's house in Shenandoah, Miami was cracking under the strain of another crisis. The Mariel boatlift, the mass exodus of Cubans from Fidel Castro's regime, began in April 1980 after an economic crash forced the dictator to declare that anyone who wanted to leave could do so. But when President Jimmy Carter decided to throw open America's doors, it was all the invitation Castro needed to empty his prisons and mental health institutions and offer them a one-way passage to the promised land. By the time the US finally stopped the boats departing from Mariel Harbor six months later, over 125,000 of Cuba's worst undesirables had landed on our shores without money, homes, work or prospects. As Miami's under-staffed and over-stretched authorities struggled to cope, Castro sneered: 'I have flushed the toilets of Cuba on the United States.'

The damage was far more than he could have anticipated in his wildest dreams, and it was long-term.

To think they once called Miami the 'Magic City'. It was now the reputed drug and murder capital of the United States and the image projected to the rest of the globe was that it was a lawless town spiralling out of control.

Yet in the middle of the chaos, the Marielitos, the cocaine cowboys and the killings, Andre somehow maintained a sense of calm. Amid the insanity his house was an oasis of civility and he was able to keep his head when all others were losing theirs. Maybe it was his 1960s perspective but he couldn't have had a lower profile if he'd tried.

His was no 'Scarface' mansion with white leather sofas and glass-topped tables. Andre's wood-frame house was decorated with souvenirs from travels around South America and the Caribbean. And the neighbourhood ambience was never shattered by the sound of gunfire. The only noise that came from his house was the reggae music that filtered gently out into the tropical sunshine through the open windows.

For the Colombian and Cuban smugglers who moved the cocaine into Florida it was a welcome stop. He knew their personalities, knew they liked to show him their macho nature, but for the most part, he knew they trusted him. It was effortless for him.

His 'clients' came from all walks of life.

There was the businessman transporter who drove all the way to Miami from Chicago in a top-of-the-line Jaguar sedan. Once he'd received a package he'd dilute it carefully with Andre's light non-toxic cut, then load up the trunk of the Jag and head off back north to Chicago, only to return a few weeks later. His wife, from a prominent mid-western family, did not suspect the source of his high income.

There were the distributors for Canada and California, slipping into the house after nightfall. After a quick transaction and a test of the merchandise they were back on the road again, disappearing into the night almost as silently as they'd arrived.

Among the Cubans who came to distribute the coke was Rafael Fernandez, who, by virtue of the fact he stood at six feet four inches tall, was a rare sight indeed. He could have been called 'Cyclops' because after playing around with a gun during a particularly raucous party one night he'd carelessly shot his own eye out. Perhaps it was because his disability impaired his senses or the fact that he was aware of the distinct possibility that he might be arrested, but Rafael harboured a level of paranoia that was off the scale.

He was in the dark about Monique's occupation but when she came over one day after finishing her shift on the beat in one of the city's toughest districts I saw an opportunity to have some fun.

While the big Cuban was feeling confident enough to relax after concluding his latest deal with Andre, I crept outside the house and, crouching under the window he was sitting near, set off the squelch on a police radio. Thinking the house was under siege, Rafael took off faster than a frightened rabbit and fled to the rear. If that had been your typical Cuban drug dealer he might have shown his displeasure at being humiliated like that, but Rafael was able to see the funny side of it . . . eventually.

I was so used to sharing the house with Colombians and Cubans that it was something of a surprise when I came back from Monique's one day to see two blond-haired Americans sitting in the living room.

It took me a moment to recognize Ed, the moody ship's captain I'd met before. His companion must have been Kelly, the replacement cook. A look of recognition flashed across his face. She eyed me up and down. She had long hair and a gorgeous, sun-kissed face. She couldn't have been older than twenty-seven. He clearly hadn't done badly out of the quick-change love switch.

Since I'd discovered Andre's secret little operation I'd been suspicious of everyone who came to the house or who had an association with the preacher's son. If they claimed to have a legitimate occupation I suspected it was just a cover for their real vocation – the business of selling drugs.

Ed was no exception. He might have been a serving captain on a research boat but I wondered what his role was in this little empire.

He introduced me to Kelly and shot me a look that seemed to say: 'I know you last saw me with my wife but it's no big deal, okay?'

'So,' he said. 'Your accountant friend. He's going to sort my finances out.'

'That's right. Michael Lewis. He'll look after you.'

'Good. I've not paid any taxes for ten years. I need help keeping the IRS off my back.'

Why's a guy like this so concerned with being an upstanding citizen? In this house?

After the coolness he exuded on our first meeting, he seemed more congenial this time around and we sat and chatted for a while.

Ed told me how the research vessel belonged to a former US ambassador to Jamaica. He explained he was the son of a top Hollywood producer, but had dropped out of high school to travel the world. Having grown up in Tinseltown, he'd moved east to New York and had somehow popped up in Greenwich Village as the young manager of the Electric Circus nightclub – the hedonistic venue that defined the modern discothèque and played host to renowned performances that helped cement the reputations of the Grateful Dead, Janis Joplin and Jimi Hendrix. I'd been there myself back in the sixties, and it was an amazing place.

A long-time lover of the blues, he'd then landed a job with the Smithsonian Institution and had been paid to travel down to the Mississippi delta to make a series of recordings with some of the genre's most legendary performers before they died and their contributions to American culture were lost for ever. It sounded too good to be true. I wondered if these were all part of the cover story but he talked with such a passion it was impossible not to be convinced.

'And after that I spent a few years in Morocco, finding myself, before I became a ship's captain – all self-taught I hasten to add – and settled in Bogota.'

After working out the years he would have been out of the US, and given he seemed the same age as me, I took this as code to mean he'd dodged the draft. When I countered with my own experiences, including serving in Vietnam and eventually going to law school, I could swear I noticed him tense and bristle at the mentions, as if these were bones of contention with him.

Kelly chipped in. She was a sailing fraternity groupie, from Connecticut, who'd moved to Fort Lauderdale for a taste of adventure. That's when she found herself on the same boat as Ed and, as fortune might have it, then as his lover.

'So how's business?' I asked.

'I've been sailing that route for years now yet no closer to making my fortune. So many other sailors cash in by smuggling.'

His reply might not have been an admission of anything but I got the impression he was sensing an opportunity, if he hadn't already seized it.

That seemed to be the common denominator with everyone who passed through Andre's house. None of them struck me as your typical smugglers. They looked more like entrepreneurs, trying to carve a piece for themselves out of a corrupt system. We were all living in a time when the only people objecting to the drug trade were the government and we were still a long way from the day when the effects were fully understood. I couldn't see a downside.

Then one day the phone rang. I was in the house alone and when I answered a hysterical woman was crying down the line.

'It's Chris,' she wailed. 'He's dead.'

'I'm sorry. Which Chris?'

'Pardon?' the woman replied, incredulous.

There were two Chris's in Andre's network: Black Chris, a childhood friend who had dark hair, and White Chris, a blond distributor. Last names were rarely used.

'Just Chris,' the woman wailed. 'I found him in bed this morning. He is blue. He's dead.'

It transpired Chris had been in Belize and had taken an overdose of prescription pills he'd been able to buy over the counter. When Andre came home I passed on the news.

'Black Chris or White Chris?'

'Dunno,' I said. 'His girlfriend didn't say.'

'Must be White,' he said, calmly. 'Black Chris would never have a girlfriend.'

The irony was that Andre and his eclectic cast got me thinking again about law. Ed hadn't been the only one to ask me for advice. When many of them found out what I did for a living they couldn't resist asking me for some legal help. These guys could have been on the FBI's Most Wanted list if the Feds had any clue, but that didn't mean they didn't have the same problems as your average law-abiding citizens.

One Cuban wanted help on a tax issue; a client from northern Florida needed advice on a house sale. Legitimate stuff.

Gradually I began to think about resurrecting my practice. It came not a moment too soon. One day the Bar Association, the regulators of the legal profession, got in touch to inform me I'd been the subject of complaints from my old regular clients. It's the duty of every lawyer to zealously work on behalf of their clients and I'd been neglecting those duties. They were putting me on probation for ninety days. To the outside world my once lucrative practice had evaporated; my income had shrunk to nearly nothing.

The notice of probation gave me an idea of how low I'd sunk.

I had two friends who were ex-prosecutors. When I explained my predicament they offered me space in their office I could rent. It was a chance to get back in the game. On the day I went down to check out my new premises it felt odd putting my suit back on.

It was also time to move things forward with Monique. It seemed crazy that she would have to keep coming round to Andre's when she had her own place just streets away in Coral Gables. It felt like a natural progression. Andre couldn't have been less concerned. He'd had so many room-mates come and go and he was delighted for us both.

I believed it was time to put my mini adventure on hold and rejoin the real world.

That's what I was thinking when Ed called me up a few weeks after I'd moved in to Monique's apartment. He said he wanted to speak to me about the accountant I'd mentioned but asked to meet alone. He came round to the house while Monique was at work.

He seemed calm but clearly had an ulterior motive. Eventually he got to the point.

'Andre says you might be the man able to help me.'

'I can try. What's the problem?'

Ed looked me straight in the eyes and coolly uttered the words that would propel my life into the stratosphere.

'Can you help me launder six million dollars in cash?'

4. The Six Million Dollar Man

You don't wake up one morning and think: 'Today's the day I'm going to become a career criminal.'

But sometimes life just works out that way.

It had been six months since my first introduction to Ed and Kelly and in that time I'd got to know them a little better.

Ed explained he'd borrowed five thousand dollars from one friend and a small yacht from another. With her Fort Lauderdale nautical connections, Kelly had handpicked a crew reliable enough to be trusted with the operation. They'd sailed to Jamaica and collected nearly half a tonne of premium grade dope. As Andre had promptly sold their first shipment, they'd turned the importation of marijuana into a regular business, cutting their teeth by brazenly smuggling their illicit cargo into Miami on the former ambassador's research vessel. Such a boat was the perfect cover. Customs never considered for a moment that something so credible would be used as a front. So far they'd never been searched. They were able to dock in the harbour, wait a couple of days and then casually retrieve the cargo. It was borderline genius.

The money was his profits from that initial operation on the borrowed boat, and those of his associates. Understandably he was jumpy at having large amounts of cash lying around and wanted somewhere safe to hide it, preferably far from the prying eyes of the US government.

Straight away I knew what he was asking me. It didn't matter how you dressed it up: it was an illegal activity. But people's attitudes were different then. I viewed the narcotics trade as a victimless crime and the government's attempts to crack down on this booming industry as an infringement on our right to live our lives the way we wanted. Additionally, being put on probation by the Bar Association was a kick in the guts. So they wanted me to get back to being an effective lawyer, did they? Well, here was an opportunity to start providing a service to a new client.

Although he looked the archetypal Californian, the combination of growing up with a silver spoon in his mouth and an unwavering inner confidence in his own abilities belied any impression he gave of being laid back. Ed had a forceful nature and although I found him fascinating and likeable I suspected he wouldn't suffer fools gladly or tolerate people messing him around.

Maybe if I'd taken a moment to consider the risks I wouldn't have taken this on, but I saw it as a challenge. And if I was going to do this I needed to know what I was doing.

While Andre had found a comfortable operating level and was content to stay low profile, Ed seemed to be looking to his next deal and had a restlessness that was slightly unsettling.

He'd come to me because Andre had told him I'd done substantial legal business in the Caribbean.

'That's true,' I said. 'There are countries down there that are the ideal location for businesses.'

Three years previously I'd represented a chemicals company who were keen to take advantage of some cost savings by relocating abroad. I'd discovered that in Puerto Rico firms could save as much as 95 per cent in tax by relocating there, providing they transferred their manufacturing operation to the Caribbean island. I'd made several trips there and to the British Dependent Territories, where local governments were offering factory shell units and turnkey industrial parks to tempt foreign investment. From my dealings with Caribbean bureaucracy it had been impossible not to notice that what took a day to process in the States took a week on the islands due to the chronic inefficiency of small provincial island governments. It used to drive me mad, not to mention my clients who were paying my fees throughout the delays, but now I could see there was potential to exploit such a diabolical system.

I told Ed I'd see what I could do.

Despite my relaxed views I knew I had to be careful. I resolved not to furnish Monique with specifics. Sure, she knew I did legitimate work for many of Andre's associates, but this was a different story. The less she knew the better.

In any event, I told myself, if I did manage to pull this off I wouldn't really be committing a crime. Ed had a problem that needed solving. I was a problem solver. It was simple.

In my newly acquired office, I worked the phones. I was confident I could make some inquiries without alarming the lawyers I shared space with – who were both former prosecutors-turned-criminal-defence lawyers. In any event, we had established a 'don't ask, don't tell' policy, so everyone was keen to keep their business to themselves.

How do you go about cleaning six million dollars in cash?

I had no idea, but I knew whom to ask.

George Phillip was a cousin of mine through marriage. He also happened to be a fraudster who'd recently conned Fidel Castro's government out of nine million dollars.

George was something of a colourful character. Expelled from an Ivy League university as a freshman for stealing rare books from the library and attempting to sell them in New York, he had also evaded the draft for Vietnam by convincingly pretending he was gay. We went to law school in Miami together, where he went to resume his education, and briefly worked together at a global law firm, but he soon opened his own legal practice determined to make his fortune as an international lawyer.

The slow progress towards success didn't sit well with him, though, and he began to fantasize about committing the perfect crime. How else, he reasoned, could one make a million dollars the first year out of law school? After studying the obscure Trading with the Enemy Act, he construed it to mean that crimes committed against nations who were hostile to the States went unpunished in America.

One of America's greatest enemies at the time was Cuba, where a trade embargo had existed since 1960, when the government started to seize land owned by US citizens. George figured that if he pulled off a stunt to defraud the Cuban government of cash he wouldn't be prosecuted in the States. Unfortunately he failed to look at our other criminal statutes. A little bit of knowledge is a dangerous thing.

Unwavering in his opinion of himself as a crime genius, he came up with a scheme to con Cuba out of millions in a bogus coffee deal. His plan was straight out of a script for *Mission Impossible*. To help him execute his daring scheme, he assembled an eclectic bunch of accomplices. There was a fireman, a cop, a well-to-do Haitian gentleman, a German coffee salesman and a Dutch woman who happened to be a part-time heroin smuggler but held herself out as an import-export specialist.

The plan was, in theory, brilliant. Cuba was selling coffee to Russia for hard currency but, since it had insufficient domestic production, it quietly bought coffee elsewhere, relabelled it, and passed it off as home-grown. George then formed a corporation in the Dutch-owned Antilles, because as Americans they would not be able to deal directly with the Cuban government otherwise. They travelled to Germany and purchased a cargo ship that would transport the supposed coffee from the Dominican Republic to Cuba. A deal would be struck with the Cubans where for nine million dollars they'd receive several tonnes of coffee beans delivered to their door. Once the bogus corporation could provide proof that the coffee was on its way from the Dominican Republic the money would be transferred to their account by a Canadian bank that had actually lent the funds.

By bribing Customs officials in the Dominican capital Santo Domingo, it would appear the coffee had been loaded on board the ship, backed up by the necessary paperwork. A port official would also be paid to allow a crew on board. The cash would be transferred but the beans would never arrive. By the time the Cubans suspected something was up the empty vessel would be sunk at sea, leaving no trace of cargo or crew.

Incredibly everything went almost to plan. Their problem was they failed to bribe one necessary port official and the crew who were due to scuttle the ship weren't allowed on board. When the fraud was discovered not only were the Cubans furious but so was Canada, where the bank that processed the deal was based.

George brazenly returned to his law office, convinced he was untouchable. Even when some of his associates were arrested and kidnapped by Cuban intelligence agents in Jamaica and given swingeing twenty-year sentences at hard labour in Cuba, he continued to believe he'd escape prosecution. He was so confident that, rather than keep his head down and enjoy his ill-gotten gains, he dabbled intermittently in cocaine trafficking.

If George had read up a little more on criminal law he'd have known that wire fraud, where communication devices like fax machines are used for criminal means, carries a five-year prison sentence. At the same time as Canadian authorities were preparing a case to have him extradited to face those charges, he was seeking to sell eight kilograms of cocaine, ironically, to a coffee salesman who just happened to be cooperating with the

DEA. To compound the felony, when he was finally arrested, the police who searched his home found the cocaine in his garage. He was sentenced to eight years for the cocaine with a concurrent three years for the fraud.

While in prison, he constantly complained about his lot, not grasping the old paradigm – if you do the crime be prepared to do the time. I told him that since he feigned homosexuality to avoid military service he should consider this imprisonment the functional equivalent of national service. He disagreed.

By the time I needed to speak to him he had served his time and was setting up a consultancy business, while no doubt at the same time working on his next scam. Despite his prison ordeal, George was irrepressible and I figured he'd help if he could. He didn't disappoint me.

After a brief catch-up over the telephone I explained to him Ed's little problem. George knew instantly what to do.

'You need to go to Anguilla and speak to my good friend Henry Jackson,' he told me. 'Henry's the constitutional adviser to the government down there. He's the top lawyer, leading politician and he even writes the island's laws.'

My word, I thought, he makes him sound like Henry Kissinger.

'But the good thing is that he's also corrupt. For a fee, he'll pretty much do anything, but not for anyone, mind you. Luckily for you, I know the password. Go down there, explain how you know me. He'll charge fees but just pay them. He'll set everything up.'

I was grateful. I knew Anguilla. It was a tiny British Dependent Territory, the most northern of the Leeward Isles in the Antilles, and a less obvious location for international cash transactions you couldn't hope to find. The beaches were beautiful but there were no six-hundred-dollar-a-night hotel rooms. It was more off-beat than even, say, the neighbouring West Indian island of Saint Christopher, or St Kitts as it was more commonly known, which had gained a reputation as a location for offshore investment. Maybe that was the beauty of it.

I also knew Henry Jackson – George's contact in Anguilla. On my excursions to the Caribbean I'd met Henry on official business. He was essentially a lawyer based in St Kitts but had an office on both islands and floated between the two. He'd represented government-owned factory sites for the chemicals company for which I'd helped negotiate a tax holiday. Yet as well as being a lawyer, Henry was also a founding member of a new political party that had swept to power only that year, and was a rising star in the administration.

As Anguilla was one of the British Dependent Territories, the small island was largely autonomous. Henry assisted in drafting laws on everything except national defence and foreign relations, the governance of which was still retained in London. He had always struck me as someone beyond reproach.

That was to be my first important lesson in laundering – that some of the biggest professionals in the world could be involved in it. Never in a million years would I have thought of going to someone like Henry Jackson. But, with George's help, I was going to gain a pass to this secretive world.

George was also clear in how best to launder Ed's cash.

'With Henry's help you need to set up some bogus corporations in Anguilla. Invest the money in the name of those corporations into the banks down there. Then you start moving the money around. Because Henry's a detail man, he'll make sure nothing in the paperwork traces the companies back to you or your clients.'

'I can't thank you enough,' I said, genuinely grateful for the advice.

'Yes, you can. Any fee you get for pulling this off you split with me!'

'Of course. One other thing.'

'What's that?'

'How exactly am I going to get six million dollars in cash out of the country? I don't really want to take it through American Airlines. That's the kind of thing that might just be frowned upon.'

George laughed. 'You're not kidding. Listen, speak to another buddy of mine, Jimmy Johns. He's an old World War Two bomber pilot based out of Fort Lauderdale. He has his own charter company that operates a Learjet fleet out of the airport. Make sure you mention my name and make sure you tell him it's not cocaine you want him to carry. He will take you anywhere but he doesn't transport drugs.'

When I ran through the outline of the plan during my next meeting with Ed I could tell he was already getting impressed. He approved the plan with hardly any questions asked, leaving it to my judgement to sort out. The respect felt good.

Next I rang Henry. I had been slightly nervous because I wasn't entirely sure George's personal approval would carry much water. Now that he'd been tainted with a drug charge and a spell in prison I wondered if his former associates would claim not to know him.

My fears were unfounded.

'George Phillip!' Henry exclaimed. 'How is the old scoundrel?'

I didn't go into detail with Henry over the phone. He suggested it was better if I came down and met him in Anguilla. He'd help register the companies, look out some locations for potential factories we could invest in and assist with the bank accounts we'd need to deposit the cash in.

When I broke the news to Monique I had a trip to the Caribbean planned she was delighted. She had been keen for me to build my business back up. At this stage it was easy telling her what I was doing. I kept the facts to a minimum. Technically at this stage I still hadn't crossed the line, had I?

Flying in over the flat landscape of this tiny island I was simply happy that I seemed to be delivering what I'd said I'd do when Ed approached me for help.

After a short taxi ride to the island's capital of The Valley I met Henry in his Anguilla chambers. He greeted me with a big smile. He was in his early forties at the time but it seemed a taste for the finer things in life had left him looking at least ten years older than that. He offered me his broadest smile and a big bear hug.

'Ken, how have you been? Welcome again to Anguilla.'

We settled down in his spacious chambers, lined with the names of all the shell companies that he had created, and within minutes were getting to work setting up the company registrations I would need to pull this stunt off.

I formed one corporation for every client who would be making the trip down with me. Henry summoned his secretaries to help and soon we had a small army of helpers, pulling together the necessary documents to make it look as legitimate as possible.

We formed offshore companies with local place names – ambiguous companies allegedly looking to acquire industrial units in Anguilla – with the secretaries holding one share of stock in each new company. That way nobody would ever be able to identify the real beneficial owner. While I was at it I opened an account for me under the name Jose Lopez. You never know when it might come in handy.

The one safeguard I insisted on was in putting my name and the clients' beneficial ownership details somewhere in the files that would only be stored in Henry's chambers. If anything happened to me there had to be some link the clients could use to show they had claim on the companies, and therefore the accounts and the cash.

Once that was done we walked literally across the street into one of the tiny island's many banks. This one, though, was different.

Henry explained the advantage of using this particular institution. It was entirely locally owned, no US connections, not a single branch, agency or representative office in the US. That meant that even if investigators in the US learned that something was up with our companies the US courts or government had no chance of being allowed to scrutinize the accounts.

'But of course,' he said with a smile, 'we have one correspondent relationship with a major bank in Manhattan. If you deposit money in here on a Thursday, by Monday it will already be earning interest in the States.

'The president here spent years working for a major US bank here in the Caribbean. Now he's set up in Anguilla he often has huge deposits. The source of funds is of little concern to him.'

The bank accounts established, I slipped Henry an envelope of cash Ed had given me for the purpose – and made my return to Miami.

His fees were eighteen hundred dollars – triple what US lawyers would charge for setting up corporations back home.

Before we'd settled, Henry had said: 'Do you want me to tag something on to the fee and I'll kick it back to you?'

What should I have expected? In the international world of laundering and smuggling, kickbacks were par for the course. It didn't feel right to me though.

'No, thanks,' I said. 'I don't work that way. I'm being paid well by the client.'

Now it was time for the real fun to begin – the small matter of smuggling six million dollars in hard cash out of the US.

5. The Mickey Mouse Account

'One thing's for sure. You can't go down there dressed like that.'

Sitting before me were Ed, Kelly and three members of their crew who had helped ship in the marijuana that had earned them their massive payday.

Also there was Benny Hernandez, a Cuban-American distributor who, through Andre, had moved the dope through the US and Canada.

Ed was dressed in a collarless shirt with shorts, while Kelly was in an eye-catching top and colourful pants. Their companions were two hardcore saltwater sailors called Peter and Marcus, who were hired by Kelly, and Sam, a former Marine and Vietnam veteran. Peter was a ship's captain from Seattle, while Marcus was a crewmember from Detroit. Both looked like they'd just stepped off a yacht in deck shoes and cut-off jeans. The other two men were in need of a haircut and a shave.

'What do you mean?' said Ed, glancing around at his assembled posse, who had gathered at his house in Coral Gables to discuss the finer details of the operation. Monique was on duty and I hadn't felt comfortable meeting the whole gang at Ed's Coral Gables home.

'This,' I said, leaning in towards Ed, 'is a multi-million-dollar deal. We ought to look like it. It might be the Caribbean but we need to look kosher.'

'What do you have in mind?'

'You all need to be in business suits, preferably navy blue or black. That goes for you too, Kelly – either a suit or smart dress.

Gents must be in crisp dress shirts, preferably white, and ties. And you'll each need a briefcase too. Each case will carry bundles of hundred bills.'

I could hardly believe what I was saying. It was as if by saying it out loud it was detached from my mouth in some way. What I was organizing was bulk cash smuggling on a grand scale. Anything over the $10,000 limit US Customs allowed in any one trip in and out of the country could earn you a five-year prison sentence, and a probable microscopic investigation of your life.

Marcus, who seemed several years younger, looked put out.

'Is this really necessary?'

'Listen, we are business people travelling to Anguilla to rent factory sites. If we look like anything different we'll attract suspicion. If you people go wandering through international airport Customs dressed like you've just walked off the beach, they'll suspect you. If you are going to do this, you have to do it right. Plus,' I added, 'it's not like you can't afford a new wardrobe.'

'Ken's right,' Ed piped up, nodding. 'We have to do this.'

Ed's endorsement was as welcome as it was pleasantly surprising. I must have been giving off a good impression that I knew what the hell I was doing. Outwardly, I might have been appearing every inch the calm, calculating lawyer, but inside my guts were wrenching. This was high risk.

'Incidentally,' added Ed, 'how exactly are we getting there?'

'It's all sorted. Jimmy will have the Learjet waiting for us at Fort Lauderdale.'

I'd previously sounded out Ed that this mode of transport was a possibility but confirmation of the luxury travel sparked a murmur of excited chat. Now I had their attention.

Just as he had done with Henry Jackson, George had come through with his suggestion to call up his old mate Jimmy Johns.

I'd met the former Army Air Force pilot at the general aviation airport where he operated his charter company, a place far more remote than the much larger Fort Lauderdale-Hollywood international airport.

As predicted Jimmy didn't care to know the nature of our trip, nor what we were carrying. For $7,500 he would take us to Anguilla, wait for everything to be concluded and fly us back. The whole trip would take less than a day. It sounded too good to be true and I started to feel uneasy when the sixty-year-old veteran announced, rather nonchalantly, that he'd never flown into Anguilla before. I had planned everything so carefully I didn't want to leave anything to chance.

'I'm sure there won't be any problems. Might mean we have to stop in Sint Maarten for fuel, but that's all.'

Clearly my thoughts betrayed me.

'But you've got nothing to worry about, right?' Jimmy said, eyeing me suspiciously.

'Of course. Only a bit of cash.'

'Like I said,' replied Jimmy. 'I don't care what it is so long as it's not contraband.'

With Ed happy at those arrangements and the corporations and bank accounts in place in Anguilla, we were ready to roll.

A date was set for the following week, a Thursday, in early autumn. We agreed to meet early, at 6 a.m., at Ed's house in Coral Gables, where a black limousine was hired to ferry us for what would be a thirty-minute ride to the airstrip.

In the build-up I busied myself with routine legal work, fussing around my house trying to do anything to take my mind off what was coming. I trimmed my hair to a more respectable and anonymous corporate cut and had my best dark suit cleaned.

Monique sensed my unease but I dismissed her concerns by putting it down to the fact I was a bit ring rusty from being out of work for so long. She knew I was helping Ed and Kelly with something and knew I was going to the Caribbean again. However, maybe because she had an inkling, she didn't probe too hard, for which I was grateful.

I still had no reason to believe this scheme would come off.

There were a million things that could go wrong if I stopped to consider them. Even innocuous things like a blown tyre on the journey to the airport or an illness on the flight could have the authorities swarming all over us.

The night before the trip I slept little, not through panic, just a nervous excitement about how it was going to play out. It was the height of summer and even at night the temperature remained unbearably high. Feelings I'd not experienced since Vietnam returned, the sensation of entering a dangerous game, where my skills were being pitted against those of an enemy. In this case the adversaries were Customs, the DEA and the local police.

I thought through everything, trying to second-guess where something could go wrong. Eventually I resolved that to a certain extent it was now out of my hands. The rest was up to fate, and the pilot.

If I had any lingering fears that my clients weren't taking this as seriously as I was, they were extinguished as soon as I saw them arrive. They had followed my advice to the letter; each dressed impeccably in a sharp suit and meticulously groomed. Kelly looked the picture of sophistication, her figure perfectly fitting into a business outfit. Gone was the sailing groupie. In her place a steely businesswoman looking every inch an equal in a man's world.

'Well, Ken,' said Ed. 'Do we pass?'

'Perfect,' I replied, greeting each of them with a firm handshake.

Each of the clients was holding their matching attaché cases tightly, understandably, given the cargo.

'I'm assuming all the cash is in there, double and triple counted. They will check it meticulously.'

'It's all there.'

Although still early morning it was clear it was going to be another scorcher. Our limo was by then waiting. It was time to catch a flight.

Jimmy met us just metres from the plane and the sight of it gleaming in the morning sunshine was enough to dispel some lingering nerves from the passengers. For others it merely heightened the anxiety and confirmed that this was real.

After I discussed the flight preparations with Jimmy, he gave us the go ahead to board. It was as relaxed as I'd hoped. Security was non-existent and there were no baggage checks. Ed filed in behind me, followed by Kelly and the rest of the gang, and we strode purposefully in a regimented line out across the tarmac towards the eight-seat jet, looking for the world the business delegation we were pretending to be.

As Jimmy made the final checks for take-off, I dared myself to relax but my in-built cautiousness made me think otherwise. I knew nothing was certain until we were in the air. Only then would I know that we'd overcome the first hurdle. The best way to catch a launderer, I figured, was to catch him leaving the country with the cash in his hands.

As the engines started up and we taxied to the end of the runway, we were inching further away from the possible clutches of Customs.

The rest of my party were now in high spirits, whooping and cheering that we'd made it this far. Yet it was only as we soared into the sky and I saw the canals and beaches of Fort Lauderdale below me that I allowed myself to breathe out. We might just pull this off.

The journey time to the east Caribbean was two and a half hours, and once we'd left American airspace it was a party flight.

Ed cracked open bottles of spirits and his crew were quickly in a celebratory mood.

Jimmy was happy enough to let anyone who fancied a chance at flying the plane to join him up the front left seat. The others were more interested in knocking back the liquor, but, feeling confident that this operation was going to come off without a hitch, I settled in beside him and took over the controls. I had learned to fly in the early 1970s, while I was still at law school. I knew another Vietnam veteran who had joined the coastguard after the war and he had given me lessons. My instructor might have survived the Viet Cong but he died tragically when a student flying a helicopter collided with his plane at Opa-Locka airfield in north-east Miami. I didn't get many chances to fly after that.

It was a thrill to once again take over the controls of an aircraft but just as I was being lulled into feeling I was on some kind of pleasure flight, Jimmy announced that, because fuel was running low, he wanted to touch down in Sint Maarten.

This shook me out of my comfort zone.

'Don't worry,' Jimmy shouted over the constant roar of the engines. 'You don't need to get off the plane if you don't want to. It's just a fuel stop. No one will check you out.'

I was grateful for the reassurance of the experienced pilot but the unintentional pit stop brought the tension back.

I'd filled Ed in on the likelihood of such a manoeuvre beforehand but, like me, when the reality hit him that we were landing on another island, just five nautical miles from our destination, I could tell he was getting anxious too.

As the engines whirred to a gentle hum at Sint Maarten, I explained the situation to the clients and tried to be as calm as possible.

'It's a routine stop. We have to refuel here because we don't have enough to get us back to Miami and there are no fuel facilities in Anguilla. Please stay put.'

Sam and Peter looked at each other blankly, then to Ed for direction. He still sat in his seat with the belt fastened. No one was going anywhere when they had a million dollars sitting at their feet.

Mercifully, it played out exactly as Jimmy said it would. It transpired Sint Maarten didn't even have a Customs department, due to the fact that the island was divided among two former colonial powers and, for convenience sake, it was abolished.

After what seemed like an eternity we were in the skies again, this time for a mere fifteen minutes as we hopped across the Anguilla Channel to our final destination.

Once again the clients' spirits were high. They knocked back more alcohol and their noise in the back of the plane was distracting. Jimmy shouted that he'd never landed on the island and needed to fly over low and slow, to determine the suitability of the runway, and rule out obstructions, animals on the field, and any number of issues which could result in a problem on arrival. He pitched the Learjet into a barrel roll, flipping the plane on its axis and back upright again.

At first the gang didn't know what the hell was happening. There was near hysterics as initially some thought we were out of control.

But the manoeuvre had the desired effect. Ed and his friends were stunned into silence, not least because they were amazed that not a drop of liquor had been spilled by the stunt. Jimmy had got his message across. We landed without a word and taxied in from the runway. This time there would be Customs checks to navigate but I was banking on Henry Jackson to have smoothed the way through for us.

Not for the first time on this adventure, I needn't have worried. Henry himself was standing just behind the small Customs shed. The little building that passed for a terminal had two solitary officials who were there to inspect our bags, with a supervisor standing over them. The first man took Ed's case and opened it, just as passengers from another small plane also came through Customs.

What happened next will live with me for ever. He took one glance at the money, neatly packaged and layered like you'd see in a spy film.

As he gingerly lifted a couple of the bundles to satisfy himself that cash was the only thing in the briefcase, the supervisor butted in.

'Close it up, close it up,' he hissed and, gesturing to the tourists who were entering the room, added: 'We don't want everyone to see it now, do we?'

Surely it was the only place in the world where millions of dollars of cash would be welcomed with no questions asked!

'You see, Ken,' Henry smiled. 'Just like I said. Come on now, your cars are waiting.'

En route to The Valley in two 4x4 all-terrain vehicles, Henry explained to me the philosophy of the island's inhabitants to foreign investment.

'Some people might consider this dirty money but, you see, here it has created a whole new middle class. The teller who will later deposit your cash used to be a fisherman. His wife was a maid, cleaning the homes of wealthy foreigners while his brother went to Puerto Rico to find work and sent money home to his family here. Now they all work in the banking industry. They are upwardly mobile, trading in their rundown shacks for a house near the beach. They can afford nice cars, spend in our restaurants, it all has a knock-on effect.

'Money like yours created that. That's why we are happy to take it.

'We are a small country. The people here lead simple lives but are good, God-fearing souls. On such a small island there are eighty churches. Do their congregations not deserve a little prosperity? The positives far outweigh the negatives.'

The jeeps stopped outside what looked at first glance like any normal shopping centre and we all got out. Closer inspection, however, revealed it was more like something out of a science-fiction movie. There were no shops. Instead banks and trust companies filled the units. Inside secretaries sat poised ready to answer the phones.

Henry must have sensed my suspicions.

'It's a good arrangement. You register the companies here and these people will field the calls for you. To the outside world it all looks legitimate. You cannot buy anything there. It is all banks and trust companies. That's where they answer the phones and pretend you have a business there.'

Just as we were about to proceed to where we needed to go, Ed pulled me up.

'Wait,' he said. 'I've been thinking about something you said earlier. I had an idea last week.'

'What's going on?'

'I'll show you later,' he said with a grin.

Back in the bank I sat with Henry to open the accounts; we watched as clerks pushed the entire six million dollars into counterfeit detectors and money counters. It's fair to say I'd never once wondered how long it would take to count six million dollars in cash. In reality it takes an eternity, especially when you're itching to get on a plane back home again. Once certified as genuine and the figures confirmed, they bound and bundled the notes and removed them to the vaults. In their place certificates of deposit, in the names of the shell companies, were created, showing the money was now earning 9 per cent interest.

'That's it, Ed. It's done,' I told him. 'You and your clients are now legitimate investors who are already receiving a return on your money.'

Ed looked at the certificate and for a moment I wondered if the thought was crossing his mind that he'd just traded his fortune for some magic beans.

'Beautiful, Ken.'

The certificates were to stay in the lawyer's files for the companies in Anguilla.

There was one more thing, I told him. He had been worried about having his signature on any documentation relating to the accounts. I asked him if he wanted to set up a mechanism here to withdraw the money, should he need to. He didn't have to. He didn't even need a signature on the account card.

'I've thought of that,' he smiled. He produced from his pocket two toys, a tiny Mickey Mouse and Minnie Mouse.

'What are those?' I was puzzled.

'Rubber stamps,' he replied, as if it was the most obvious thing in the world. 'One for me and one for Kelly. Can I use these on the accounts?'

I laughed. 'I don't see why not.'

Signature stamps were acceptable, so why not an image?

Moments later the transaction was concluded with the signature of a picture of two of Disney's most famous characters, confirming the handover to two accounts totalling over two million dollars, approved by the bank president on the spot. That's what I call being user-friendly.

'What sort of crazy place is this, Ken?' Ed remarked as we left the bank. 'That a bank would allow you to do that?'

'The kind of place where we want to do business,' I replied.

The cash banked, we celebrated in a nearby bay-front restaurant where waiters donned snorkels and flippers to retrieve lobsters fresh from pots in the bay. As we toasted our success, Henry patted me on the back as he watched us sip fine champagne from nearby French Saint Martin. I'd offered him a glass but he was happy with his German beer.

'You know something, Ken? A lot of people have come here and they have opened up corporations and they say to me, "I am going to do this and I am going to do that," and they never do.

'But you, my friend, have actually done something. You have delivered what you said you would do. You did it! I hope this is the start of something special.'

I sat back, permitting myself to relax after a day spent living on the edge of my seat. Savouring the bubbles on my tongue as the waves lapped gently on the shore, I raised my glass in Henry's direction.

'I'll drink to that, Henry. I'll drink to that. Thanks to you.'

By the time we got back to Miami the money had been sent by courier to the bank's corresponding account in New York City at a high interest rate. To all intents and purposes, it was the bank in Anguilla's money commingled in the bank's account and it was already making a profit on the difference between the interest they obtained from the bank in Manhattan and the 9 per cent they were offering us on our investment.

And the beauty of the transaction was that there was no evidence we had even been there. The certificates of deposit went back into Henry Jackson's office so we came home without any paperwork whatsoever. We never even had to state the official reason for depositing the money. There were no such rules then on Anguilla.

To say there was a celebratory mood on the plane on the way home was the understatement of the year. The gang were very happy. Ed seemed impressed.

'I got to hand it to you Ken,' he said. 'We pulled it off.'

I just smiled, basking in the satisfaction of a job well done. Ed then returned to a subject he'd brought up several times already.

'So, what's your fee gonna be for all of this? You might be more crooked than most but you're still a lawyer and I've never met a lawyer that didn't want paid.'

This might sound hard to believe but I hadn't even thought about the money. That's not why I'd agreed to help Ed out.

Sure, since my practice had dwindled away I certainly didn't have a lot of it to play with. But from the outset it was never about the cash. For me, it was for the adventure, and to serve a client, albeit a criminal one. Laundering had always been more about beating the system than making myself rich.

I tried explaining this to Ed one more time.

'Come on. You must have some idea. You've been amazing and we need to sort out a rate for future jobs . . . because, believe me, there will be more trips like this, buddy.'

'Okay,' I said finally, 'if you insist. I'll take your car.'

Ed had a beautiful red Fiat Sport Spider convertible.

'You're kidding?' Ed laughed.

'I'm not. You asked for a fee. My fee's the Spider. You said you're getting rid of it anyway.'

I'd had my eye on that car ever since Ed announced he was intending to sell it. To me it was perfect – stylish without being flashy. Compared to the Mercedes and Ferraris that everyone else connected to the drug trade travelled around in, this was considerably lower profile, was cheaper to run and wouldn't look like I'd suddenly come into a lot of money.

I got back to the house by midnight that same day. I had been on the road for eighteen hours. My jacket was off but after a day in the baking heat of the Caribbean my shirt was clinging. Monique was sitting in the kitchen when I came home. I bounded in with a smile as wide as it would go.

'How'd it go?' she beamed, getting off her seat.

I grabbed her and twirled her round.

'We have cause for celebration,' I announced.

'Wow! What happened?'

'I just helped the clients move all their cash. Everything went like clockwork. Couldn't have been better. This could be the beginning of a nice niche.'

I put Monique down and went to the refrigerator to find something to open. She was buzzing with excitement, her brown eyes sparkling.

'What's going on?' she asked. 'Is this with Ed? Tell me what went on down there?' She laughed and hit me playfully, almost childlike in her frustration for answers.

'I just set up accounts that will earn Ed and his friends a lot. But it means there will be business for us. And it could lead to big things. I feel great.'

'That's amazing.' Monique was the most animated I'd ever seen, practically jumping up and down as she produced two glasses for the wine I'd taken out of the refrigerator.

'I had no idea your work made you this excited,' she exclaimed. 'You should take on new projects more often.'

'I'm planning to, sweetheart,' I said, as we clinked.

I spared her the gory details of the transactions, preferring to stick to the facts – that I'd helped Ed invest some cash. I'd just facilitated it. Everything had been above board. She seemed to accept it. It was enough that the experience had transformed my attitude.

I went to bed several hours later, my mind buzzing, my dreams vivid.

6. The Cheap Thrill – Being Shot at and Missed

I'd only just started to savour the cool splash of water on my face when the shout came.

'Incoming!'

A whistle gave the first warning but had barely registered when the explosion ripped through the camp. The tree above me shook, sending more water cascading on top of me.

Damn, they are early tonight. It was normally sundown before the first rockets came. Typical it would happen when it was my turn for the shower.

It sounded as if the first missile had narrowly missed the base. The next might not be so wayward. Around me men were frantically diving for cover. Instinct told me I should join them. But the water was so cooling. I'd been looking forward to this since the morning's first sortie from the base.

'Rijock! Are you out of your mind?'

One of the young lads looked at me incredulously as he tore past for the cover of the tent. Like most of the troops he couldn't have been more than nineteen. All he had to rely on was his survival instinct.

I splashed the water over my face once more. Another whistle was followed by a second blast, much nearer this time. The Viet Cong rockets were getting closer. I thought again about moving but then decided to stay put. If it's my time, it's my time.

I awoke, drenched in sticky sweat, the fan whirring overhead.

The image had been so real I could almost smell the smoke.

It had been a long time since I'd had dreams of Vietnam but recent events must have shaken some memory banks.

I squinted in the half-light. Monique lay sleeping beside me. I got up to get some water. An old quote from Winston Churchill came into my head: 'There is nothing more exhilarating than to be shot at without result.'

After successfully flying out of the US with six million dollars in cash and getting away with it, I knew exactly what he meant.

The only time I'd felt that exhilaration was serving in Vietnam. Now *that* was high risk. Getting shot at on a near daily basis, especially after dark, facing a dedicated, hidden enemy whose sole purpose was to destroy you. That was constant pressure.

In that environment, sundown at base camp nearly always spelled rocket attacks. The Russians had made twelve-foot-long missiles that they sold to the Viet Cong. They could destroy a building and everyone inside but by the time they'd fired them they'd disappeared back into the jungle.

The time I stayed out there under fire I'd only just got into the shower when the rockets started. I say shower but really it was a five-hundred-gallon aircraft fuel tank filled with water and wedged in a tree. It was basic but it was all we had. I had two years' service in Vietnam and Cambodia and considered myself one of the lucky ones. I was older and at least I'd had an education. Most of the guys I served with were just kids and there they were going out in tanks and armoured personnel carriers, fighting for their lives.

One time we were out in the field and had just finished breakfast when one of our own bombers flew overhead and dropped a huge load of tear gas near to our position. Everyone was coughing and spluttering. Tear gas makes you throw up, invades the mucus membranes and stays there all day. It was a sickening experience.

Coming home it was impossible to leave the images behind. They stick in your psyche. Once I went to see a movie and a car backfired and I hit the ground. I wasn't alone. Other vets told how it took them months to get out of the habit of running naked outside with a bar of soap when it started to rain, so used were they to taking a shower when they could.

But while there were images I wanted to erase, I was starting to realize that there might have been experiences I yearned to feel again. The bulk cash smuggling run I'd just pulled off was intoxicating, mind blowing. I'd never felt so alive since Vietnam; taking risks does give one a rush of sorts. Unfortunately, it is an addiction.

I'd always known that I'd end up in that conflict. Like anyone raised with John Wayne movies, stories told by veterans and the whole Wild West glorification, I wanted to experience military life. The fact that the North Vietnamese Army and the Viet Cong were Communists also resonated, for my family had fled Russia after the 1917 revolution.

Although my father served in World War Two, he persuaded me not to enlist during the peacetime years that followed the great conflict. His view was that while I might have no option but to fight should the nation go to war, I should concentrate on my education until then. Years later, however, when the Vietnam War dominated the news, he changed his tune and still opposed my enlisting.

At college I maintained a student deferment, which kept me out of the clutches of the Draft Board. As it was, going to college probably saved my life, because I could easily have been a casualty if I had gone to Vietnam between 1965 and 1968. Instead I started graduate school, in New York's Greenwich Village, studying Economics, the day after my college graduation. I did want to further my education, but I was reclassified as 'available for conscription' by the Draft Board. It was time.

While many men my age were doing all they could to avoid the draft, I went to my local army recruiter and enlisted. By doing so I was granted a couple of months' grace before I had to leave and spent the time working in an electronics factory, enjoying what I knew would be my last days of civilian life. In hindsight perhaps it was a mistake because by the time I went on active duty in January I had to take basic and infantry training in the dead of winter up north, where it was bitterly cold.

When I got to my unit in Vietnam, assigned to the First Infantry Division, I was sent to an armoured cavalry unit, which generally meant I was going to ride, and not walk, through the jungle. Before long I discovered my college degree might further save my life. Only 4 per cent of enlisted men had a college education so the commanders considered me a valuable commodity. This was 1969, when anti-Vietnam protests were dominating the news back home and the military was anxious to tell its story to the American people. My captain offered me two choices: either to assist with courts martial, the military trials for offences committed by the troops, or go into the field to write about what was going on there. The articles would be published in local military newspapers, and many would later appear in *Pacific Stars & Stripes*, the military newspaper for Asia. It was an easy decision to make.

My typical trips involved joining one of the three cavalry troops and riding with them for several days in the bush, on top of an armoured personnel carrier. These vehicles were designed to carry soldiers inside but in the jungle we rode on top – the best way to survive a land-mine blast. The drawback though was that you were then a sitting duck for snipers. My mission was to document any remarkable stories from the frontline as well as any efforts to win 'hearts and minds' with the local population.

My first exposure to journalism was easy, while also messy

and hazardous, but it sure beat carrying an M-16 in a rifle company. In the rainy season it was wet and cold and extremely muddy. Dry season brought endless dust. There was no comfortable season. After each assignment I returned to base camp to write up the articles, while at the same time hoping the near nightly rocket attacks would not hit the building where I slept.

When the unit lost its chaplain's assistant, I was asked to fill the role and found myself out in the field helping to conduct memorial services for men killed in action.

Later, I was attached to the Squadron Operations unit in the field, the people who actually direct the movement of the cavalry units. Working with the officers who were directing and fighting the war, I learned how they operated in hostile territory. I didn't appreciate it then but now I could see that the military arts of misdirection, disinformation, camouflage, could come in useful. Working in a hostile environment turned out to be an excellent preparation for my future occupation.

When the First Infantry Division went home, I extended my Vietnam tour, and was transferred to the Twenty Fifth Infantry Division, also in a cavalry unit, where I served for several months until it was time, after 400 days, to go home. I did get a free, all-expenses-paid trip to Cambodia at that time, due to the invasion of the enemy sanctuaries across the border. At the frontier, some engineer unit had posted a sign, stating that this was a shortcut to enemy headquarters. That's what we call gallows humour.

I might only be one smuggling trip into my laundering career, but I already knew that if I was going to stay ahead of the game I would need to use those tactics I'd learned in the military.

7. Meeting the Mob

The sun was so hot the mercury must have passed 90 degrees.

Two days after our Caribbean adventure, the sidewalk tarmac was like walking on a rubber mat. The perfect day to take delivery of a new convertible. I drove our new wheels back to the house. Monique came outside to see it. She was ecstatic, if a little curious.

'Who gets paid with a car?' she exclaimed.

I shrugged.

I handed her the keys so she could take it for a spin. As I watched her dart in and out of the quiet suburban streets of Coral Gables, I wondered what twists and turns my life would take. In some ways I felt I was buckled up for a ride in the fast lane, but I wasn't entirely convinced I was the one in control of the wheel.

In less than a week, Ed had called and invited me round to his house for a party. He said there were some people he wanted me to meet. It would be mutually beneficial.

Ordinarily Monique would have been with me – after all we were practically neighbours to Ed and Kelly – but not this time.

'I'll go on my own, honey,' I tried to reassure her. 'It's just more business. He's suggesting I take on another client. It's a friend of his who is looking for some legal help.'

Monique had no real reason to doubt. I wanted to spare her the details.

But, as I drove round to Ed's house in the fading evening light, I was conscious of a feeling that I was compartmentalizing my life, legal and extra-legal work. I had only completed one deal but already I sensed I was opening a chapter. Should my relationship with Ed lead to more business, I considered, I was going to have to keep even more from Monique. She had no need to know.

The party was a far cry from the laid-back events at Andre's house. In the kitchen two of the gang I recognized from our trip to Anguilla were tooting cocaine with a couple of stunning Fort Lauderdale-type women.

The dope fumes wafted from room to room while disco music blared. Already intoxicated by the last few weeks, I cranked up the feeling with a few shots of hard liquor and strutted about feeling pumped up to the tips of my fingers.

Ed collared me and led me through the throng to where I could see Benny from the Anguillan trip standing next to a suave Cuban, who was leaning against floor-to-ceiling bookcases that took up the entire wall. For a high-school dropout, Ed had an impressive collection of books.

He caught me gazing admiringly at his library.

'I thought you said you dropped out of high school,' I said.

'I did,' he countered. 'I've taught myself everything I know. When you're sailing around the Caribbean you have plenty of time to read. I'm interested in everything – politics, travel, music, history, even cooking. I devour knowledge.'

'Oh, yes,' the Cuban interjected, laughing. 'Such a great intellect. And he puts it to use smuggling drugs into America!'

'This is Charlie,' Ed announced, holding out his hand theatrically.

'And this is Ken. The man I've been telling you about.'

By now Ed had his arm around me pulling me towards him in an over-aggressive man hug. 'This is the man who set everything up in the Caribbean. And he's my lawyer.'

Then, grabbing me even tighter, he declared: 'He's my brother.'

I wasn't sure if his effusive praise was a blessing or a curse, but I laughed it off.

Charlie smiled, shaking his head at Ed's antics, as if indicating he had seen it all before. He seemed affable.

'I've heard a lot from Ed about what you did.'

'How can I help you?'

'Come, let's talk,' Ed suggested.

He motioned us into a small room where I noticed he had a bank of personal computers, a rare sight at that time. Two other men I'd only glanced at earlier joined the three of us. Ed shut the door.

For a moment it felt like an interrogation. The two newcomers looked like Italian Americans, with greased-back hair. One sported a moustache so thin it looked pencilled on. The other was jowly and overweight. They looked menacing, and from their expressionless faces I got the impression they didn't do small talk. No introductions were forthcoming.

Benny, who'd been quiet during the trip to Anguilla, now did most of the talking. Charlie was his lieutenant. I found it slightly amusing that drug gangs adopted the same ranks as the military.

Benny was the son of a famous former political prisoner in Cuba who had spent ten years in a hellhole of a prison under Castro. Since his release, Benny's father had become a port captain here in Miami, piloting huge commercial vessels into the port of Miami.

Benny and his brothers had been smuggling dope into south Florida since they were teenagers. They also had the contacts to distribute their contraband throughout the northern US.

Recently though they had been branching out into cocaine after realizing it was much more lucrative. But, as Benny explained, they still retained their core business of marijuana, adding hashish oil – a concentrated resin from the plant. By painting the oil on to their regular pot, users made a much more potent substance. Apparently it was in demand in Canada.

Ed explained that Benny and his crew would smuggle either the dope or cocaine into the US in boats, or occasionally via light aircraft. The contraband came from Colombia and was air-dropped into one of six hundred islands in the Bahamas, where someone would be waiting in a fast boat with a radio to locate the falling package. It would then be ferried to Tampa or Fort Lauderdale as fast as possible, hoping to avoid detection and arrest.

Once Andre had cut the drugs, they had an ingenious way of transporting them – hidden inside secret compartments on panel trucks that then used interstate highways, en route to the northern US, where much of the market was.

For the first time Benny acknowledged the two men.

'Freddie and Enzo operate in Canada. We have a good mutual arrangement.'

He leaned in. 'They have links to the Cotrones. Very powerful.'

The Cotrone family? I was no expert on the Cosa Nostra but even I'd heard that the Cotrone syndicate controlled large parts of Canadian organized crime. Didn't they have links to the Bonannos in New York?

These guys dealt with the Mafia? With drugs from Colombia? What was I getting mixed up in? I knew one thing. Organized crime could mean greater scrutiny.

As Benny went on, he said his family also owned a retirement home, while he owned a Corvette dealership. In its own way, each was the perfect legitimate cover for any illicit business.

After listening to them detailing Benny's experiences as a smuggler, I was at a loss to see what I could bring to this enterprise.

'What do you need me for?' I asked. 'Seems like you've got everything under control.'

'What we want,' Benny said, 'are boat documents. I think you can register them in the UK and they are untraceable to Miami. Also you can set up offshore companies – even ones connected in some way to our own – and register vessels in states where we can conceal ownership.'

I nodded. 'I can do that for you.'

Benny smiled.

I glanced at the mobsters but they looked bored, as if keen to rejoin the party.

Ed patted me on the back. 'Looks like I've got you another trip to Anguilla, Ken.'

As Benny continued to talk, Ed vanished momentarily and came back with a small bag.

'Here,' he said, handing the bag to me. 'Take it.'

'What is it?'

'Your fee. You earned it.'

I opened the bag to see bundles of hundred-dollar bills, neatly wrapped.

'But you already gave me the car.'

'Don't be ridiculous Ken. This is for your next project. Ten thousand dollars. Is that enough?'

'Of course.'

If I'd been harbouring any belief that my involvement with this caper would be limited to one cash run it was out the window. I was now locked into their operation.

Monique was asleep by the time I got back to the house. She looked so peaceful, her bare chest gently rising and falling as the ceiling fan whirred overhead. I stashed the money in the bottom of the closet and silently slipped in beside her.

As I lay there in the darkness, I began to plan ahead. I had a lot of thinking to do. I was in this now. It was going to take some careful work to make sure it was done properly. And without drawing attention to myself.

The Mafia? If I'd thought about it, what other organization would high-level smugglers deal with? It was well known the Mob controlled sales and supply in many areas. Still, the confirmation took some getting used to.

If the Mafia were distributing the drugs, where were they originating? The Medellín cartel? Was I helping bankroll one of the biggest and most ruthless cartels on the planet? Or was it one of their competitors? Where was the cocaine coming from anyway?

And what of the strange meeting in the room? The cash payment? Was it to show I was part of this now, implicated as much as them? Or to bind me to all the players, a sort of retainer, but coming from career criminals that I did not know?

Enjoy it, I told myself. This might not last. If things get too intense I can walk away. Simple.

As my fears calmed I thought about more pressing issues. The probation from the Bar Association was over. But technically I was under some form of observation. If I didn't get back to running a legitimate practice people might start asking questions.

Yet how could I practise law and diligently represent my clients at the same time as I laundered cash for what seemed to be a burgeoning narcotics gang?

In the morning Monique kissed me goodbye as she left and I hurriedly dressed for work. In the office that I shared with the former prosecutors, I set about organizing my affairs.

I'd resolved that my firm would be your typical 'door practice' – that means I handled any business that walked in off the street. Routine litigation? I could handle that. Need a realtor for a house purchase? No problem. Got several million in dirty cash you need cleaned? I'll see what I can do. Just don't ask for a receipt.

I dug out all the active files I had from existing clients and neatly filed them in the cabinet I had in my office. I figured if I ever did anything to attract the attention of the authorities and the office was raided there would be plenty of evidence of a nicely functioning law firm. No records could exist for anything I did with Ed, Andre, Benny or anyone else who came to me for my sideline business. A paper trail could hang me. Therefore, let us keep everything either in my head or offshore.

I found that my legitimate cases were boring in the first place but after the laundering began they became even duller. The monetary gains from legitimate commerce were minimal; the gains from laundering were obscenely high.

Looking through the files of my regular clients I wondered how I'd managed to survive for so long. Man, this was far more intellectually challenging. To think that I had been busting my balls on a daily basis for such minimal rewards while in just over a week I'd earned a new Fiat Spider and a fistful of dollars. I was a Vietnam veteran looking for something more and it had found me.

Now all I had to do was sit and wait for the phone to ring.

It duly did.

'Rijock?'

It was Charlie.

'Let's take a little business trip.'

8. The Sint Maarten Run

'My God,' Charlie said after we'd parted company with Henry Jackson to firm handshakes.

'Benny said it was simple. But I never thought it would be like this.'

As we walked out into the blazing sunshine, he was shaking his head in disbelief, but a broad smile broke across his face.

'No offence but regardless of what Benny said I didn't trust you until now.'

'None taken,' I said, smiling. 'I imagine in your line of work scepticism is a necessity.'

My second trip to Anguilla with a new client had been executed with the same success as the first. With only one companion there was even less interest at the Anguillan Customs and, after I'd travelled down to set up the bank accounts and set up the registrations for the companies Benny wanted, everything had been in place.

We'd deposited a somewhat paltry sum of less than a million.

The more trips I made to Anguilla the more knowledgeable I became about the practices of this quaint little tax haven. And the more I got to thinking about ways to make these little operations safer for all concerned.

I'd felt much happier travelling down with only several hundred thousand dollars. Despite the success of the last outing, the idea of taking to the skies with millions could still have turned the hairs on my head grey long before my next birthday.

In addition, when we'd once again landed in Sint Maarten for a pit stop, I had an idea that I wanted to see if I could put into practice. It would be costly for the clients if every time they wanted to deposit money in their offshore bank accounts, they had to hire a private jet. But what if there was a way to carry out the cash in bulk through regular scheduled aviation routes?

It wasn't long before I was able to test out my plan. After our first success I seemed to have Ed's unqualified trust. Soon he had another half a million he wanted to clean.

I suggested breaking it down and giving me an initial $150,000 for a trial run. I figured a Thursday flight late in the afternoon would give me the best cover. That was a time when many American northern city dwellers headed south to the Caribbean for weekend jaunts, gambling and sunshine. All things being well I should be able to mingle with the tourists and perhaps security would not be quite as diligent.

At Ed's house one morning, soon after I had agreed to his request, I counted out the notes to make sure it was all there. Then I counted it again. On this trip I would be travelling alone and, as I was going to be personally liable, I wanted to be doubly careful.

I took it home and started to think how I was going to carry this on board a plane. Removing from the bills all wrappers or bands that might show up on a scanner, I dug out an old beaten-up overnight bag and emptied it on the bed. At the bottom of the bag I spread out the notes. Then grabbing some underwear, slacks and shirts I covered the cash.

Next I had to select my outfit for travel. Opening the wardrobe, I flicked past the suits, past the regular pants and chinos, past the polo shirts and smart casual wear until I came to the most garish Hawaiian shirt. Perfect.

I teamed it with a pair of worn safari shorts and dusted down an old pair of sneakers. Topping it off with a weathered Panama-style hat, I checked myself out in the mirror.

I looked like the dumbest tourist that ever stepped off a plane. It was ideal. I smiled. It couldn't have been further from the suited swagger of our first trip to Anguilla.

Arriving at Miami international airport by taxi, my cockiness evaporated. I felt less bullish.

Inside, the concourse was as hectic as I expected. That much was good but it wasn't my fellow travellers I was focusing on. It was the armed security guards and police dotted around the departure building. I stood transfixed just a few feet inside the doorway, staring at the cops in fear, as if they could smell the dirty cash in my bag.

I might as well have had a sign on my hat saying 'money launderer'. I had to snap out of it. If this was going to work I had to act as casual as possible. Any cause for suspicion would land me in it big time. This was no time to act nervous.

In the restroom I splashed water on my face and stared into the mirror.

Come on Ken, you've been in worse situations.

All you're doing is taking slightly more cash out of the country than usual. There are a thousand explanations you can give but none of them will work. Your lawyer skills won't help you here; use your survival skills.

I strode back out into the concourse with a renewed sense of purpose. I had bought a ticket earlier in the day, paying cash, for the evening American Airlines flight to Sint Maarten, returning the following day. At the security check I waited until a crowd formed before going through the x-ray machines. Although I knew the primary aim of this screening was to look for firearms and metal objects, I stiffened with apprehension as I placed my bag on the conveyor belt and watched tensely as it slowly disappeared from view.

The security guard beckoned me to walk through the metal detector but I paused, waiting to see if a commotion was made about the bag, as if an alarm would sound whenever obscene amounts of cash were smuggled through.

This was it – the moment of truth. Another line to cross before I became a fully fledged currency smuggler.

I could feel the tension building in my neck, my cheeks started to flush. I wanted to turn and run but something inside made me step forward and, as if on autopilot, I walked through the scanner.

Nothing happened.

No alarms, no flashing lights, no beeps. Of course there weren't. There was no way such primitive machines could detect paper money and, in any event, this was long before magnetic strips and other security features had been added to hundred-dollar bills.

I walked through without as much as a second glance from the security officer. The adrenalin started pumping. I purposefully picked up my bag and, chest puffed out, left the security behind me. I was clear.

Or so I thought.

Boarding the plane brought the anxiety back. What if I had been followed to the plane to make sure I was actually leaving the States? What if this was the moment Customs would pounce? Paranoia set in once again.

I eyed the vacant smiles and faked sincerity of the welcomes by the cabin crew suspiciously and edged my way down the aisle. My seat was at the back of economy. Although the island flights were pretty basic, they had a few seats that passed for first class at the front. Although I had enough cash on me to buy the entire first-class section and had grown accustomed to luxury travel, for this venture I had chosen cattle class to stay low profile.

I sat in an aisle seat next to an elderly couple. The man sitting next to me was overweight with a puffy face and glasses. He smiled politely. I forced one in response and made some remark about how good it was to get away for the weekend after a hard week at work.

I was hoping I was giving a passable impression of a man without a care in the world but was more convinced I might just as well have been saying: 'Look at me. I am a man with nothing to hide. I am not doing anything illegal and there is nothing in this bag here that hints at any criminal activity.'

Being a lawyer had never been so stressful. Before take-off I sat rigid in my seat, convinced that until the plane was safely in the air there was still a chance I could be apprehended.

I've never been so grateful to see the flight attendants give their routine safety announcement and found myself listening intently as if it was my first time in an aircraft. It meant the plane was taxiing to the runway and I was nearly home and dry.

After what seemed like an age, the engines roared into life and I felt the reassuring pressure of being pushed back into my seat. As we levelled off, I slunk further into the seat back and breathed out. A huge smile spread across my face. Relief washed over me. The thrill I had felt when we soared into the air with Ed and his gang returned but seemed even greater because this time I'd taken the cash through the eye of the tiger.

This was why I was doing it. This was why I was putting my career, life and liberty on the line. The thrill was just too intoxicating. I was hooked.

I now had no doubt that this trip was going to work out as successfully as the others. And, although the stakes were slightly lower and the amount of cash I was smuggling far less, in many ways testing out this trial run was going to mean more to my working life than hiring the Learjet.

We landed at Sint Maarten and my experience with Ed's gang told me there wouldn't be a problem. Since I'd been amazed at the lack of security I'd discovered that this tiny island – divided in two with a French-governed north and Dutch-owned south – was practically the only Western country that had dispensed with Customs since the seventeenth century. Unsurprisingly it had become a safe haven for smugglers and launderers, and a hotbed of corruption. I was later to meet up with smugglers who had set up residency there, and operated their Caribbean smuggling business, Colombia & Jamaica to America, from this offshore location.

Striding off the plane, I walked through passport control, flashing my birth certificate as identification. I knew that passports weren't required in the Caribbean and, although I had it in my pocket if necessary, the nod from the immigration control officer reinforced my belief that I'd found the ideal transit point in which to bring the clients' money. If I could ghost in and out of this island without a passport stamp it would never look like I was here.

Emerging from the airport, I caught a taxi to the island's capital Philipsburg, on the Dutch side. I found myself a discreet little Caribbean businessmen's hotel on Front Street. Safely alone in my room I found a crawl space above the water closet and stashed Ed's cash in there.

Once settled, I felt relaxed enough to go for a walk. Chancing upon a small casino I went in for a flutter. I believed I'd earned it. As I watched the nylon ball bounce erratically around the roulette wheel I thought of the gamble I was now playing where the stakes were truly high – my life.

It wouldn't always be this easy, would it? How did I know the combined forces of the police, the DEA and Customs weren't monitoring Ed, Andre, Benny and the rest? All it would take was one weak link.

'Twenty-one,' called the dealer. 'You win, sir.'

He pushed a stack of chips my way. Surely with the way my luck was going I should stick the lot on – even gamble some of Ed's money? I could double his cash.

No. I had to be careful. The last thing I wanted was to attract attention.

I smiled.

'Must be my lucky day,' I quipped and collected my chips.

I cashed them and strolled nonchalantly back to the hotel. I had entered a dangerous game. The rush was greater than any cocaine high but I had to control the feeling. If this house of cards was to come crashing down, it wouldn't be today, and – I resolved that night – it wouldn't be by any mistake I made.

The following morning I retrieved Ed's cash from the dropped ceiling and took a cab over to the French side of the island, to the port of Marigot, that sector's capital. From there I took a water taxi for the short hop over to Anguilla. My companions were local workers commuting to their jobs as maids, cooks and other services.

The benefit of taking this route was that there was no record of me setting foot on the island. A taxi driver took me to The Valley and I returned to the bank where only weeks before we'd deposited six million dollars.

The business completed, I then visited the offices of lawyer Henry Jackson and set up additional corporations. Now I wanted to find out how easy it was to register a boat there. Our corporations gave us the same rights as UK citizens and, as the island was a British territory, the documents for registering vessels there were sent by slow boat to far-off Cardiff for processing. While the paperwork was crossing the Atlantic the boats could set sail under false names and have the drugs delivered, earn those obscene profits, and disappear from the registry as fast as they entered it.

Armed with this goldmine of information, I returned to Sint Maarten and caught a flight back to Miami that afternoon. I had time to stop off at a jewellery store in Philipsburg and bought a beautiful necklace for Monique. Another advantage of this lucrative line of work was that I could spoil her. Plus, the island offered competitive cut-price deals that made jewellery 30 per cent cheaper than in the US.

On the flight back I set some rules for myself. It seemed wise never to stay on in a place where I moved money. That way there would be no hotel receipt, no ticket for travel. I could slip in and out like a ghost. I resolved that all my trips to Anguilla would be as brief as possible, business only, with no overnight stops.

Travelling back was a breeze. Once again, aside from my boat registration documentation I had no paperwork linking me to Anguilla and the cash I'd just deposited. And the beauty of being a lawyer was that when I came back into the US, if I was stopped by Customs and asked for the reason for travelling, I could say: 'It was business and I am an attorney.' I did not have to identify the client, or even the legal services that I had performed, and where.

That should have stopped any further line of questioning.

I'd also hoped that my surprise gift for Monique would limit unnecessary questioning from her about the clients. But I should have known by now that, being a police officer, she was naturally inquisitive.

'You're making so many trips to the Caribbean maybe you should open up an office there,' she said.

'Well, I told you, it's a tax haven. Everyone wants a piece of it. It beats doing real estate week in week out.'

Her eyes narrowed as she peered at me.

'I just hope you're being careful.'

'I know what I'm doing. It's just legal work. You wanted me to get back to work and I'm working. It's all for our benefit.'

She was sitting at the kitchen table. I walked up behind her and gave her a reassuring kiss on the top of her head, pausing to breathe in the lightly scented perfume in her hair. I loved

Monique dearly and saw my future with her, that much was true. Yet, while I didn't know where this adventure would lead me, and for how long, I was still sure that the only way I could protect her was to tell her as little as possible. Technically I wasn't lying to her. That's what I told myself.

She seemed to accept it, for now, but I wondered how long I'd be able to keep this side of me secret.

I was pondering this when she threw me a curve ball. She had a cop pal called Paddy Montana. He'd been accused of stealing jewellery from a house eviction and was due in court. The union weren't helping him and he needed a lawyer. Could I?

'A cop?' I asked, incredulously. 'Wants me for a lawyer?'

'Yes. I said I was sure you'd help him out.'

Monique stared up at me, her dark eyes glistening. What else could I do?

I grabbed a cold beer from the refrigerator and sat out in the garden in the shade.

I thought about it. A lawyer for drug dealers and now police officers?

Could my life get any crazier?

9. Spinning the Plates

Children were playing in the street by the time I left to head down to my office. They must have already finished school for the holidays.

It was nearing Christmas, but in Miami it was still a pleasant 72 degrees, the winter sun bringing with it a freshness that was most welcome after the long and sticky summer. It was also a far cry from the biting chill that enveloped my native New York at this time of year.

It was ten years since I'd relocated to the Sunshine State, after Vietnam, and life could not have been more different than I'd imagined when I'd first headed south.

My family had arrived in the US from Russia in 1923 – a lucky escape because the next year immigration was tightened and, during World War Two, everyone in the small village they'd left was executed by invading German forces, as part of Hitler's liquidation of the Jews. I grew up in a small, peaceful town just north of New York City, with a typical suburban childhood; my father took the train into the city each day where he had a business importing men's clothing from the Far East. While I was in Vietnam, my parents moved to Miami Beach, following other relatives who'd relocated to Florida. On my return, it seemed logical to join them and I enrolled at law school in Miami.

Ruth and Robert, my mother and father, must have been wondering what was going wrong with my life. After seemingly having everything in place, with a good job, wife and a nice apartment, I was now divorced, out on my own and living with a divorced single mum. My sister Michele, a real-estate agent, would now have to be the respectable one. If I was economical with the truth with Monique I was even more so with my family.

Busy, was how I described my day to day. That way they were protected.

But although they were in the dark about my life, to any of our neighbours in Coral Gables, who had been decorating their houses with tinsel and lights since the day after Thanksgiving, I looked like any normal professional living with his partner.

Monique worked as an economic crime detective at that time and neighbours would have seen her leaving in civilian clothes. Meanwhile, I did everything I could to appear Mr Average, journeying as routinely as possible to my office downtown.

What the neighbours didn't know was that I was now the gatekeeper to a burgeoning criminal network. News of my ability to make bad money disappear and reappear as sparkling clean investments earning top rates of interest had spread. Once Ed and Benny started bragging about how the boats they used for smuggling were being re-registered thousands of miles away from the seas they were sailing in, everyone wanted a British company with a name that suggested the vessels were legitimate charters.

I was now registering the boats myself. Benny had a whole fleet he'd wanted renaming to keep one step ahead of Customs and, as everything with Henry Jackson was generating a fee, I'd endeavoured to find out a way to do it myself, using his secretaries only when necessary.

The bulk cash smuggling trips were becoming as commonplace as brushing your teeth. I didn't need to be on every one. These days I was going down a day before to do some prep work and set things up.

Benny was soon shipping millions to the tax havens. On his

last trip I was waiting for him in the control tower at Anguilla, such was my familiarity with the staff there. When Benny disembarked he was with someone I didn't recognize. The dark-haired, brooding stranger appeared less respectable than my client and was paying no regard to the dress code we'd all adopted for trips to Anguilla. He *looked* like a trafficker.

Benny introduced him as Rick Baker, one of his lieutenants. We shook hands but I felt uneasy and exposed to a newcomer who had first-hand knowledge of my methods. I needed to better enforce my new rule: new clients can only introduce associates before a transaction takes place. That way I wasn't divulging trade secrets before checking them out first.

I'd deployed that tactic when Benny had introduced me to his brother Carlos. I was happy to do business with him because I trusted Benny. However, when he'd shown up shortly after that with Freddie and Enzo, the goons who claimed to work for the Cotrone family, to talk about registering a company, I drew the line, inventing some excuse why I wouldn't be able to help them. No hard feelings, but I didn't want to be a lawyer with the Mob as clients.

In any event, I had more than enough things to keep my mind occupied.

Through some other contacts I'd made in the Cayman Islands I'd met a boat surveyor called Samuel Matthews who, for a much smaller fee, was happy to give me the necessary documents to register a vessel. He even came to Miami and Fort Lauderdale to perform his duties; apparently he had relatives in Florida.

I'd watched Henry do it enough times to see what I needed to save the clients some money and, once I had a builders' certificate from Samuel, I could go to the office in Anguilla to register the boats in the UK. In the same way that automobiles are valued by their service history, for a documented vessel you needed to prove all the previous owners since it left the builder. This wasn't easy but the fact that boats could be registered from major British dependent territories was a major tactical advantage for traffickers. By the time the paperwork was laboriously sent across the Atlantic, I already had the updated registration documents.

Should Customs even board a boat and consider it suspicious, when they contacted the British government for the most recent ownership information they would most likely be told the documentation was in transit. By the time the details I'd registered arrived in Wales, that boat could have been used once or twice to smuggle drugs into the US. They were even considered expendable at that point, should the risk level be too high.

After a few months testing this theory I began to look at alternative means of registration. After some research I flew from Miami to Philadelphia, hired a taxi and made the short hop across the border to Delaware. There I headed to an obscure little bait and tackle shop where I'd heard I could be supplied with US boat registrations.

With fake bills of sale I collected from Samuel and anonymous corporations I came away with Delaware registrations.

By the time I got back to the airport in Miami, Benny was waiting for me so he could take the brand new registrations to his captain to use, should they get boarded. By now, boats could go out with a Florida number, switch to Delaware on the high seas, if necessary, and even return with UK documents. They were practically untraceable.

Benny had told me that even if Customs were suspicious about a boat, even if they tore it apart, by the following week that vessel's identity would be switched and it would start its next voyage as a new ship, with a new name painted aft, and perhaps a new colour scheme.

The other beauty of Delaware was that I could form corporations using a business services provider, who would sign the necessary documents as the officers. The newly formed corporations – with no paper trail back to the clients – were listed as owning the boats used to smuggle in the cocaine. As an added bonus, Delaware boasted zero sales tax, which meant they were saving money registering it there over Florida where the sales tax was substantial – no small saving on a six-figure yacht or motor vessel.

My plan with the new corporations, when formed in the US, was to let them expire before I ever needed to file the company's first annual report. That way I would never have to designate who the real officers were. So companies formed in June one year would have fifteen months of trading before I had to file a report. By then I would simply close the corporation down and start a new one elsewhere.

With an ever-expanding client network to satisfy I was content that I had the business know-how and the expertise to keep the cash flowing in.

My newfound confidence also convinced me to start laying down some ground rules. If my services were going to be in demand I needed to make sure I could trust the people referred to me.

I had this in mind that morning when I set off from home for a meeting with Charlie Nunez. After seeing for himself the set-up in Anguilla he wanted an offshore account of his own. He wanted to talk business that didn't concern Benny.

From there I was heading to court. Then it was over to Andre's house where he wanted me to meet a chemist who manufactured his own form of crystal meth, to discuss helping him move some of his illegal profits.

Next I needed to arrange the surveyor to visit a boat Ed wanted to use for his next smuggling operation, while also working out when my next trip to Anguilla would be.

And all the time I had to ensure that I was busy with bona fide legal work so as not to arouse the suspicions of law enforcement, while also not letting slip any of my activities to the criminal defence lawyers whose office I shared.

My brain was running at one hundred miles per hour. Everywhere I turned there were client problems to be solved. Everyone around me seemed to be living a normal life. It seemed like I was the only one with something to hide. Even routine became stressful when I stopped to think how it would fit in with my criminal activities.

The holidays would bring Monique's children to stay with us soon. Katherine and Luke had stayed with their father while she concentrated on building her career. Their arrival would bring a new kind of stress but I believed that I could handle it. I was the one keeping the authorities away from my clients and their money. That was my primary role. If I slipped up and didn't do everything right my clients would go to prison and I could end up with a bullet in the head. These men were friendly enough when the coke was lined up and the party was in full swing, but if anything happened to jeopardize their little empires I would pay the ultimate price – especially now that I knew who they worked with.

It was pressure, but despite all of this it didn't seem like a job. It was more an adventure, trite as that sounds. I was fulfilling a role that nobody else was. Like Henry Jackson had said, people might have whispered about it but nobody was actually doing it.

Henry had been the find of the century but I already knew I had to be constantly innovating to stay ahead of the game. If I put everyone's business through the same route it would only lead to a pattern of behaviour that would be easily tracked by any number of agencies that would love to call a halt to our not-so-little operation. What I needed were new schemes and new places to hide the money.

I liked Charlie. The Cuban – six feet two, athletic and only in his twenties – was still relatively inexperienced. But I'd seen enough in our trip to Anguilla to know he was bright with a head for business. He'd started out as a small-time dealer but after linking up with Benny had risen through the ranks and was now the kingpin's right-hand man.

We met in a small café near my office and he spoke with a seriousness that belied his tender years.

'I know the risks,' he said solemnly. 'My brother was accused of ripping off a Colombian gang who he'd convinced he could sell their marijuana. They thought he had cheated them and he was shot in the face. Only his friend's reactions saved his life. The bullet grazed his neck. He got out of the game after that. But his scar is a reminder.'

I didn't know if he was telling me this as a threat, but if I needed a reminder of what was at stake, this was it. Despite the implications, Charlie was a likeable man and someone I was prepared to help out. He had been raised by his mother who had fled Cuba with her two sons. He was intelligent enough to hold down a legitimate job but, like so many Cuban exile kids growing up in Miami, fell into drugs because it offered a fast route to wealth.

I could relate to that. Since I'd agreed to help Ed launder his cash, I had seen the potential to make ten thousand bucks a week, minimum – five times what I'd been earning as a legitimate lawyer. After wearing army surplus clothes during my time at Andre's I could now dress in expensive suits, treat Monique to dinners in swanky restaurants and pay cash for anything we wanted. I kept ten thousand dollars in cash in the house for emergencies and stashed the rest in my Jose Lopez account in Anguilla.

Charlie had a lot of connections and I could see even then

that he was ambitious enough not to be content with being Benny's lieutenant for too long. He had his own cash and wanted somewhere secure to stash it. He listened intently to the advice I gave him. He was becoming a big player but his head was screwed on. He wasn't a gung-ho cowboy with a death wish. I figured a part of him was envious of his brother's decision to leave the trade, but he realized that while this was the only life he knew he had to make the most of it.

Leaving him, I digested the business in hand. If Charlie wanted his own corporations in Anguilla I could double up the trip with a new boat registration for Ed.

I just had time to swing by the office to collect the paperwork for the police officer Paddy's case before we were due at the court around the corner. I got there to find the elevators out of order and, cursing building management with every step, doggedly climbed the stairs.

It was a sweaty and out-of-breath lawyer who greeted the nervous-looking officer outside the court. His difficulty was that he'd been supervising a particularly unpleasant eviction of Cuban immigrants when a piece of furniture had gone missing.

The Cubans accused him of stealing it: it had minimal monetary value but was apparently a family antique. The officer claimed he'd merely picked up the item when he arrived to forcibly eject the family from the house and thought it was of no value.

He insisted it was a mistake rather than a misdemeanour.

Though his guilt was obvious I agreed to help him out, first of all as a favour to Monique, second, because it added credibility to my legitimacy as a lawyer and, third, because I was curious to see what it would be like defending a cop on a criminal charge.

I'd already discovered that the force's internal legal affairs department didn't take too kindly to a civilian lawyer handling their case and they didn't seem to grasp that any disciplinary procedures would have to wait until the court case was over. I'd been to one court hearing with him and had encouraged him to put his hands up to curry favour with the judge. Today we would learn his sentence.

As we waited in court for his case to be called, it was notice-able how much of the prosecutor's time was taken up with small-time dealers. After a succession of low-level hoodlums were disposed of and passed us as they left the court, my client turned to me.

'Lowlife scum, these people,' he hissed. 'Every crime we tackle is down to drugs. Murders, thefts, assaults, shootings – all drugs. We should string them up. You'd see this city clean up overnight.'

He meant it. There was real contempt written on his face. I shrugged and faced forward, feeling my face flush again.

He could have no idea that his own lawyer, the man sitting next to him, was helping to bankroll the enterprises he despised. But that didn't stop the waves of guilt flooding over me. Beads of sweat formed on my brow that had nothing to do with the stuffy courtroom or the quick dash I'd just had to perform.

I couldn't think of anything to say that would sound remotely convincing.

A bailiff announced the arrival of the judge.

Saved by the bell, or the wheels of justice.

After what I felt was an impassioned plea for leniency on my part, the judge stopped short of making an example of the officer and let him off with a fine – a good result. The system would later seek to revoke his police officer's certification, though.

A relieved Paddy shook my hand fervently outside the court. Panic over, I appreciated his gratitude but, conscious that I had to be in Shenandoah across the city for my appointment at Andre's, I made my excuses and took off.

My friend laughed when he saw me harassed. It was changed days from the times we used to hang out together and our only stresses were whose turn it was to light up the barbecue.

'You're a man in demand,' he said, when I filled him in on the upturn in business I was enjoying.

'You're legitimizing them. It's perfect.'

'I only did it to help Ed out,' I explained. 'Who knows where it will end?'

'Enjoy it, my friend,' Andre said, smiling. 'But be careful.'

He leaned in.

'This can be a lucrative game, but remember. Trust no one. Ed will be the first to roll over if things get ugly.'

'You can't be serious,' I said, looking straight at Andre. 'Are we not in this together? United we stand . . .'

'Divided we fall,' Andre retorted. 'I just want to make sure your eyes are open.'

'That sounds like a threat.'

He shook his head.

'Just some friendly advice, amigo. Come now, there's someone to meet you.'

David Vanderberg couldn't have been further from a typical drug baron if he'd tried. A graduate chemist from North Dakota, he had turned his back on a conventional career – something I could relate to – to develop a particularly pure and potent form of methedrine, or crystal meth, a powerful form of speed, on his own organic farm.

As he sat there proudly telling me how he refused to allow pesticides on the farm he ran with his wife Mary, oblivious to the irony that he was concocting an artificial stimulant to sell for profit, it struck me how the business attracted people from all walks of life; lawyers, doctors, accountants, scientists were all lured into the game, whether as participants or even as launderers.

Like he did with many suppliers, Andre organized the distribution of the substances and passed his share of the profits back to David.

The chemist wanted some money moved overseas. It was straightforward and he was someone I could easily add to my ever-growing list of clients.

'You'll be here for New Year's, won't you?' Andre shouted at me as I was leaving.

'You bet,' I replied before getting in my car to drive the short distance to my final appointment of the day.

It was with Ed. From the minute I walked into his house I could tell he was tense. His eyes were bloodshot and he looked like he'd been sampling too much of the product he traded. From his initial shipment of marijuana, he'd now branched out into the far more lucrative white powder. I could see it was making him edgy.

'You're a busy man. Pleased for you,' he said, as if trying to be polite but I could detect an edge to it. 'I've been trying to get you for a couple of days.' He seemed put out.

'Well,' I said, 'since we came back from Anguilla your friends all want the same thing – offshore corporations, bank accounts. You started it.' I tried to laugh.

'Yes,' he replied but he seemed detached. He appeared more stressed than I'd seen him before. His face looked drawn and gaunt and his usual self-confidence seemed dimmed.

'We brought a boat in two days ago but Customs are sniffing around it,' he said, as if anticipating what I was going to ask. 'For the moment it's not safe to bring the dope off. Kelly's found some potential boats in Fort Lauderdale I need someone to give me a quick survey on. Do you know anyone? Someone we can trust?'

Immediately I thought of Samuel Matthews.

'I do. He's a surveyor who's helped me on boats for Benny.'

'Good,' Ed said, without even looking at me. 'And listen, Ken. I'm happy that things are taking off for you. But remember it was me who put these people your way. Your first loyalty should be to me.'

'It's not a question of loyalty, Ed,' I countered. 'If someone comes to me with a problem I try to help. That's all.'

I explained that the more enquiries I made benefited everyone and told him about the Delaware registrations.

He wasn't listening. Whatever the root cause of his dark funk, I made my excuses and headed home. I had too much to be getting on with. But in my car I started to seethe.

Was this arrogance brought on by success? I was the one who'd legitimized his little empire. Maybe it was being born with the silver spoon in his mouth. He expected everyone to drop everything for him.

I had too much on to worry about Ed's problems. The following morning I needed to be getting on with planning my next bag run to the Caribbean.

I was in my office the next day doing just that when the phone rang. It was Charlie.

'There's someone I want you to meet. Are you free for lunch today?' he said.

'Sure. Who is it?' I asked.

'I'll explain when I see you. A very big fish. If you do a good job for him it could be lucrative – for all of us.'

'Sounds intriguing.'

'Meet me at the Red Snapper at 1.30 p.m.' My rule only to accept a new client with a personal recommendation from an existing one would never mean they were completely kosher but it could prevent some undercover agent turning up claiming to have a referral. I didn't know who was watching and which of the gang was under surveillance but I needed safeguards.

The Red Snapper was a waterside seafood restaurant near the

marina that was a bit off the beaten track, making it a popular hangout for smugglers, especially once the sun went down.

At lunchtime it attracted a business clientele and was the perfect cover for discussing matters less than legal.

I arrived and found a table. It was a few moments before Charlie arrived, alone.

'Where's your companion?' I asked, puzzled.

'He's making his own way here. He won't be long.'

'So, who is this guy?'

'His name is Bernard Calderon,' Charlie said, leaving the moniker hanging in the air as though I should have known instantly to whom he was referring.

My blank stare told him otherwise.

The biggest cocaine smuggler into Miami, he told me. I could detect the admiration in his voice. Originally from Paris but based in Vancouver for years before coming to Miami, Bernard had a boat company in Miami Beach called BVTA – Boats and Vessels to America. I'd seen the sign.

Charlie was just about to expand on the background story when the deep-throated roar of an engine outside the restaurant distracted us.

Pulling into the parking area was a blue Jaguar XKE convertible with the top down. In the driver's seat was a deeply tanned man who looked in his late forties or early fifties, with receding hair. When he stepped out of the car, his slim physique suggested healthy living.

Beside him, now easing herself out of the passenger seat, was a breathtakingly beautiful, young Asian woman, slender and dark skinned, her eyes shielded from the hot rays by oversized sunglasses.

'That's Bernard,' Charlie said, under his breath.

Reading my mind, he added: 'And that's his wife.'

The couple weaved their way into the restaurant and we

stood to greet them at the table. Close up, the Frenchman looked more weathered than healthy and his aquiline nose and thin features suggested that his looks weren't the first thing that had attracted his stunning companion.

Charlie made the introductions.

'Bernard. This is Ken, our lawyer. Ken. This is Bernard. And his lovely wife Tao.'

In a European style, she offered both cheeks by way of greeting, while Bernard grasped my hand in both of his in an over-zealous welcome.

'Monsieur Rijock. It is a pleasure to meet you,' he said, in a thick French accent that made me question how long he'd been living in Canada.

We sat down to lunch and I soon found this man engaging and likeable. You would never have thought he was a kingpin masterminding a multi-million-dollar enterprise. He spoke like a businessman, not a trafficker, to such an extent at times I nearly forgot our reason for meeting.

'Monsieur Calderon,' I asked him. 'Charlie tells me your business is in boats.'

'Mais oui. My beautiful wife, here,' he said, gesturing to the fragrant Tao, who smiled on cue. 'Her father manufactures the most impressive Chinese junks in Taiwan. I ship them to Miami.'

'They are sailed all the way here?'

'Non, non. The boats are dismasted and transported on huge container ships and delivered to the clients in Miami.'

'Impressive,' I said, as Charlie and Bernard exchanged glances and smiled.

After the niceties were completed, however, the Frenchman moved on to why he sought my expertise.

'I want what you are doing for Ed, Charlie, everyone else. I want to move my money from overseas and I like the idea of these Caribbean territories you are exploiting. But tell me,

Monsieur Rijock, what I also want are – how you say – economic citizenships. I don't just want bank accounts in these countries. I want passports. I understand in some of these islands nationalities are available at a price.'

This was true. Since one Caribbean country had become independent the tiny nation was effectively selling economic passports. If you bought a condominium there and paid the government a $50,000 fee you could get yourself a passport from a country with the added bonus that it was a member of the British Commonwealth. That meant no visa was required to go into another Commonwealth country so, with his new passport, Bernard would be able to fly into Canada and come into the US quietly without the inconvenience of getting a new visa every time.

I could see why it would appeal to him. Given our relationship with Henry Jackson – the Henry Kissinger of the region who was practically unimpeachable – I saw no reason why I couldn't make this happen.

As the lunch went on, I started to wonder if the subject of how he really made his millions was strictly off-topic. Eventually, however, the Frenchman confirmed his line of business and, in doing so, demonstrated a sense of humour I was discovering was rare with drug lords.

Bernard smiled. 'Business is booming, despite the close attention of the US Customs, the DEA and the police,' he said. 'There seems to be such demand for this stuff. I don't touch it myself. To me it is as though we are in the business of growing potatoes. Everybody likes potatoes, everybody wants potatoes; who are we to deny them their simple pleasures, eh?'

We laughed.

Lunch concluded with the promise that I would seek out the answers to Bernard's request and get back to him. More problem solving.

As we departed, with more double kisses and warm hand shakes, I couldn't help feeling that this could be the beginning of a beautiful friendship.

'What are we doing for New Year's?' Monique asked me not long after I'd walked in the door.

'I'm easy,' I replied. 'But Devon's throwing a party. We know a lot of people going.'

Devon was one of the criminal defence lawyers I shared space with. After the year I'd had – where I'd seen my life change beyond all recognition – I wanted to sign it off with a bang.

The week before the bash I was hanging out with Andre when he produced a small block of gelatin that was perforated into tiny squares. I recognized it as LSD.

He let out a little whistle.

'Windowpane acid, my friend. You gotta try this.'

I'd grown up around LSD in the sixties but latterly had steered clear because I always felt it accelerated the ageing process. But seeing it there, practically beckoning in Andre's hand, I was tempted once more.

We took a long and vivid trip that night and the feeling was so great Andre gave me some to take away with me. I figured New Year's Eve might just be the occasion for another all-nighter. I dropped the square jelly not long after we arrived. In a short time I was on another planet. I can vaguely remember a doctor who was a guest at the party peering into my eyes, saying: 'You must be on some kind of medication.'

No shit, doc.

I recall bringing in the New Year before a resigned Monique decided it was best if she drive me home. I was in no fit state.

It was an apt way to end a far-out year. As I drifted to a dreamful sleep I could only wonder what the next few months would bring.

10. Sympathy for the Devil

We were airborne again. Ed and Kelly from the original Anguilla gang, Andre, who came along for the ride this time, and one more travel companion – a neurotic and eccentric movie scriptwriter.

This time, we weren't flying south for the sunny climes of the Caribbean. We were heading west, to the beaches of California and an unlikely meeting with Hollywood producers for a bizarre project that involved the Rolling Stones, a famous bluesman and a Hollywood studio.

When Ed first brought up the idea of this trip I thought he'd been smoking too much of the marijuana he and his crew had been smuggling into the country along with the coke. Since he'd told me previously of his love for Mississippi bluesmen and his commission from the Smithsonian to preserve the legacy of the genre for ever, he'd been particularly keen to impress upon me the importance of Robert Johnson's place in the history of music.

Johnson was one of the blues giants – his 'Cross Road Blues' tune was revered by the Stones and Eric Clapton. He had died in mysterious circumstances at the tender age of twenty-seven, the supposed victim of strychnine poisoning from a spiked whiskey bottle which may have been given to him by a jealous husband, furious that the singer was flirting with his wife.

Although he only recorded some twenty-nine songs in a twenty-four-month period his legacy far outlived the impact he had during the 1930s.

It was Johnson who, popular legend tells, formed a pact with the Devil, trading his soul for a mastery of the guitar that no mortal could match. Selling souls was certainly a concept that many of us who had entered the cocaine industry in Miami in the 1980s could relate to. His story would certainly make a good movie. And that's what Ed was now planning to do.

Flushed with riches, he was looking for a new venture to invest in and had somehow acquired the rights to a screenplay on Johnson's life. Given how little was known about the enigmatic blues legend, it's a wonder that Miami screenwriter Gray Allison had managed to compile a story at all. Yet, not only had he done so, he'd also at one stage optioned the rights to the screenplay to the Rolling Stones, who were also great fans of the blues, and of Johnson in particular.

Those rights had expired before any movie could be made. But, sensing an opportunity – and with his background as the wayward son of a Hollywood professional – Ed saw a chance to combine his twin passions and bring Johnson's story to the big screen. He told me he was on the verge of doing a deal and was intending to meet the producers who would make the movie possible.

So far, so plausible, but when he told me the people he had lined up to help turn his dream into reality I started to harbour serious doubts. He'd got in touch with two people who claimed to work for one of the biggest producers in Hollywood. Not put off by the type of productions it was famous for, Ed's enthusiasm only increased when these two fly-by-night producers then claimed they were confident of landing Prince to play the lead role. Funnily enough, Prince, who was by then making his name as a controversial talent who could cross over from R'n'B to the mainstream, wasn't much younger than Johnson was when he died. But when Ed enthused about the project I swear I could see stars in his eyes. He'd got the fever for it.

Ed was insistent that he wanted me to come along. By now I was seeing myself as his lawyer for all business, not just laundering, and I thought, what the hell, I might as well add entertainment law to my ever-expanding portfolio of expertise.

First he sent me to Delray Beach, north of Fort Lauderdale, to meet a retired entertainment lawyer to learn a few pointers about showbusiness. One of his tips was to read *Variety* to keep abreast of what was going on.

The next thing we're on the move, first to collect a bemused Gray from his condominium and then on to the plane to California.

For once I didn't have to withhold the truth from Monique. She just raised her eyes and saw it as another of Ed's impractical schemes to make money. Dealers, like the rest of us, have dreams sometimes – but they can fund them.

We landed in Hollywood, with the screenwriter in tow, trying our best to look like legitimate Miami businessmen, with sharp suits and shades. We stayed at a top Beverly Hills hotel but I had some trouble rousing the screenwriter for our meeting in the morning, as he habitually slept with eyeshades and earplugs. He was a bit unusual.

When the time came to meet the producers, it became clear it might take a miracle for this project to get off the ground. As we made our introductions to the two men at their office on the Pacific Coast Highway, I turned to Andre and whispered: 'These guys look like hustlers not producers.'

The wise guys could just as well have been on *Miami Vice* they seemed so much like your typical dopers. They certainly talked a good game and made the right noises and Ed came away from the meeting feeling energized and convinced it was going to happen. I had my doubts, but wanted to appear optimistic.

During the all-day meeting, ideas about who would play

which part were being bandied about and Ed was getting more and more excited. The producers were predicting that a soundtrack featuring Eric Clapton, the Stones and others performing versions of Johnson's songs could be even more profitable than the picture itself. They were happily agreeing to all of Ed's demands, which basically amounted to his name appearing as 'Executive Producer' on the credits.

After hours thrashing out the details, the meeting ended with the producers making assurances that their lawyers would finalize the contract and send it east for us to sign. Ed and Kelly hit Rodeo Drive to celebrate with a massive spending spree in designer stores. Then we hit the bars on Sunset Strip for an all-night drinking binge.

We had to be up early to catch the plane back to Miami. We dropped the screenwriter off at his Coconut Grove home. On the way, Ed was keen to brainstorm new ideas on how we could further clean up his dirty cash — and come up with ways to avoid detection from the increasingly vigilant Customs and coastguard.

As it happened, I had a suggestion for another scheme that I was intending to run by Ed and my other clients.

'You know that accountant I put you in touch with to sort out your taxes?'

'Who? That Lewis guy?' Ed seemed bored.

'Yes,' I said. 'He could have a method of legitimizing some of your money without it ever leaving the US.'

Now I had Ed's attention. 'I'm listening.'

I told him how Lewis had clients who sold food items in bulk. They had large stockpiles of product and huge sales teams to shift the goods. Nearly all of the business was done in cash. The boss of this firm — in return for a large fee — was offering to effectively hire some of Ed's team as salesmen. The new employees would be paid purely on commission.

The employees wouldn't actually turn up for work but they'd be put through the books as if they were high-performing salesmen. For a year the new recruits would be selling things left and right. The sales records for the employees would be fictitious but covered because the firm has sufficient inventory on hand. The clients would appear to be super salesmen.

It could even be that some of the sales were overseas to bogus companies in Third World countries, where it's very hard to get proper records.

The firm pays out the commission on the sales and the employee/client pays tax on the commission to keep everything above board. I told Ed he could pump as much as he liked into the firm and it would come out as taxable earnings.

'After two years,' I said, 'they could even use their clean funds to purchase their own legitimate business – say, a restaurant – and you can launder more cash through that.'

Ed beamed. 'A restaurant, you say?'

He shot Kelly a look. She said nothing but returned a smile that suggested they were now operating on a non-verbal level.

'This is brilliant,' he said, sitting forward in his seat. 'I love it. Can you do this salesman thing for Kelly and me?'

'Don't see why not. It's been done before. The firm has fallen on hard times and needs the injection of cash to get it back into profit. You'll be doing them a favour.'

I went on: 'The added bonus if you and Kelly do it is that it also shows a means of support on your house. No one can question where you get the money because it's all there in the books. And I take it you don't mind paying a little something back in tax from those obscene profits you're making.'

'Not at all,' said Ed. 'Well done, brother.' He liked to say that we were as close as brothers, but I always doubted his affection. After all, I had been warned early on that he would be the first to cave.

He sat back in his seat. But he was relaxed for barely a split second. His face turned gravely serious again.

'Right,' he said, sitting forward once more. 'This could be a way to launder some cash but what are we going to do about the boats?'

Ed explained he'd lost one after a Customs seizure. Although no drugs were found it was enough to show that they were attracting attention. He was worried that if he didn't throw Customs off the scent he wouldn't be able to keep trafficking.

Kelly piped up.

'What we need is something that Customs will never touch if they board the boat; something they won't think to look into.'

Ed nodded but there was silence for a few moments while everyone tried to think of a solution.

'I think I might have it,' Ed said. 'Safety gear.'

We all looked blankly.

'Safety equipment is the one thing on a boat that is hands off. Nobody would touch that.'

Our response continued to suggest we needed more convincing.

'If we could hide the gear in some kind of safety thing – like a life raft – Customs would never think to look there. If they raided us at sea, even if they ripped the boat apart and found nothing, they'd still not seize or destroy any safety gear because what would happen if the boat sank in a storm? They'd be in big trouble.

'If we could create something totally bogus but perfect for storage, I think we could be on to something.'

Kelly nodded, leaned over and planted a kiss theatrically on his cheek.

'You're a genius.'

Andre and I looked at each other sceptically. The idea might be good on paper but we saw it working as successfully as Ed's movie plans.

My suspicions on the film front were confirmed just a couple of weeks after we returned from California. Doing what the retired lawyer had advised me, I was leafing through the latest edition of *Variety* when I spotted an interesting news item. Two Hollywood producers, who had been caught and accused of massive fraud, were sacked from their studio and were now the subject of a million-dollar lawsuit.

No prizes for guessing which producers.

The news was a setback for Ed, because he had grown up in Hollywood and dreamed of being a success there. I half expected him to try his luck with a different studio and keep pushing until he found a partner but he seemed resigned to his fate and appeared keen to move on.

Clearly it was going to take something bigger than that to deflect him off course. It wasn't long before I discovered his latest scheme. A few weeks later he called me round to his house excitedly. When I arrived he greeted me holding up what looked like a big white torpedo, with big lettering and stickers down one side.

'What's that?' I asked, forgetting the conversation on the way back from California.

'It's the Stayfloat,' he replied, as if it was obvious.

It certainly seemed like something that you would see on a yacht. Along the side of the tube were all manner of genuine-looking insignias and patented trademarks and the name of the manufacturers in Florida who designed it.

'It is an emergency flotation device,' he announced, as if he'd just invented the wheel. 'It is to be carried below decks so that should the boat ever capsize in a storm these sealed tubes will keep it from sinking and the vessel will right itself.'

'Will it actually do that?' I asked.

Ed observed me incredulously.

'It will be full of coke. But Customs don't know that. They

only know that if they touch these they could damage the boat's chances of surviving a big storm.'

'Where did you get it from?' Genuine respect now crept into my voice.

'They were designed and built for us at a factory down in the industrial district in Hialeah. Pretty realistic, huh?'

I had to agree. This was impressive.

'I'm going to store them in containers under the deck. Customs are welcome to break into the containers but I'm sure once they see they are flotation devices they won't want to touch them.'

I watched him turn the plastic tube over in his hands, caressing it and admiring his brilliance. I had to hand it to him though. If he applied his considerable talents to any other line of work he could quite easily have been an industry leader or someone who made a real difference somewhere to society. He'd just chosen to apply his skills to furthering the profits of drug producers.

He smiled at me.

'Come on,' he said, putting his arm around me. 'Let's get a drink.'

As we went off to the kitchen, a thought struck me. The fact that he was comfortable showing me his schemes highlighted the unusual attorney–crook relationship that, for the most part, we now enjoyed.

Until I had met Ed I had tended to put a wall up between myself and those I performed professional services for. But we were both up to our necks in illicit enterprises which were involving increasingly innovative covert operations.

In the same way as the Mafia kept everything in the family, so we too were now demonstrating the same closeness, at the same time gradually blocking off anyone – former colleagues, neighbours, even family members – who might get wind.

Ed got me a beer and we clinked bottles in celebration.

'I've got another thing to tell you,' he said, a self-satisfied look spreading across his face.

'What's that,' I asked.

'Remember you said we could invest in a restaurant?'

'Not sure I said that, just that it could be an option after you laundered some of the profits.'

'Whatever. Anyway, that's what I'm going to do – invest in my own restaurant. Kelly too. It will be our hangout. Think about it. A secure place we can eat, drink and plan our next move. Miami will never have seen anything like it.'

He was borderline brilliant but at that moment believed he was bullet-proof.

Although such a restaurant could potentially be a focal point for the DEA and Customs to monitor his every move, it wasn't that bad an idea. It was a venture to pump money into, I told him, and another way to clean the cash.

'That's what I like about you, Ken,' he said, smiling. 'Always thinking about work.'

For a while after that Ed and I were practically inseparable. It made for some interesting excursions.

As much as possible the city of Coral Gables, the upscale Miami suburb where Monique and I had made our home, celebrated the union with its sister city Cartagena, in Colombia. The cities are officially twinned through their beauty and elegance. But the other thing the third oldest city in the new world – after Havana and Santo Domingo – has in common with Miami, aside from long sandy beaches, is the amount of cocaine that floods its streets each year.

That's something the city fathers were keen to play down, but my clients and I were keen to explore Cartagena as a party destination.

In my first summer after starting my new career as a launderer and as Colombia geared up for the annual celebrations, Ed, Andre, Benny and some other key players proposed to fly down for the annual Caribbean music festival in Cartagena, held over five days in two huge bullfighting arenas.

I had a more novel idea. I paid a visit to the mayor's office and convinced him to make me the city's official representative for the twin cities programme. I asked if, in my official capacity, I could take a delegation down to Cartagena as ambassadors for Coral Gables.

Astonishingly, my wish was granted and, armed with an official city flag and an illuminated proclamation, we partied for five days, staying up all night, fuelled by the country's main exported commodity. We got our hands on a large quantity of coke, which sold for an impossibly cheap three dollars a gram, and having obtained the necessary equipment, created our very own freebase in the hotel room. It was a trick we'd perfected on Andre's kitchen range and shows the level we were going to find that extra high. Then freebase was the most addictive way to abuse cocaine. Notorious as the drug that caused American comedian Richard Pryor to sustain life-threatening burns when the heat source he was using to smoke it ignited his clothing, it was relatively simple to produce.

It involved mixing powdered cocaine with baking soda and water and heating it in a test tube. The end result was cocaine base, literally the precursor of cocaine hydrochloride. Then it was a case of serve immediately.

As one friend joked: 'You will never see a piece of freebase lying around someone's house; if you have it, you smoke it.'

The rush was extremely intense, and one that users wanted to repeat over and over again. The other benefit, if there was such a thing, was that, unlike with cocaine powder, you did not lose your appetite for food. As the base required users to employ an extremely high temperature heat source when turning the base into vapour before it was inhaled, there was always the chance you could set yourself or possibly the whole room on fire. We might have been getting out of our minds but I never forgot my volunteer fireman training and was careful to remove anything flammable before we got down to business. The last thing I wanted in Cartagena was five fried bodies in a hotel room I needed to explain.

We partied hard but, making sure we fulfilled our ambassadorial duties, we paid a visit to the mayor of Cartagena and presented the document to him.

I'm sure if the mayor of Coral Gables knew his official diplomats, and their lawyer, were actually traffickers, he might have thought twice about endorsing us, but it demonstrated how effortlessly my clients and I were able to slip between mainstream America and the illicit world.

We had a great time and, when it was time to go home, I decided it would be good to take back a couple of bottles of the white rum Tres Esquinas, which wasn't readily available in the US – 'three corners', striking because of its triangular bottle. I handed one of the bottles to Tony, one of Ed's cohorts who, like me, had served in Vietnam. I passed through Customs without incident, but Tony was not so lucky. Still the worse for wear from the excessive partying, he was hauled to one side. Clearly he'd forgotten about the alcohol inside his bag and, when the officers opened it up, the pungent aroma of a broken bottle of drink hit them instantly.

The Customs officer asked him: 'What was the purpose of your trip to Colombia, sir?'

Still drunk, Tony slurred: 'Fun and sun.'

He was to discover that US Customs don't have a sense of humour when it comes to liquor being brought into the country by intoxicated travellers.

They detained him for twelve hours, for questioning and to

let him sober up, which was a shame because we got straight off the plane to yet another party. It was a tradition among our clientele to hold Friday the 13th parties. In that year – 1981 – there were three.

While Tony dried out in the slammer, we held a massive outdoor party at Andre's, buying large quantities of beer from all over the world, and filling up children's paddling pools with ice to keep them all cool.

For the first time in five days I saw Monique. She was working as a sergeant in the white-collar crime division. The irony of the situation – where she was now investigating professionals committing crimes – was not lost on the rest of the gang. Her new role meant longer hours and we'd started to see even less of each other.

'Sounds like you all had a good time,' she remarked when I regaled her of our exploits in Colombia. 'I wish I could've been there.'

'There'll be other trips,' I said, trying not to make a big deal of it.

'Hmm, maybe,' she replied. If I'd been more switched on I might have detected the first signs that while we'd always kept our professional lives as separate as possible, our social lives were heading that way too.

Instead I grabbed another cool beer and was distracted by the commotion that greeted Tony's arrival at the party, several hours after the rest of us.

I left Monique standing as I rushed to hear about his ordeal. The beer continued to flow, the music played and as line after line of cocaine disappeared I really couldn't see a downside to this enterprise.

11. Trouble in Paradise?

'Paradise Lost' proclaimed the banner headline.

Time magazine had long been known for its front pages but this one in particular caught my eye on the news-stand as I walked through Miami airport.

The cover was a picture of the Sunshine State, with 'South Florida' in bold letters, of the type you would see in any tourist brochure. However, closer inspection showed that making up the letters were images that Florida would not want projected around the world.

Villains – some of whom might have met untimely and violent ends – wads of cash and drug seizures were seemingly replacing flamingos, beaches and palm trees as archetypal images from America's southern state.

Instead of the lush green colouring afforded to the cover graphic of north Florida, the south was lit up in danger red, with a burning intensity over my own Miami; Mr Sun, usually so smiley, was wearing a stern frown.

Inside was a picture of a policeman leaning over the body of a man whose throat had been slit, his wallet emptied. Another photo showed a speedboat, loaded with a half-ton of marijuana, skimming across the waters of Biscayne Bay. And in another was a group of Cuban refugees, living in a tent underneath a highway overpass.

South Florida was labelled a region in chaos. Apparently an epidemic of violent crime, a plague of illicit drugs and a flood of Mariel refugees had engulfed the state, and Miami in particular, like a tidal wave. The prosperous but somewhat sleepy destination favoured by retired Americans everywhere was in danger of being destroyed by gangs and dirty cash.

Time listed a catalogue of statistics. In the most recent FBI list of the ten most crime-ridden cities, three of them were in south Florida, with Miami in the unenviable position of top spot. Behind it, West Palm Beach was fifth worst and Fort Lauderdale eighth. Miami also boasted America's highest murder rate – 70 per 100,000 residents – and it was predicted that rate would rocket higher still. About a third of these murders were drug-related.

Of all the marijuana and cocaine that flooded into the US, an estimated 70 per cent passed through south Florida. Drug smuggling, it said, could have been the region's major industry, worth between $7 billion and $12 billion a year, topping even real estate and tourism.

Apparently there were so many drug-related fifty- and hundred-dollar bills flushing around the system in Miami that the city's Federal Reserve Bank had a surplus of $5 billion. Drug money, the article went on to say, was responsible for corrupting banking, real estate, law and even the fishing industry, where boats were more interested in landing what were called square groupers (marijuana bales) than the scaly variety.

If nothing were done, the whole region, *Time* was effectively saying, would be going to hell in a handcart.

I shrugged, rolled up the magazine, shoved it into my bag and strode out into the fading evening sunshine. I'd just returned from Sint Maarten where I'd exploited another loophole in the tax havens.

Rather than my usual trip to Anguilla, I'd chartered a small private plane to Road Town, capital of the British Virgin Islands, and told the pilot – a contact of Andre's called Trevor Gilchrist – to stay in the plane. From there I hired a small jitney bus and had the driver take me to the offices of an accountant named William O'Leary. An associate of Henry Jackson's, O'Leary had a shelf-load of newly formed companies. I took one company off the shelf, bought it and then it was back on the bus, aboard the plane and then out of there before anyone knew I had ever set foot on the island.

From Miami airport I just had time to grab a taxi home, then a shower and a quick change and I was heading straight over to a party Bernard was hosting on Miami Beach.

With Monique working, as usual it seemed these days, I arrived to find the house empty and glanced at our new black 3-series BMW sitting outside the house – the one visible sign of wealth in our otherwise low-key existence. On a whim we'd decided we needed another car. We went to the dealer and told him we'd had our eye on the 318i. The salesman was ready to give us his pitch on finance payments when I opened the brief-case and said: 'If it's okay with you I'd rather pay cash.'

Monique had been giddy with excitement when he'd handed us the keys – a concession that masked the imperfections in our relationship.

'This is great,' she had said, beaming. She long suspected what was funding our new lifestyle but was choosing to turn a blind eye. I wasn't sure how long I could keep the full truth from her but I was grateful she wasn't asking questions.

She wasn't the only one. Everyone in Miami was in on the game. Even the car dealer, who'd just gleefully sold one of his executive motors, was in on it. Under normal circumstances he should have reported the suspicious payment – but he was happy to take the cash, no questions asked. He had offered a disguised loan arrangement, with the cash under the waterline, but I had declined.

I got changed and glanced at the bottom of the closet. Cash was bulging out of suitcases in bundles of hundred-dollar bills.

It looked as if I'd just robbed the Federal Reserve. I wondered how many of those bills were tainted by drugs, as the article had said. All of them?

Monique's job might have been the excuse I could give why I'd be going to Bernard's party alone. But the truth was she'd already made it clear she didn't want to come. She'd never met the Frenchman but knew enough about his business interests to know she would be better served steering clear.

'I have no idea who's going to be there,' she'd said a few days earlier when I enquired about whether she'd be joining me. 'And I don't want to know.'

So instead I arrived at Bernard's on my own to find the party was just getting into full swing. It wasn't the best environment for a cop like her – but many of her colleagues in the squad would have given their right arm to be there.

It was a rogues' gallery of smugglers and distributors from all over North America and Cuba. Cocaine was being chopped up on a glass table. Charlie was there with his crowd that attracted groupies, and whichever direction you looked beautiful young women were hanging off the traffickers as though they were rock stars. The champagne was on ice, the beers were cooling in the bath, the music was pumping and the rooms were full of people, all with a vested interest in the trade.

As I looked back into the house I mused over something Monique had said about the people I now seemed to spend every waking hour with, or working for. Were they clients, were they friends, were they semi-clients? The lines had been blurred so much I wasn't sure any more.

Not long after I'd started with the big city law firm, the head of the DEA in Miami stated there are criminal defence lawyers and then there are attorney criminals. Whichever way I tried to dress it up I was now an attorney criminal, wholly committed to the clients to get their cash and launder it.

Life was a constant conflict. On one side I was a lawyer practising law, even representing police officers – a regular person in
the community. But the flipside was that I was also quietly representing people I knew were career criminals. My attorney–client
privilege meant nothing now.

I don't know why I was thinking of this stuff now. Maybe
that magazine article had shaken me up, brought up a few home
truths.

It was Bernard who shook me out of my contemplative
mood.

'Kenneth.' He approached me with two glasses of strong
drink, handing me one. 'My friend, how did you get on today?'

'Good. Everything is as you asked.'

'C'est magnifique. Come, let's celebrate. You look like you
could do with a pick-me-up.'

We joined the throng. The truth was that by then my business with Bernard was fitting in nicely with the work I was doing
for the existing kingpins. I had been forming charter company
after charter company in Anguilla for him and his partners as
fronts for boats they were using to smuggle cocaine and pot.

Practically each week he would have more funds for me,
either to invest in offshore accounts, or to fund the registration
of overseas corporations. In Anguilla the US dollars could be
exchanged for New York drafts, cheques drawn upon the island
bank's correspondent account in Manhattan. Bernard would
have those instruments couriered to a bearer share corporate
account in Panama. Later the money would travel to such places
as the Republic of China (Taiwan) and France. It meant I could
piggyback his jobs on to trips I was making to Anguilla for Ed,
Benny or Charlie, who was increasingly branching out on his
own.

It had now got to the stage where I was performing so many
tasks for different clients and their associates that I could marry

up trades between the companies formed for the different client groups. If one group needed a cashier's cheque for five hundred thousand dollars and a second client of mine had funds offshore that it wanted repatriated, in cash, to the US, the solution was easy.

I called it The Switch. I purchased the cheque offshore, in the tax havens of the Caribbean, for one client with the funds of another, and paid the client who wanted his funds back in the US with the money the other client needed to send offshore.

If I do say so myself, it was smart because that way I wasn't even transferring funds anywhere. I wasn't even exposing anyone and there was no risk of losing any of the money.

Recently I had even managed to fit in some legitimate work during my trips to the tax havens. Ray Stevens was an American businessman who relocated to the Dutch Antilles and owned a luxury condo on Miami's Brickell Key that I had helped him purchase. His circumstances changed and when he had to move back to the States he rented out his villa to a couple; within just a couple of months his tenants had fled, abandoning the property. Ray asked me to check it out, which was easy enough to do as I was heading down there for my usual weekend trip for George and some other clients.

After completing my illegal activity for the day I popped round to inspect the beautiful, ocean-front property. Although it was still in reasonable order a couple of things caught my eye. A small closet was stuffed with camouflage clothing and radio and navigational equipment that could only have come from a small plane. Could it be that the house had been used as a 'front' property for a cartel?

Ray was relieved that his property was intact and he soon rented it out again to a respectable businessman. But I turned over the equipment I found to US Customs who vowed to investigate. Well, I wouldn't want anyone to think I wasn't fulfilling my duties as an officer of the court, now, would I?

And off the back of all of this, I was making a handsome profit for my services.

I was performing a high-wire act but so far I was pulling it off. With each trip I got bolder, with each scam I wanted to devise a better one.

What could go wrong?

After toasting the success of our working relationship with Bernard, I walked over to the table and casually hoovered up two fat lines of cocaine in quick succession, then, topping up my glass, walked out on to the balcony. The thumping music from the party behind me filtered out into the darkening sky. Out in the bay lights twinkled against the twilight. Customs were out in force, but it was like a finger in the dyke trying to stem the flow of drugs into Miami.

I felt the rush explode in my brain. Everything seemed brilliant again.

'Hey, what are you doing out here on your own?'

I turned. It was one of the girls who worked as a crew member on the smuggling boats. She couldn't have been more than twenty-five, had long, shiny blonde hair and was dressed to kill in a figure-hugging white leather skirt and tube top.

'I was just getting some air,' I said.

'Come on in, you're missing a great party.'

She grinned, took my hand and led me back into the party, her heels clicking on the tiled floor. As I followed, now buzzing from my cocaine high, I thought once again of the magazine article I'd seen coming off the plane.

Paradise Lost? What the hell were they talking about?

12. Where Did I Put That Fifty Thousand Dollars?

'Excuse me, Mr Rijock, sir? There seems to be a discrepancy in the amount you wish to deposit today.'

William was a teller at the bank I'd used before and he was clearly apologetic for disturbing me.

'Really?' I queried. 'That's annoying. Tell me how much it is short and I'll make up the difference myself.'

I had already produced my wallet and started flicking through some cash, irked that either my new client or I had been careless with their accounting. In all the time I'd been laundering I'd never been out by even so much as a dollar. Although I hated carrying large bundles of cash on my person – save for the several hundreds of thousands of dollars I packed into a case for my regular Sint Maarten runs – I often made sure I had about a couple of thousand dollars on me in case of emergencies.

I pulled out a bundle and stood ready to thumb out an amount. The teller looked at me, the concern still etched on his face.

'So,' I repeated. 'How much are we out?'

'Er,' he paused. 'Fifty thousand dollars . . . exactly.'

'What?'

I was incredulous. What kind of stunt was this?

'Check it again. You must be making a mistake. Or the calibration of your counting machine is out. This is impossible.'

'We have double-checked, Mr Rijock, sir. You said you wished to deposit three hundred thousand dollars. We only have two hundred and fifty thousand here. There is no problem with the machine.'

This couldn't be, I thought. Not today. No, no, no. The initial mild annoyance at my own professionalism being questioned had now been swept away by a full-on panic. What the hell was going on?

I started to pat my pockets, frantically pulling out the bills and receipts and other bits of paper as if I seriously expected to find fifty thousand in hundred-dollar bills hiding in there. I opened up my bag and parted the loose items of clothing to find only the leather bottom of the case.

I raised my head at the teller, who stood there, expecting me to produce the errant cash.

'Well?' I said.

'Sir?'

'I don't have it. The mistake has to be with your machine. I need to see the president, someone senior, someone who can clear this up.'

'Of course,' he replied, giving me the kind of mockingly sympathetic look a doctor gives a patient when they're telling them there's nothing they can do.

I looked around me, eyeing my fellow bank customers suspiciously. Had someone picked my pocket, got to my bag when I wasn't looking?

I could feel the heat building. God, I needed to lay off the coke. It was making me paranoid.

But what if it wasn't the drugs? What if someone had dipped me?

This was ridiculous, the cash had never left my sight. Plus how would anyone have been able to get some of the money but not all?

Still, my near daily fix didn't help in moments like this.

I started staring at the floor, stepping back carefully from my spot as though not to disturb the crime scene. I looked to the door but it was crazy to think there would be a trail of cash leading out into the street as if they'd all fallen from a hole in the pocket of my shorts.

Wait a minute . . . not out of my sight? Well, the cash hadn't been, except for when I'd stashed it in the ventilator shaft above the sink in the bathroom of my hotel room.

Surely this couldn't be. I checked my watch. It was still 10 a.m. Among the debris I'd pulled from my pocket I noticed I still had the room key. I hadn't checked out yet. Was there still time to go back to the hotel and check the room before the cleaners moved in?

I banked the cash I did have and headed back to the hotel.

Pushing my way past startled pedestrians on the street on my way to the water taxi rank, I tried to work out what could have happened.

This had been no ordinary trip to Sint Maarten. True, the route was the same, the deposit routine and the length of stay customary. But this had been the first time I'd worked on behalf of a new client.

My mind went back to that party at Bernard's ocean-front condo on Miami Beach just a few weeks before. It was at that party that I'd discovered how Bernard's little operation worked. I'd watched stunned as he went round each of his associates in turn whispering in hushed Spanish: '*Tengo un regalo para usted*' ('I have a gift for you').

I understood the Spanish, but not the code. Charlie deciphered.

'That means their delivery of a Chinese junk has come in to Miami.'

'What?' I queried, naively. 'All these people are into sailing traditional junks?'

Charlie smiled and explained. When the ships passed through

the Panama Canal, they picked up a little cargo. By the time they arrived in Miami the dealers got not only their boat but also a shipment of Colombia's finest. It meant Bernard had new stocks he could sell. Each boat, Charlie said, could be carrying a cargo of cocaine worth as much as $10 million, maybe more.

I let out a whistle.

Later that night, Bernard had introduced me to a fellow cocaine smuggler. Alain Lacombe had been a French Canadian like Bernard, although older and plumper, but he'd also struck me as someone with whom I could do a lot of transactions. Like Bernard, he'd seemed very businesslike in his demeanour. Our host had been raving about my qualities as a lawyer who could clean money without a trace.

Lacombe had suggested he wanted a trial run with a modest $150,000 to open an offshore account. Bernard had also given me another $150,000 to cover some boat registrations and a few deposits. It had been effortlessly simple and was just one example of the clients I was acquiring nearly every month.

Had I now lost $50,000 of a new client's money? What would this mean to my relationship with Bernard?

The Dutch-owned hotel had not been one I'd stayed in before but I'd often passed it on the way to a few of my more regular haunts and considered trying it out.

The trip back took an eternity. I got to the harbour to find not one single water taxi waiting. Usually they were queuing up.

As I paced up and down I went over the last two days. Had I counted the cash? Had I been preoccupied with keeping the bundles separate?

Both Bernard's and Lacombe's cash had been bundled in neat blocks of hundred-dollar bills. Routinely I'd removed the rubber bands and wrappers and loosened up the notes while trying to keep them in their bundles. I always removed anything solid in case the airport scanners detected anything unusual.

How was I going to explain this? As if it were possible, my agitation grew on the short ferry ride from Anguilla back to Sint Maarten. A fellow traveller tried to strike up a conversation. Ordinarily I enjoyed these casual acquaintances because I felt it helped draw suspicion away from me from any watching undercover cops or DEA agents. Today, though, I scowled.

'Cheer up, buddy,' one elderly tourist chirped up.

I growled. He thought better of it.

Back in the room I grabbed the chair next to the dresser, put it in the bathroom and unscrewed the air vent.

I peered into the steel air duct. Nothing. It looked empty. I shoved my arm into the steel tunnel and felt around the darkness. Still nothing. In my haste last night had I pushed some notes around the corner? I jumped down, went to the wardrobe and pulled out a hanger. Quickly I fashioned a straight rod with a hook on the end, climbed up and probed around in the vent. Again, nothing.

I jumped down and sat on the bed. For the tenth time I checked my briefcase, forlornly hoping I'd find a secret stash I'd somehow overlooked.

Nothing. Where had the cash gone? How was I going to explain this to Bernard, let alone Lacombe? It was one thing to mess up for a client but I had the added shame of embarrassing Bernard because it was on the basis of his recommendation that his friend had placed his faith in me.

I felt sure Bernard would not have short-changed me. We'd only been working together for a short while but in the deposits I had made for him he had always been scrupulous.

Maybe this had been some sort of test. Had there really been $150,000 in the first place? Had Lacombe been checking to see if the money had been deposited at all? If I'd reported back that the money had been safely deposited and presented him with a fake receipt, would that have been proof that I was a conman?

Perhaps when I reported the shortfall it would be evidence that I wasn't corrupt. But as I got on the plane back to Miami I knew I could never admit losing the dollars.

I met Bernard over lunch and reluctantly told him what had happened.

He shrugged. 'It is Alain's money?'

'It was. Your deposit was as discussed.'

'No problem then,' he said, and carried on eating. To Bernard Calderon, $50,000 was loose change.

In any event he had more pressing matters he wanted to discuss. He was still desperate for me to arrange economic passports for St Kitts.

'I have just come back from a very interesting meeting in Panama with some Colombians. It was very fruitful. And should secure supplies for many months to come. What will help smooth relations is if I can deliver the passports they desire.'

I said I'd do my best to arrange them.

From out of his pocket he took a small collection of photographs and handed them to me. He continued eating and, through mouthfuls of sea bass, said: 'These are the people who want the passports.'

I flicked through the pictures. There were three of them – mug shots of Colombians who looked like they would kill their own brothers for a nickel. My heart froze. I recognized one of them. It was a member of the Ochoa family, a highly placed lieutenant in the Medellín cartel.

So this was where Bernard was getting his cocaine. My speculations about the source of the coke had been correct. I was caught between Colombian lords and potentially the Mafia. Good going, Ken.

I nodded and calmly stored the photographs in my case, hoping that Bernard was too preoccupied with eating his grilled fish to see that my hands were shaking.

'Okay, leave it with me,' was all I could think to say.

We finished lunch and parted before walking to our cars. Watching Bernard roar off in his Jag I sat in my car and contemplated what I was on the verge of getting myself into.

Aside from the Ochoa brothers, the most notorious of the Medellín cartel was Pablo Escobar. Their empire was estimated to be worth tens of billions of dollars and responsible for the deaths of thousands of people, like those murdered by Griselda Blanco.

What would happen if I refused this request? What would happen if money from a deal that involved the Cotrone family went missing? I'd managed so far to avoid dealing directly with Freddie and Enzo, but what if they were the real beneficiaries of a transaction I organized through Carlos Hernandez? My life would be on the line.

I was still feeling on edge as I drove home. I turned into our street and again froze.

Outside our nondescript little home were two police cars. It wasn't unusual to have a squad car pull up at our home; Monique was a cop after all. But something about this, today, made me uneasy. Seeing those pictures that Bernard gave me brought everything into sharp focus.

Were those cars a coincidence? Was it just friends visiting Monique? Shouldn't she be at work anyway? For a moment I thought about driving past the house, keeping on going.

But something – maybe the same reckless curiosity that got me into this life in the first place – made me park the car and, as calmly as I could, walk into the house to see what twist the fates had in store.

It wasn't quite what I feared. Monique was sitting at the kitchen table. Sitting with her were two male detectives.

'Hi, honey.' Monique greeted me with her usual enthusiasm, getting off her chair and embracing me with a kiss.

'I was hoping you'd stop by. This is Barney and Dan. They were hoping you might be able to help them.'

'Mr Rijock,' the first cop said, extending his hand. Did police officers ever slip out of their rigid formality?

'Our friend Paddy told us what a good job you did representing him. We have our own legal disputes we'd like to run by you.'

'Oh, is that all?' I said, relieved. 'I thought I was in trouble there for a second.'

'No, no. Nothing like that,' the second cop said. 'Have you just run a red or something?'

Everyone laughed. I joined in nervously, jaw twitching.

'Something like that,' I said, thinking of the pictures sitting in my pocket. 'Maybe just the sight of you guys naturally makes people feel nervous.'

It turned out Barney and Dan had some low-level litigation matters that needed a lawyer's expertise and once again they had been left without legal representation.

I listened to their stories and promised to help them out, adding them to my list of things to do. After all, a lawyer can't be choosy about whom he works for. Sure we can decline work, but the more legitimate clients I had on the go the better – and what better endorsement for a legal practice than cops? This I could deal with.

It was only when they left that I started to relax for the first time since my lunch with Bernard.

'Why are you home today anyway?' I asked Monique when we were alone again.

'Have you forgotten? I'm taking the afternoon off because John is bringing over Katherine and Luke.'

'No, no, I haven't forgotten,' I fibbed. 'I just thought it was later on.'

Monique's children were with us for the summer holidays. As

if life wasn't complicated enough I was now going to be playing full-time parent to teenagers. Katherine and Luke were good kids and I appreciated what a lift it would be for Monique to be reunited with them for an extended period.

She enjoyed a strained but civil relationship with her ex-husband John but it had been extremely hard for her to be parted from her kids while she tried to carve out her career.

Because we'd been seeing less and less of each other these days she continued to put no pressure on me to get married, which was at least some relief. Since I'd got deeper and deeper into the laundering, it only reinforced my attitude that we shouldn't be legally bound. Should anything happen to me, Monique could be liable, lose her job, be arrested or at the very least lose everything if the courts decided to pursue a case to recover proceeds of crime. She might not see it now but, in the same way she had made a tough decision for the sake of her children, I had to do this to protect her.

The kids arrived that afternoon and we set about trying to be a family, however unorthodox. We'd had them to stay with us periodically, but this was eight weeks of concentrated parenting. Already I'd found it strange experiencing what it was like to be a father back to front – when the children were already adolescents.

Any worries I had about whether having the children stay with us would interfere with my work were dispelled. I already had my routine and was well practised in keeping any sensitive information from Monique, so I just extended that policy to include the kids.

In fact, when I returned from my regular trips to the Caribbean we enjoyed a normal family life. We barbecued at the weekend, took trips to the malls and Coconut Grove.

To anyone poking their nose in we were an average family; the lawyer, his police officer wife and their two children.

So I was fairly relaxed when Monique informed me that she and John had agreed that Katherine and Luke would extend their stay with us indefinitely, continuing to attend their private school and making Coral Gables their permanent home.

'Sure,' I said, to Monique's obvious delight. 'What harm can come of it?'

13. Your Fee, Señor Rijock

It was Charlie who recommended them.

He'd been itching to leave Benny and his brother and branch out on his own. Now he'd got himself involved with the Martinez brothers, slightly rougher around the edges than the Cubans I'd usually prefer to deal with.

Sticking to my rule of only accepting new business personally recommended from an existing client, I found it hard to say no when Charlie introduced me to Joey, the youngest of the brothers.

I didn't appreciate it then but Joey was the acceptable public face of the Martinez family. Although I would later discover he demonstrated characteristics that today would be indicators of a deeper personality disorder – a short attention span, easily excitable and, what seemed to be a prerequisite for a member of his family, a quick temper – he seemed calm, intelligent and willing to listen to advice when we first met.

Although they were relatively young, the brothers seemed to have an impressive little operation. Their front was a real-estate business, which meant they could lay their hands on several short-term safe houses that they could use for their illegal trafficking before moving on to the next property.

Joey was handsome and sharp – and could easily pass as a commission-hungry realtor. He could be charming too. During our introductory meeting with Charlie – who had delivered Bernard to me after all – Joey impressed me by bringing the conversation on to Vietnam, a subject still close to my heart.

'Charlie tells me you were in 'Nam,' he said. I nodded.

'My brother Enrique was there too. It sounded brutal, man. He came back a changed man.'

'Really?' Strangely enough, after experiencing years when civilized society did not want to acknowledge that that fifteen-year conflict had ever existed, since I had been involved with the trade everyone had a Vietnam story to tell.

'Where was he?'

'He was a Marine. Served two years and was eventually recruited by the CIA for some black ops.'

'Is that so?' His story could be true and, as Charlie was personally vouching for these people, I saw no reason to distrust him.

His request was simple and, for me, straightforward. As with many clients he wanted some offshore corporations formed and had some boats they wanted disguised. Routine work. Set up vessel registrations for cocaine smuggling from the Bahamas into Florida.

As we got up to leave I spotted a flash of metal in his waistband. He was carrying what looked like a semi-automatic pistol in his jeans. This wasn't uncommon. I had even taken to hiding a .45 automatic in my house in case of emergencies; mostly to safeguard against any thefts when I was carrying a lot of cash. I was naturally cautious, however, of cowboys who saw flashing a firearm as some kind of macho statement. These were the kind of hoodlums who exchanged fire in a crowd and settled scores by peppering restaurants with bullets. I had tried to limit my involvement with drug bosses to intelligent, albeit flawed people like Ed, Andre and Bernard.

I raised it with Charlie when we were alone.

'What's the gun for? Is he a wanted man?'

'Don't worry,' he reassured me. 'That's just Joey. He likes to show off. His bark is worse than his bite.'

That's what I was afraid of.

I completed the work for them as ordered. It should then have been a simple task of collecting my fee and we could all get on with our lives.

That was the plan.

But, as I described in the prologue to my story, the reality was I now had a bag of uncut cocaine as a payoff that I didn't know what to do with. And I couldn't reach Andre, my port in a storm.

I drove through the streets of Kendall like a ninety-year-old Sunday driver. Steady as she goes. Nothing to see here. It was a battle to keep the car within the limit when every impulse in my body was screaming to put my foot down.

Why the hell did I accept that bag? I could have left it there. Who cares if it's poor form? Who cares if it causes someone offence? It's nothing compared to the offence I was committing now. Half a kilo of cocaine? That's fifteen years minimum mandatory in a state prison, with a bunch of career criminals. Fifteen fucking years.

Sweat was pouring off my brow, yet I had the cool air on max. Hunched over the wheel, my eyes darted from side to side and into the mirror for any signs of a patrol car, any signs I was being followed.

How long had that black car been behind me? Didn't Feds drive blacked out saloons? It must be the Feds. They could have been watching that house for weeks. Those stupid gun-toting hoods – they will have attracted attention from the cops, the DEA, the FBI, everyone.

I was a dead man already.

Keep it steady. I was crawling along in the middle lane, observing every rule in the highway code. I was the perfect learner driver. Signalling at every turn, driving bang on the limit. I now knew why drivers delivering cocaine on the interstates stay five-to-seven miles per hour under the limit; to stay under the radar.

Finally I was approaching Coral Gables. My only saving grace was that it was the middle of the afternoon. Monique was at work. The kids were at school.

The kids?

My God. The kids. In all this excitement I'd completely forgotten about them. How the hell was I going to hide half a kilo of cocaine in the house without anyone finding it?

I pulled up into our street. Paranoia had now completely taken over. I drove past the house three times checking all the time for cars that could be cops or the DEA staking out the house before I felt brave enough to park up.

Even with the engine off I sat there. What if there was someone in the house? How would I explain the bag?

Eventually deciding I'd make this up as I went along – after all, that strategy had got me this far – I got out of the car. As calmly as I could I walked to the trunk, nervously looked around and lifted the bag out.

I might as well have been carrying a dead body in a rolled-up carpet I felt so conspicuous. Yet all I was doing was carrying a perfectly normal looking bag into my own house. What was suspicious about that?

'Hello-o, I'm home,' I called into the silent house. That was the first time in my life I'd ever done that. Good job no one was home. That alone would have given me away.

As I expected, and hoped for, there was no response.

Like a teenager trying to hide evidence of a party as the parents are walking up the path, I darted from room to room trying to find a place to hide this toxic time-bomb.

Nothing was suitable. No closet so unused it could sit undetected for a day. At one point I even considered hiding it in the kids' rooms. They were so messy they couldn't even find their own stuff. Then I realized that would make me the sickest parent in town.

No, the only place was under the bed, our bed. Monique hardly went under there and even if she did she'd just think it was a bag I was using for my trips to the tax havens.

I shoved it as far under my side of the bed as it would go. For good measure I placed an old pair of sneakers strategically around it. If they were displaced, I figured, I'd know someone had found it.

Surely it would be safe for twenty-four hours?

The following day I called Andre to ask how successful he had been in finding a buyer for this stuff.

'Sorry, buddy. My man's out of town. It's going to take a couple of weeks before I can find someone who'll take it off you. You okay to hold tight for that long?'

'Two weeks! Two weeks! This is Miami. I can't believe you're telling me you can't find someone who wants half a kilo?'

'The people I deal with deal in far bigger quantities, brother. They're doing us a favour. It will be fine. Stop stressing.'

'That's easy for you to say. You don't have two teenagers rifling through your belongings.'

Andre just laughed. 'I'll call you.'

'Yeah, do that.'

This was not in the job description.

Strangely enough, despite my sometimes out-of-control cocaine bingeing, and Monique's fondness for the stuff, we never kept our own supplies around the place. With her being a cop and me a lawyer I didn't want to give the cops any reason to come, for want of a better expression, sniffing around.

That was one of my golden rules. A rule that was now smashed to pieces.

I spent a nervous fortnight worrying that someone would stumble across the bag or find it and try and use it for something.

The last thing I wanted was the children taking it into school or to a sports event.

Andre was true to his word and in two weeks found someone who would buy it for $10,000 – the going rate in a flooded market.

I went to retrieve the bag from under the bed when everyone else was out of the house. Just before I pulled it out I paused.

Wait a minute. I hadn't left that shoe like that, had I? It looked like it had been moved, deliberately. And, when I pulled it out, I saw the bag . . . it was half open. Surely I had left it closed tightly?

Had Monique found it? Thought it was a secret stash she could dip into? The package was still sealed so that ruled that out. Had the children discovered it but were too scared to say?

All I knew was that I wanted it out of the house now.

After the sale, Andre counted out my share of the proceeds and handed it to me. I had agreed to share it with him. After all it was a windfall, and if you cannot share a windfall with your friends, you are not much of a friend yourself.

'There you go, Ken. That wasn't so bad now, was it?'

I glowered at him. 'I don't mind being a bag man. It just depends what's in the bag.'

Andre laughed.

14. The Elevator Exit

It was a Thursday much like any other.

I was in my office, tidying up my legal affairs for the weekend so nothing would delay me from making my usual flight. At home, the clothes I would change into later were already laid out; a Hawaiian shirt and a pair of old shorts, carefully selected to ensure I blended in with the other tourists heading down to Sint Maarten.

In a battered and unremarkable artificial leather attaché case in my bedroom, the bulk of $200,000 in cash was packed, ready to be washed, cleaned and eventually invested for my clients without a trace of its origins. The remainder I would carry on my person, artfully concealed.

The only difference was that today I had a slight complication.

Another job had come up. I had to retrieve a ship's captain who had been caught with 800 kilos of pure cocaine hydrochloride.

Two days earlier Bernard had called me with a problem.

'They have the ship,' he told me. 'Jean-Luc too.'

US Customs had boarded one of his vessels after it entered the Miami river. Once on board they broke into the pilot's house and discovered the drugs.

They arrested everybody, including Bernard's captain Jean-Luc Lenoir. Jean-Luc, an equally charismatic Frenchman, was a loyal associate of my client. Since Tuesday, however, he was looking at a long stretch in prison.

That kind of statistic was enough to test the loyalty of any man.

Jean-Luc's bail was set by the judge at $12 million, the estimated wholesale value of the cocaine. It sounds unreasonably high but that's because the court doesn't want smugglers to walk free. Therefore, even if he wanted to, Bernard was unable to pay for his captain's freedom. For a start, who has $12 million lying around? Moreover, you have to show you earned the money by legitimate means. Unless you're a legitimate millionaire how can you turn up at a court with that kind of money?

Bernard's instructions were clear.

'Get him out of there,' he told me. 'Use whatever pretext you can. There is a fifty-thousand-dollar reward if you can help.'

Since then, Jean-Luc's girlfriend Pascale had called me. Glamorous, slim and effortlessly attractive, Pascale was a typical dealer's girlfriend, lured to the criminal world by the promise of unfathomable wealth, live-fast-die-young pretty boys and the ever-present threat of danger. Unlike most smugglers' molls, however, she wasn't running off at the first sign of trouble and seemed to be sticking with Jean-Luc for the long haul.

Pascale told me that Bernard had fled the country, terrified that now Customs had seized the boat and arrested Jean-Luc it wouldn't take long until they went looking for his boss.

To add to the confusion, since his arrest, Jean-Luc's bond had been reduced and then the Miami state attorney seemed to be dropping all the charges. What was going on here?

My instructions were the same. I had to get Jean-Luc out of the clutches of the state attorney's office by any means I could think of. But this wasn't going to be easy.

When Pascale told me they were dropping the charges against Jean-Luc, for a second I wondered if there was a problem with the evidence. That wasn't the case. When you catch someone red-handed with millions of dollars' worth of cocaine there's no chance they are walking free from court.

I started to smell a rat. Normally it takes twenty-one days to press charges. This case was being expedited with lightning speed. Someone was in a real hurry.

It could mean only one thing. Jean-Luc was to be given immunity from prosecution in exchange for testifying against Bernard and his whole operation. And if Customs traced the drugs to Bernard, that could lead them to me. Not a good thing.

For years Bernard had been defying the attempts by police, Customs and the DEA to find out who was flooding Miami Beach with cocaine.

I'd formed a number of corporations down in the Caribbean and Bernard had taken over the registrations. And the beauty of the British overseas territories in the Caribbean, other than endless white beaches and ten hours of sunshine every day? There it is against the law, punishable by a fine or imprisonment, to lead an inquiry into who owns such a corporation. I always thought that was twisted, yet brilliant.

Now, however, the house of cards could come crashing down.

After I got the call from Bernard, I couldn't go near Jean-Luc until I knew exactly what the exposure was. For a while I thought we would have to sit tight. There was certainly no way I could deal with him. I didn't know if he was cooperating with the authorities. If he rang me I didn't know if I would be taped.

I took my orders from his boss. And when a slightly agitated Pascale rang me to say the charges were being dropped I had to step in. I had to act, not just as an advocate but also as part of a criminal conspiracy whose only motivation was to safeguard their illicit operations.

So late on Thursday morning, instead of clearing my schedule to make my usual overseas laundering trip, I was heading down to the criminal courthouse downtown to find out what was going on. By the time I reached the court, I found the case had indeed been dismissed.

Jean-Luc was technically a free man. But all that meant was that the state attorney had him in his office upstairs and was about to give him immunity in return for his soul – and everything he knew about Bernard.

The dilemma facing Jean-Luc was simple: the charges had been dropped, there was nothing pending; but he now had to testify or go to jail. And they can leave you languishing there for years until you decide to cooperate. A Hobson's choice if ever there was one.

Now I really had to act fast. For all I knew Jean-Luc could have been upstairs already giving an interview to the attorney. The whole organization could be about to be blown to bits. That's always how it works. You take a lower echelon person in the organization, offer him immunity and use him to take care of everyone else up the ladder. The reverse of the domino theory. It generally works, but not on my watch.

By the time I got upstairs the interview was about to start. I barged my way into the large conference room where they had Jean-Luc. There were fifteen different agents and prosecutors – it was like a rogues' gallery of law enforcement. In front of Jean-Luc was a stack of pictures and diagrams of boats.

There were no introductions. It was clear from the faces of the prosecutors no one wanted me there. I was the fly in their ointment. Time was against me. I said the first thing that came into my head.

'I'm this man's lawyer. I can't let him testify.'

'Why not?' asked the state's attorney, shooting me a look that told me I was as welcome as a rain cloud on a sunny day. 'He has been given immunity.'

I glanced at all the faces staring at me. I recognized two federal prosecutors. That was my chance to buy some time.

'He can't testify unless he gets federal immunity. These are all crimes under state and federal law. If he is going to testify, I need to make sure he has immunity for crimes under federal jurisdiction.'

They begrudgingly gave me that, but I was now completely running out of options.

I had to rack my brains. Then I had an idea. The trouble was I had no clue if it would work.

'This man is a French national,' I said. 'He's been all over the French West Indies. As you have a French law enforcement agency official in here, from the Sûreté, I cannot allow my client to testify unless he has immunity for crimes under French law.'

My request was met with blank faces. No one challenged me. Could I be the only one who knew there was no such thing under French law? I had called their bluff and it seemed to be working. While the prosecutors deliberated, I got Jean-Luc out of the room.

Just when it looked like we were getting away, there was a commotion. The state attorney wanted to get a judge to make a ruling on the French stunt I pulled. This was it. I'd be defeated.

Everything happened at lightning speed. I went with the prosecutor upstairs where a judge would surely see through my paper-thin ruse. But my luck was in. The only judge available was still in court – sentencing a defendant to death and explaining his reasons why.

If there's ever a situation when you can't interrupt a judge, this was it.

The attorney had no choice. Jean-Luc was a free man. He was able to walk out of that courtroom on the understanding that he, and I, would be back the following morning for the ruling on French immunity. To say Jean-Luc was euphoric was an understatement. From a situation where he had either been betraying his entire organization or staring at a very long prison term for refusing to testify, he was now free.

He'd gone from the frying pan into the fire. He just didn't know it yet.

I grabbed Jean-Luc and took him to the parking lot, bundled him into my car and took off. The captain was in the same dirty clothes he had been in when he'd been arrested two days ago but he was on cloud nine. His joie de vivre had returned. In ten minutes we were back at my office but I knew we wouldn't be allowed to go that easily. I was convinced they would stick to me like glue.

I was sure that if Jean-Luc had been in that room for half an hour longer before I got there, it would have been over. There would have been enough to get an indictment against Calderon and, by association, me, as well as many other clients. After all Calderon was a distributor of cocaine to a number of major Miami-area traffickers.

Jean-Luc had been making all the right noises but there's no doubt he would have saved his own skin. There is no honour among thieves.

By the time I got back to my office, there was another surprise in store; and once again luck was smiling on me.

Christine, the secretary who serviced our offices, greeted me on our return.

'There are a bunch of cops outside,' she said. 'I recognize two of them and I'll bet there are more across the street.

'This has nothing to do with you, has it?' she asked with a raised eyebrow.

Christine's parents were both cops, an incidental fact she'd mentioned when I'd first met her and one that I could never have predicted would pay such rich dividends for me in the future.

The cops were staking out the office.

There was only one thing to do. I called Pascale and asked her to meet Jean-Luc and me downstairs from my tenth-floor office in a restaurant on the second floor. My plan was simple. While I distracted the cops outside, Jean-Luc and Pascale were to duck out of the building by a side entrance and make their escape. Where they went after that was up to them. In effect, my job was done but it would be expedient for all of us if they now disappeared.

Pascale showed up and there was an emotional reunion with Jean-Luc. I looked at the clock. I had less than three hours to get my flight to Sint Maarten. Even amid the drama of the day, there was no question of me not getting my usual flight.

With it being the middle of the afternoon, the restaurant was deserted and, being on the second floor, we were out of sight of prying eyes. I recommended to Jean-Luc he use one of the side or rear doors to make their exit. As the two lovers disappeared down their rabbit hole with a wave, it was time for me to play a starring role again.

I grabbed a couple of random litigation files from my office, went downstairs, and casually walked past the car where the cops were waiting. My heart was beating hard as I pretended not to know they were there. I was convinced they'd see it pounding out of my chest.

I walked down the street but could sense I was being followed. Glancing back I saw two men in dark clothing. Instinctively I quickened pace, but I had to fight to maintain an air of normality. I'm sure other cops continued to watch my office for any sign of Jean-Luc. Rightly, they suspected he might try to flee the city and wanted to put a tail on him to make sure he showed up at court the following morning.

I wanted to create the impression that I was going about my business as a civil court lawyer, while Jean-Luc waited in my office for my return. As long as Jean-Luc and Pascale had left the building undetected we had a chance of pulling this off.

It was a five-minute walk to the civil court. A last furtive look back before I entered the building confirmed the men were still following me and, keen not to lose me inside, had closed the gap.

I'd spent twelve years practising law in the civil courthouse. Once inside I made straight for the elevators. There were two side by side. I managed to shut the doors behind me and pressed the button that would take it to the sixth floor.

The ride took seconds but I wanted it to last an eternity. For that brief moment I felt safe. I didn't know for sure that Jean-Luc and Pascale had made it out of the building without being spotted. Even if they had, I didn't know what their plans would be. Pascale would have been smart enough to grab anything of value from their apartment, knowing it was unlikely she'd ever be able to return. Where they went from there, however, I hadn't a clue.

If they were tailed it was a certainty the cops would make sure Jean-Luc kept his appointment with the court. If he testi-fied, Bernard was in deep trouble and I was now horribly exposed. The odds were that this would end badly.

Exiting on a floor crammed with offices and courtrooms, I didn't wait to see if my shadows had taken the other elevator. As soon as I came out I went back down the back stairs. I jumped two at a time, my clumsy steps echoing up the stairwell. Amid the clatter I tried to listen out for the sounds of people following me.

In the basement I pushed through the doors, out into the underground car park. It was where the judges parked their cars and the place was virtually deserted save for the occasional driver returning to his motor. I doubted the officers knew about this exit.

I half-walked, half-ran, to the exit of the car park and, once back out on the street, shook off any pretension of calmness and legged it. The sweat was now running down the middle of my back but I didn't care. I ran like hell, not checking to see if anyone was coming after me.

I sought refuge in the first place I could see – a dry cleaner's a few blocks away from the court. I heaved for breath as I tried to compose myself.

With any luck, the officers who followed me to the court would be waiting for me outside, convinced I would soon complete my errands and return to my office. I knew they would consider me crooked for helping to bring out a suspected smuggler but hopefully they wouldn't think I was as devious as this.

Once I got my breath back, I crossed the street to a pay-phone and called a friend. I needed help. I explained I couldn't get back to my car – that was too risky. Could he come to the dry cleaner's, pick me up?

It was now after 3 p.m. My flight was at 5.25 p.m.

I was grateful for my military training and my insistence on always over-preparing. I ran into the house, changed my clothes in about sixty seconds, grabbed my case with $200,000 and made for the airport.

To a casual observer, I may have been a curious sight; one minute running into my house, decked out in a respectable suit, the next emerging dressed in a Hawaiian shirt and shorts.

In keeping with my weekly routine, I had earlier bought a ticket with cash, and now filed in behind the other tourists heading for the Caribbean. It was only when I had time to catch my breath that the fear gripped me.

Not only had I revealed myself as a crooked lawyer in front of federal, state and international prosecutors, but I was also in the middle of another operation.

There I was, about to smuggle a bunch of cash out of the

country . . . hours after springing a smuggler from custody. Would the agents looking for my client search me?

There was never any question I wouldn't have made this flight. If I hadn't been able to deposit that cash safely in a bank in Sint Maarten, my other clients wouldn't get their money on time. They were depending on me. If I hadn't made it to the bank on Friday there would have been a delay getting that money into the system.

It wouldn't have been fatal but I had worked hard to build up a reputation for punctuality and I didn't want to let my clients down.

Even after a day full of them, there was time left for one more surprise.

As I arrived at the departure gate, I looked across the hall. Passengers for the flight to Panama City, which left ten minutes before mine, were filing forward to board.

Among them I spotted a tall, thin, unshaven man with a pretty blonde companion. They were waving at me. It was Jean-Luc and Pascale, fleeing the country. I knew then the client was safe and my responsibility was over. I signalled back to them.

While they could relax, I still had a few tense last minutes to see out. Until my plane took off I couldn't be entirely sure that the DEA were not going to board the aircraft and haul me off for questioning.

A lawyer friend of mine was lined up to take the flak for me in court the next day. The judge would have some questions as to why not only Jean-Luc, but his lawyer, failed to show. It was fair to say a few people in that court were going to be angry.

At 5.15 p.m. the engines started whirring and before long I was airborne. It was then I sank back into my seat and exhaled. A good day. I'd just earned myself a $50,000 bonus. All's well that ends well . . . for the criminals.

15. When There's a Target on Your Chest, Keep Moving

On 14 November 1957 Joseph Barbara called a meeting.

This wasn't any meeting. Joe the Barber was a feared hitman and the boss of the Bufalino crime family. And his guests were one hundred of the most powerful Mafiosi in America at the time.

Barbara wanted to thrash out an agreement between the families to carve up the territories, settling the control of casinos, gambling and drug empires. The meeting, at his sprawling estate in Apalachin, two hundred miles north-west from New York City, was top secret.

But the Mob bosses didn't account for eagle-eyed state trooper Edgar D. Croswell, who'd observed an earlier meeting at Barbara's house and became suspicious when he heard the Barber's brother had been reserving rooms in local hotels. Setting up a discreet watch outside the estate, he was stunned to see so many luxury cars arrive, most with out-of-state licence plates. Closer inspection of the plates revealed they belonged to dozens of known criminals.

When the meeting was raided, many of the Cosa Nostra tried to escape but were stopped at a police roadblock. Others fled through fields and woods, ruining their tailor-made suits and discarding guns and cash as they ran, to such an extent that hundred-dollar bills were still being found by grateful locals scattered across the countryside some weeks later. Although nearly fifty men escaped, some fifty-eight others were arrested. The bungled meeting finally confirmed the existence of the

American Mafia, something J. Edgar Hoover, the director of the Federal Bureau of Investigations, up until that point had steadfastly refused to acknowledge.

The Apalachin Meeting became legendary in American crime history but its significance mustn't have spread as far as Canada or France. I'm sure if Bernard Calderon had known about the success of the Mafia bosses' get-together he wouldn't have tried a similar stunt some thirty years later.

After Jean-Luc's arrest and the seizure of cocaine in the Miami river, Bernard fled the country so fast even Tao had no idea where he'd gone and quick enough so that an indictment for trafficking couldn't be served.

Many of his crew were still in custody and there was the small matter of 800 kilos of cocaine seized from one of his boats to deal with.

After hiding out in Taiwan he then moved to his native France. It was a clever move, with the French government's ironclad reluctance to extradite its own nationals for anything. But although he was safe from prosecution there, he felt too remote from his empire to fully know what was going on in the wake of a seizure of such a sizeable shipment. He was desperate to know what damage had been sustained and, more importantly, whom he could still rely on.

He called a meeting of his crime syndicate in Guadeloupe, in the French Antilles, which was still, he correctly figured, under the protection of his homeland. It was the Miami equivalent of that Mafia meeting, with similarly nearly catastrophic consequences. Little did Bernard know that the DEA had got wind of his little gathering. He would never know if someone had tipped them off or whether they'd been tapping phone calls but they knew not only on which island the meeting was taking place but also in which hotel. The only problem for the DEA was that they didn't know in which room Bernard had planned the meeting to take place. Undeterred, ahead of the meeting they audaciously bugged every room in the entire hotel, not letting the small fact that such an action is illegal under French law worry them. The tapes could never be admitted under US law, but they provided a window into both Calderon's operation and his absolute arrogance.

Bernard's meeting went ahead and DEA agents sat listening as Miami's biggest cocaine smuggler was debriefed on the health of his empire and laid out his game plan.

Among the revelations that were to have an implication for me was Bernard's bold boast to his cohorts that 'When you have a problem in another country, you hire the best lawyers that money can buy and you won't go to prison.'

Had I known that Bernard was presenting lawyers like me in such a favourable light I might have made some different choices in the months to come. As it was, though, I was oblivious – about a great many things.

It was hardly surprising though that we would all be attracting the close attention of the law. The dramatic circumstances of Jean-Luc's spring for freedom signalled a new phase in the game.

I knew they would be targeting me. From that moment I accepted that, as far as the government was concerned, I was now part of the problem.

It could be argued that at this point it might have been in my interests to step back from the frontline, to keep a lower profile.

Sometimes though – when you have a target on your chest – you just have to keep moving. You are harder to hit, at least in theory.

I tried to keep this philosophy in mind when Charlie called me up. By this time Bernard had retreated back to France and was working out how best to resume his activities.

Charlie had owed $50,000 to Bernard before the boat was seized and now a neighbour of the Frenchman in Miami Beach called Tony Nesca had come out of the woodwork offering to take it to him.

I trusted Charlie but Nesca I wasn't convinced about. I had good reason to be suspicious. I didn't know it then but Nesca had previously been caught with cocaine in the Bahamas. In a desperate bid to save his own skin he had tempted prosecutors with the boast that he personally could deliver them Bernard on a silver platter.

He'd met Bernard while he'd been renting an ocean-front apartment in Miami Beach and now saw his opportunity to play a 'Get out of jail free' card.

Nesca's plan was to collect the money from me and hand it to Bernard. In that I couldn't see a problem. He was due to contact me with a time and place for the handover.

'Okay,' I said, 'come back to me when you have some instructions.'

Sometimes, as I had already discovered, the fates smile on you. They were to do so again this time. When I didn't hear from Nesca in a week instinct told me to back away so I returned the money to Charlie.

The next thing I knew Nesca rang me up.

'Hey, Ken, have you got that money? Let's meet up and I can get the cash off you for Bernard.'

'Sorry, Tony. I don't hold money for clients. I gave it back because I didn't hear from you for so long.'

He was clearly unhappy with this development. Years later I would find out why. Nesca was secretly recording me. It was a sting. If I'd handed over that cash I would have been arrested for a criminal conspiracy for aiding Bernard's attempts to evade justice.

Although I didn't know then what Nesca's true role in these proceedings was, his approach had made me nervous and I could feel paranoia building.

After sticking my head above the parapet was I safe to assume I was being followed? I couldn't be sure, but I felt it was the very least I could expect since the DEA and other agencies had a fair idea about my associates. I needed to modify my behaviour just in case. The most important thing though was to keep up the charade of being the legitimate professional, with nothing to hide. So I made sure I was in the office at 9 a.m. every day and always available. Ever since I'd become a laundry man I'd been on call 24/7 for my clients, taking calls at home and popping out for emergency meetings with demanding kingpins at all hours of the night.

These were the days before cell phones and the only way to reach people was on landlines and pagers. I knew it would be difficult for anyone to get a court order to retrieve phone numbers from a law office where there are a number of people practising so I directed everyone to call me there, not my home. After the drama of the courthouse, I knew I would be a watched man. I'd crossed the line. And I knew it.

I became circumspect about my movements. I varied my parking places, constantly changed my routine and made sure I only parked where I could see if someone was following me. As I tried to safeguard against any eventuality I started to worry about my fringe clients. Had any been arrested and released to inform on me?

How could I be sure they weren't talking to the cops? I'd seen at first hand how the screws could be put on a low-level operator to reel in a kingpin.

Who knew I made regular trips to the Caribbean?

Even setting aside the obvious risk from a sting operation, could it be possible that I was a target for a carefully staged mugging? It was unlikely but I didn't want to take any chances. From then on I always made sure I only carried cash on operations; I never carried more than a thousand dollars in my wallet; I stayed away from bad parts of town.

Although I was well dressed I was never flashy and never flaunted it. I resolved I had to do things right if I was going to stay one step ahead of the law. In those days in Miami lots of lawyers were getting into trouble and I didn't want to be one of them.

With Bernard out of the picture, albeit temporarily, my trips to the Caribbean were less frequent. This pleased Monique. I think she dared to hope it meant I might at last lead a normal lawyer's life.

Then, just when I was starting to feel the heat was dying down, Tao called me from Paris. She was upset.

'It is Bernard,' she sobbed, through her thick oriental accent. 'He is in custody.'

'What? How?'

'He made a mistake,' she said in her staccato English. 'He is in Genoa. He is asking for you.'

Tao explained that the longer Bernard had managed to evade justice the bolder he'd become. He'd gone over the French–Italian border but had been picked up by Interpol.

'What can I do?' I asked.

'He wants you to visit him.'

'Me? Why?' I was at a loss to see what I could do for him now he was in custody.

'They want to extradite him to America. He is fighting it. He needs you to help him.'

My initial instinct was suspicion. What was going on? Since the drama of Jean-Luc and with him fleeing the country I was trying to push him out of my consciousness.

'Please,' she implored. 'I will arrange you a ticket. He needs you.'

What was I going to do? If this was a genuine request how could I say no? I had no reason really to think Bernard would set me up. Where he was concerned I was already exposed, so there was nothing to lose, surely?

I decided I would go and see him, but I needed to have some sort of control.

'Okay, I'll see him, give me the details. But you have to send me the money. I'll make my own travel arrangements.'

'Thank you so much, Monsieur Rijock. Bernard will be delighted.'

Tao was true to her word and sent me the funds and I booked my trip.

Monique was less than impressed when I told her a client was facing extradition in a foreign jail. I felt I owed her that much.

'He can afford the best lawyers money can buy but he chooses you,' she said as she prepared to leave for work the next morning.

'Thanks for the vote of confidence.'

'You're not even a criminal lawyer. How can you help him?'

I tried to explain he wanted someone he could trust. Someone who knew the American justice system, someone to arrange experienced criminal defence counsel.

This was an added complication in my life I could do without.

I arranged the flight to Italy to come the day after a trip I was making to New York for my twentieth high-school reunion. The plan was for Monique and Katherine to come with me. They were to enjoy a night in Manhattan at a nice hotel while I travelled the thirty-minute drive upstate for the party at my old haunt.

The experience of meeting people I hadn't seen for two decades was more enjoyable than I'd hoped. Everyone talked excitedly about the jobs they had, the marriages and the children. For obvious reasons I kept the fact that I was a practising money launderer quiet – it's not the type of thing you can slip into polite conversation, as you can imagine:

'Yes, and so for the last five years I have been bankrolling some of the country's biggest trafficking gangs to the tune of tens of millions of dollars, the result of which means America is being flooded with cocaine. But enough about me. Tell me more about your summer house on Long Island.'

It doesn't really work. Instead I just said that I was a lawyer, that I was in a long-term relationship with a police officer and, after Vietnam, was enjoying the sun and fun of Miami.

However, as the night wore on I found myself modifying my relationship status, particularly to girls I hadn't seen since high school, and I held back details about Monique. When I was reunited with Sally, a girl I used to have a thing for when I was much younger, thoughts of my girlfriend went out of the window. It had been bothering me for a while now that things weren't really working out between us and I couldn't see a future for us. Actually, I couldn't see a future for myself. That was the reality.

Before the New York trip I had started renting an apartment in the Brickell Bay Club – the apartment building I'd lived in with my first wife. It was an impulsive thing. I'd spotted that a stunning tenth-floor corner apartment, with an impressive bay view all the way down to the Ragged Keys, was available and taken on the lease in the same day. I hadn't even told Monique about it. I had been paying the rent while I worked out what to do. If anything, it gave me something to pump the excess cash I had lying around into.

But that night, the more I got reacquainted with Sally, the more reckless I felt. I ended up enjoying a wildly passionate night with her, didn't make it to the hotel in New York and, after staying up all night, had to make a mad dash to the airport for the Alitalia flight to Milan.

After catching a train to Genoa I realized I had no idea where Bernard was being held. I called into what looked like a major police station. Helpfully they told me he was being detained in a thirteenth-century prison on the outskirts of town.

Even more helpful was a beautiful blonde Italian who offered to assist when I also said I was having trouble at the police station. She was a flight attendant who just happened to be the daughter of one of the senior police chiefs. We hit it off straight away. She offered to help me find my hotel. I suggested we do that after dinner. Some pasta and a bottle of Chianti later we were walking arm in arm through the streets of Genoa trying to find my lodgings. She came back with me to my hotel room. In two consecutive nights, in two continents, I'd slept with two stunning women. Suffice to say I didn't get much sleep that night either.

I was not the freshest when I finally made it to Bernard's jail the following morning.

I was expecting a medieval prison but this place looked like something out of the Stone Age. Huge wrought-iron gates and thick stone walls gave way to a prison block so imposing that I wouldn't have been surprised if the Count of Monte Cristo himself was an inmate.

'The food is horrible,' Bernard complained when I finally got to see him. He was always one to appreciate the finer things in life so I could understand how bad this would be for him. 'But I have my own source of food and entertainment.'

How could I have doubted him?

Bernard explained he was able to pay for better food to be delivered to him and he was paying enough for some of the other inmates in his ward to have fine dining too.

'I also sponsor the local football team.'

'What for?' I asked, failing to see why he would want to benefit a local sports club while locked inside a prison, facing extradition.

'It looks good. And the owner supplies me wine as a show of gratitude.'

'You have wine, in a prison?' I said, starting to think this Stone Age jail wasn't so bad after all.

The truth though was that, although he was living comfortably, he was miserable. Tao had only recently given birth and he was desperate to see his baby.

'So what can I do to help?' I asked.

He wanted me to represent him and help him fight extradition.

I promised to do all I could and bade him a fond farewell. Of all the kingpins I dealt with Bernard was one of the most likeable. I stayed on in Genoa for a couple of days and met up with what turned out to be a sharp, local lawyer he had engaged to work on fighting the extradition order from his end.

This was going to be a tough case. Since the boat had been seized in Miami, some fifteen people from Bernard's network had been arrested. Although Jean-Luc might be safely in Panama, among the others in custody someone was bound to cooperate.

Loyalty only went so far in this business.

16. 'Move the boat and you're dead'

On my return to Florida I set about hiring counsel for Bernard. Fortunately he had allowed me access to money from his off-shore accounts to fund his representation. It was agreed I'd return to Genoa in a month to update him.

I arranged a defence team for him in Miami and put them in touch with his Italian counsel. Then I made plans to travel to Genoa and then to Paris to keep his wife and family abreast of what was going on.

It was a trip that interested Monique.

'I've never seen Paris,' she told me.

'Well, come along.' I was happy to involve her in this excursion because all I was doing was visiting a client in jail. There would be no illegal activity required. It then transpired that Katherine, her daughter, who was starting college at Georgetown, also wanted to come.

'No problem,' I said. 'Bring her along too.'

We went to Genoa and they hung around in the town while I visited Bernard. From there we flew to Paris and while Monique and Katherine took in the sights, I travelled twenty miles outside the city to Sarcelles, a fourteenth-century village where Bernard had a four-storey villa. His sister Françoise lived there with her husband Vincent but I suspect Bernard's millions paid for it. Tao was also living there while she adapted to life as a young mother.

Françoise and Tao were fully aware of Bernard's predicament so I could be straight with them. They had a million questions about what was going to happen so I sat and talked with them for hours. Françoise said Bernard also had a son of about twenty who was in the dark about his father's true business dealings so she faced a tricky decision when the time came to tell him where his father was.

When at last I prepared to leave and rejoin Monique and Katherine, Françoise said: 'Kenneth, you have been such a friend to Bernard. We will never forget this. The next time you come to France you will stay with us, yes?'

We spent the rest of the week in Paris acting like normal tourists and seeking out places where we could browse art deco artefacts. I'd always had an interest in those stylized pieces of furniture and fittings and longed to kit out our home in that fashion.

We returned to Miami and already I was making plans to return to Italy and France. The arrangement we'd agreed on was that I would get a briefing from the Florida lawyers on how his case was progressing here, liaise in Genoa with his Italian lawyers on how his extradition was proceeding, then give Bernard the rundown before travelling to Sarcelles to update the rest of his family.

I found Françoise interesting and engaging. Some ten years older than Bernard, she told me she and her brother had been orphaned when the Germans invaded France in 1940. I didn't want to pry too deeply but I got the impression she had spent time in a concentration camp, such was the visible anguish she displayed when she talked about that time.

It became routine that I would stay with the family, except on one occasion when I turned up at the villa to be met with a frosty reception. Vincent met me at the door, quietly stepping out on to the stairway while closing the door behind him.

'I am really sorry, Kenneth, but now is not a good time. You have to leave,' he whispered urgently.

'What's going on?' I said, trying not to sound agitated.

'It is Christophe. He is here.' Christophe, Bernard's grown-up son, knew nothing of his father's arrest.

'I see. Not a problem. I'll make myself scarce.'

'I am sorry,' said Vincent. 'Françoise will get a message to you when it is convenient.'

There was nothing else for it but to get a room in a hotel in the neighbourhood and wait until they could see me.

Françoise never confirmed it as such but I could tell she had some control of Bernard's finances. Whenever I needed to pay the criminal defence lawyers' fees, she would take me to a bank and get a cashier's cheque for the amounts – often over $100,000. Due to strict French banking laws the cheques had a red diagonal line across which meant they could only be cashed by the payee and never endorsed to a third party.

Tao seemed to be bearing up well. She had a bodyguard who never seemed to leave her side. She made frequent trips to visit Bernard herself but, living with Françoise, she was well looked after considering she was up to her neck in her husband's empire – after all, he was using her father's junks to import cocaine through the Panama Canal.

The frequent European trips meant a hectic travel schedule but there were upsides to it. I could enjoy the great food in Genoa, a beautiful seaport on the Mediterranean, and got to know Paris well.

However, while the miles between us were constant, the emotional distance between Monique and me seemed to be growing. It was surely only a matter of time before things came to a head.

With making the travel arrangements, keeping on top of Bernard's case, managing my other clients, trying to run a legitimate legal practice and staying one step ahead of the law, something had to give. It was Monique.

I had been so careful to compartmentalize my life that I had nothing to share with her. Gone were the days when she would hang out with Andre and his gang. My close connections with more serious players meant she was steering clear. Now we weren't even socializing.

She had been studying for a master's degree at college and was now qualified to be a police psychologist. It was a role she found demanding and all consuming. It wasn't something she could leave at the station when her shift ended. She became more serious and contemplative.

My dalliances with the women in New York and Italy had proved to me my heart was not in our relationship any more. Maybe having her children around had something to do with it. They were great kids but although I harboured dreams of one day settling down and having a normal life, maybe having children of my own, I wasn't ready to be a father just yet – certainly not to teenagers.

Monique was dead set against marrying again and, feeling that this was the time to concentrate on her career, she seemed to be in a different place from me. I wondered how we could ever have a real future together. Maybe, I thought, it was time to make use of my apartment in the Brickell Bay Club.

I let off some steam in a bar in Coconut Grove after a particularly hectic day. It was there I got chatting to a pretty redheaded girl – I seemed to have a weakness for them. Her name was Joanne, she was a broker and much younger than I was. I was mesmerized. We embarked on an affair that was crazy and impulsive. With everything I had on my plate the last thing I needed was another woman to try and keep happy.

On the day I called time on my relationship with Monique there were no tears, no recriminations – that's because I moved out my things when she wasn't there. The first she knew we'd broken up was when I didn't come home.

The affair with Joanne was passionate and full-on – but it was also stupid. After just two weeks the girl started making noises about marriage and I panicked once again. I moved out as quickly as I had done with Monique and went straight to my high-rise apartment with its stunning view of the ocean.

Standing in the empty lounge in the dark, staring out to the twinkling lights in the harbour, I made a phone call.

'Just come and meet me at the Brickell Bay Club. I have something to show you.'

We'd only been apart for a matter of weeks but when she showed up at the parking lot it could have been years. The minute I clapped eyes on her it was clear our brief separation – combined with her newfound distrust and attitude – reignited all the old feelings I'd had for Monique.

I led her up to the tenth floor and opened the door to the vacant apartment I had been renting.

'What the hell is this? Who lives here?'

I showed her in. The floor-to-ceiling windows looked out over the ocean in two directions.

'What do you think?'

'What do you mean, "What do I think"? Are you going to tell me what's going on?'

'How would you like this to be our new home?'

She looked at me as though I was mad. But I could detect a smile forming on her lips, which she was doing her best to hide.

'Come on,' I said. 'It will be good for us.'

I have to admit, I had no idea what her reaction would be. Astonishingly she said yes and I made immediate plans to move in. I'm not sure if I then really believed it was a new chapter in our unorthodox relationship . . . maybe it was just a solution to the predicament I had found myself in. But, for a while at least, I kidded myself we had a new future together.

She shared my love of all things art deco and this was a

chance for us to indulge our new passion. With a lavish new apartment to furnish we splashed our cash on original artefacts from the 1920s and '30s. I continued to make the trips to Italy and France but returned with gifts for her or a rare item we could restore for our apartment. For a while it seemed things were back on track.

Before long the apartment was transformed from top to bottom. The furniture and furnishings were my escape from the stress of dealing with clients who were rough around the edges. But as I got more into my new hobby, the similarities were inescapable. To clean the artefacts I used a particular chemical, acetone. It was the same chemical my clients used to test the potency of their cocaine before agreeing to buy. I kept my acetone in a metal container on the patio. When Andre or Charlie came round they couldn't help have a dig that I'd moved into trafficking and queried what sort of testing I was conducting.

For a while it really looked like Monique and I had found a routine we could be content with. She loved the chance to explore Europe and I appreciated the chance to show her around.

Whenever we came back from Paris, usually on a Friday night, we readied the place for a big party. The champagne was ordered, the cocaine still seemed to be on endless supply and our friends flocked to our new home to party the night away.

When we weren't entertaining we dined in one of the four restaurants in the building. We avoided Ménage. The nightclub continued to do a roaring trade but was too high profile, attracting the next wave of professionals to its dance floor in the basement.

It felt like we had gone back in time, living the life we should have lived in our twenties, when, for me, the war in Vietnam got in the way and Monique had first attempted to settle down with marriage and children.

We fooled ourselves into thinking it was a lifestyle that was sustainable – that this was all each of us wanted out of life.

Meanwhile, as Bernard still fought extradition, there was a major development in his case. Two of the lesser defendants arrested at the same time as he was were facing trial for letting drug boats use their marina to bring in their cargo. But shortly before the trial was due to start the daughter of one of the defendants went swimming, jumped off a diving board, broke her neck and was paralysed. The judge granted a mistrial because the circumstances were so disturbing and adjourned the proceedings. A new trial was set but the intervening period allowed Bernard's lawyers to see the case against him. And I had the transcript of the first trial, which gave his lawyers a rare sneak preview of the government's entire case. That never happens in federal court.

For fourteen months, while the new trial was set, I visited Bernard and kept him up to date with what was going on. During that time his Italian lawyer had proved an expert in delaying the proceedings, but eventually even his options ran out. Bernard was being deported and brought to Miami to stand trial. Given the weight of evidence against him and his clients it seems inconceivable that they would manage to evade justice this time.

Fortunately for Bernard, the mistrial and subsequent delay before the proceedings began in earnest allowed his US lawyers to start building a picture against the government's witnesses. His team discovered that many of the key witnesses had had colourful or chequered careers. Some had been in jail, others had track records of assisting the government in return for favours. This didn't look good when set against Bernard and the other defendants who, up until then, had lived squeaky-clean, blameless lives.

A major witness in the case was Tony Nesca, Bernard's neighbour and the man who'd tried to sting me. It was seeing the details in these crime papers that had confirmed it. But when an investigator found Nesca had lied in a child custody dispute in New England, Bernard's lawyers were able to cast doubt on his credibility as a witness.

The tapes of the conversation from Bernard's version of the Apalachin Meeting were also made available to the defence lawyers. On first listen, the tapes seemed damning evidence that was sure to convict him. But then his legal team realized that the DEA hadn't sought a court order to sanction the bugging and wouldn't have got one had they done so. Such was the government's zeal to catch Bernard, it had broken French law in the process. The tapes – and all the evidence on them – would be inadmissible.

In the midst of all of this I received some alarming news. Charlie Nunez had been arrested. Since he'd struck out from Benny to run his own affairs, his organization had been shipping in cocaine through the Bahamas but had been hit by problems. In desperation they had hired a ship's captain without doing the necessary background checks. It was to prove costly. He was an undercover agent working for the DEA.

I'd always feared those gun-toting, crazy Martinez brothers would be the undoing of him and it seemed I was going to be proved right. The moment that boat set sail from the Bahamas, the DEA and Customs pounced. The load was confiscated and Charlie and the rest of the crew were arrested. Sickeningly, the Martinez brothers escaped because they weren't on the boat at the time.

I feared Charlie's arrest could have implications for me.

Only weeks earlier I'd travelled to Anguilla with Nico Nunez to look at a sixty-foot research vessel they'd used for dozens of operations. I lost count of the times I'd re-registered that boat in both Delaware and in the UK. When I went over to the harbour I noticed that there were some government agents looking at the boat so I'd left a note for the mechanic: 'Get out of here, there are law enforcement looking at the boat. Don't go near the boat.'

Nico called me up. He said the brothers had been forced to abandon the boat where it still sat moored in Anguilla.

'What are they going to do with it?' I asked.

'Nothing.'

'Is that wise? That boat is evidence. It should be destroyed.'

'No one's to touch it. The brothers wanted me to tell you specifically.'

'I wouldn't go anywhere near it,' I insisted.

'Good. Enrique says if you move the boat they'll kill you.'

It was the first time I'd been directly threatened. No surprise it was the Martinez brothers. It put me on edge but I knew I wouldn't be doing anything to incur their wrath.

Given everything I'd done for them, the implication that I'd double-cross them rankled.

It was yet more evidence of the net closing. Charlie had been one of my original clients. Bernard's case had hammered home how close the authorities were getting but with Charlie the government were edging even closer. How much longer before they came for me?

Enrique's threat showed how edgy everyone was getting.

Did I need to get out of Miami? Leave America? Should I flee to Central America? There was a war in Nicaragua. Surely I could hide out there, take on a new identity? I needn't even tell Monique. I could just disappear.

It was attractive but running wasn't an option.

I sought out Ed. He used me less and less these days because he'd wanted to move his money from Anguilla to Switzerland and I'd counselled against it.

We weren't guaranteed the same protection there but he objected to Henry's fees every time we did a transaction.

I got the impression he felt he'd outgrown me. But with the heat building I wanted to make sure we were still solid.

I went round to his house with Monique. The place was in near darkness but he was home alone. He seemed pleased to see us but his eyes were bloodshot. He looked high.

Quickly we established why. He was snorting heroin.

Miami might have been awash with drugs of all kinds but smack wasn't something you encountered often. Life in the ghetto didn't fit with the city's hedonistic party fever.

After we'd been chatting for a while, he offered the foil to us both.

Monique politely declined. She drew the line at coke and was scaling back her recreational use anyway.

I, on the other hand, was curious.

Putting the tube he was using to inhale in my mouth, I lit the foil and watched as the brown tar started to boil. As the fumes rose I inhaled gently. For a moment I felt euphoric but as quickly as the feeling came it was overtaken by nausea.

'If you throw up, it makes you feel better,' Ed said.

'No thanks, I'll leave you to it.'

Later that night I was plagued with vivid dreams. It could have been the heroin, Enrique's death threat or the stress of the arrests.

I didn't feel on top of my game. If I was going to ride out this storm I needed to be in top shape. I'd been lucky. Since living the high life I'd kept slim and my health had been good.

Now I felt poisoned. It was time to scale back.

Meanwhile I still had the problem of two major clients in the Metropolitan Correction Centre – Miami's federal prison – where people were held before they were tried. They had some exalted company in there. Manuel Noriega – the former military dictator of Panama before the US removed him from power and charged him with racketeering, money laundering and trafficking – was an inmate.

I visited Bernard and Charlie in prison but even by doing so I was taking a huge risk and drawing greater attention to myself. Although I was talking to them about their cases, the only lawyers who should have been there were criminal defence lawyers. For all that I represented these people, I wasn't a criminal lawyer – I was a civil lawyer.

We finally got some good news when, after a lengthy trial, all the defendants, including Bernard, were acquitted – astonishing when you think that 800 kilos of cocaine was found on board their ship in the Miami river.

At the acquittal, the Assistant US Attorney attempted to have Bernard improperly rearrested on other unrelated charges, pulling out an indictment he was holding in his file. But since extradition laws prohibit persons being tried for any charges other than those they are actually extradited for, the District Judge had no option but to order his release.

The Assistant US Attorney who tried the case resigned soon after. We never found out if he was pushed or quit following the indignity of letting what appeared to be a watertight case slip through his fingers. Whatever the reason, he soon turned up as a defence attorney, specializing in representing informants the criminal fraternity like to term 'snitches'.

One of the lawyers in the firm that represented Bernard picked him up at the Federal Detention Centre and drove him straight to Miami international airport where he was soon boarding a flight to France and freedom.

I had no doubt that he would be back in business. While Bernard was in prison in Miami awaiting trial, he asked me to fly to the French Antilles to check on a boat that had gone missing. While I was there he wanted me to liaise with one of his associates and assure him he would be back in the game the moment he was out of prison.

I knew then that with people like Bernard it was an obsession.

The acquittal gave his organization a new lease of life but it was one that didn't involve me. Bernard went back to the south of France and set up an empire hoping to do in Europe what they'd successfully managed in the US. It didn't last long. The French police eventually caught Bernard and his crew in what at the time was the country's biggest cocaine case. Justice was swift and they were handed twenty-year jail terms without parole. Even Tao, his dutiful wife, got ten years. She tried to appeal but the old French Napoleonic system didn't view kindly such bids for leniency that weren't founded on merit and they reportedly doubled her sentence.

Charlie was dealt a similarly harsh sentence, given twenty years for his part in the Bahamas sting. He unfortunately relied upon his lawyers' representations that they would win on appeal; he was to serve seven years, in some of America's toughest federal prisons.

The long arm of justice also finally caught up with Jean-Luc. Although he had made it to Panama he was only on the run for a matter of months before he made the mistake of going to the airport where a DEA official recognized him. Declared *persona non grata* in Panama, the French sea captain was thrown out of the country, brought back to Miami and given a two-year sentence. This time, because he was well and truly considered a flight risk, there was no magic trick I could pull. He didn't stand a chance of bail.

His goose was cooked. How many others would be roasted too?

17. Breakthrough

In the field office of the FBI in Miami Beach, Agent Dean Roberts was frustrated.

For a year he'd been asked to investigate allegations of money laundering in the Caribbean, but had so far drawn a blank.

The tax havens were out of the reach of American agencies. Under the jurisdiction of governments thousands of miles away, they were a law unto themselves. Roberts knew corruption was rife, knew they operated as refuges for scoundrels – but he was powerless to do anything about it.

Inaction had made him cranky and gruff. He longed to get his teeth into the criminals he believed were thumbing their noses at the authorities. Colleagues, who remembered him when he was more genial and obliging, now gave the forty-year-old a wide berth.

That morning Agent Roberts was about to receive some news that would dramatically change his fortunes.

His superior, Special Agent Rich Lerner, approached his desk and dropped a dossier on top of the files he was studying.

'What's this?' Roberts said, not even raising his head.

'Your lucky day.'

Lerner left him without explaining further.

Reluctantly at first, Roberts examined the files. They were entitled 'Operation Man'.

The information dated back to an incident in the summer of 1981. Police raided a yacht centre in Florida, seizing fifteen tons of marijuana and making one arrest. A decent success but they missed a key player in the smuggling operation – Eddie Romano. The gang boss might have escaped on this occasion but, feeling nervous, needed to hide $550,000.

In desperation, he asked his long-time friend Sam Malloy to install a safe in the floor of his workshop.

Malloy dutifully stashed the money but the thought of such riches so close at hand burned inside him. One night he tried to break the safe open with a sledgehammer. At first it wouldn't budge but setting at it with a jackhammer he finally got it open and did a runner.

In a motel en route north he picked up a prostitute. Unluckily for him, she was the most expensive hooker in history. When he woke in the morning he was $550,000 lighter and the girl had gone.

If that was his first mistake, his second was to return to south Florida.

On his reappearance, Romano asked to meet him at the yacht club. The gang boss wanted Malloy to join him on a little trip.

Once out at sea, Malloy was bound in chains by Romano's cronies and weighed down with an anchor. Before tossing the hapless double-crosser overboard, Romano wanted to show his friend what he thought of his betrayal.

'I want to do this myself,' he told his accomplices.

With chilling calmness, he placed a gun to Malloy's head and shot him through the skull.

The lifeless body was tossed into the water, followed by the gun.

Romano was eventually convicted of smuggling and murder.

But the half a million he lost through Malloy was, for want of a better expression, a drop in the ocean compared to his total drug profits of $100 million.

The man entrusted with laundering much of this cash was Romano's enforcer Simon Anderson. A college boy, smart and educated, he was also a ruthless killer, suspected of kidnapping and murdering three gangland figures. Carrying hundreds of thousands of dollars in a suitcase, Anderson left the US and headed to England under a false name.

His plan? To launder the cash through banks on the Isle of Man – a crown dependency meaning that it was a British-owned island but with secretive bank laws like the tax havens in the Caribbean.

Assisting him was a Manx lawyer called Alex Hennessey. They set up fake corporations and accounts under false names. What Anderson didn't know was that his dealings with Hennessey were being monitored.

The lawyer was a person of interest to Scotland Yard who were investigating what had happened to £26 million stolen from the Brink's-MAT robbery. The heist, in November 1983, was notorious in British crime folklore. When six robbers broke into the Brink's-MAT warehouse at Heathrow they thought they were going to get away with £3 million in cash. When they arrived, however, they found instead three tonnes of gold bullion, worth £26 million. It was the biggest robbery in British criminal history.

Although two men would receive sentences of up to twenty-five years for their part, most of the stolen gold was never recovered and the other four robbers were never convicted. It was claimed that anyone wearing gold jewellery bought in the UK after 1983 was probably wearing Brink's-MAT.

The case was so high profile, police were under huge pressure to get results. Scotland Yard detectives suspected Hennessey had been laundering some of the missing millions. Although he operated a tiny Manx firm, Hennessey was already up to his neck in crime, having laundered cash for American dealers through corporations registered in the British tax haven. Tailing Hennessey had led cops to Anderson.

Using surveillance, they watched as the lawyer, who also had a record for possessing cocaine, met Anderson in central London. They tailed Anderson until they suspected he was about to leave for Spain to visit a man involved in the Brink's-MAT robbery. That's when they pounced.

He was questioned closely about dealing and the source of his money. Anderson protested his innocence, claiming: 'I'm not such a bad guy. I went to college. We are all white college boys. There are no Colombians or Cubans. College boys have morals.'

An examination of his bank accounts in London then revealed deposits of £300,000 – and more than £1 million was later found in a bank account on the Isle of Man.

By this time, police also had enough to charge Hennessey. A jurisdiction issue meant that officers had to be sworn in as special constables before they could have full authority on the Isle of Man. That done, they set about arresting the lawyer.

He seemed relieved to be detained. Hennessey was in fear of his life. It wasn't surprising, given Anderson's history of violence.

Hennessey agreed to cooperate with the police in return for a reduced sentence. He flew with detectives to Florida to help with their inquiries. The police were stunned when he confirmed he was at the centre of a massive transatlantic laundering racket and knew so much information that it took months to debrief him.

Police also discovered that Hennessey had helped turn a small charity in the north of England into a front through which to flush dirty cash. Among those said to have used it to hide large sums of money and gold was Ferdinand Marcos, the deposed president of the Philippines, and his wife Imelda. In the other direction, crime syndicates with links to the Mafia also took advantage of the services offered by the UK charity.

Hennessey's cooperation helped him escape with just an eighteen-month sentence with nine months suspended after admitting handling £100,000 in money from the Brink's-MAT raid.

But, before then, he led detectives to the British Virgin Islands, to the offices of an accountant, one William O'Leary.

They raided the premises at dawn and, armed with a search warrant, seized his files. It was soon clear O'Leary was a key player in laundering drug cash from the US. Pleased with their haul, Scotland Yard alerted the DEA, Customs and the IRS in the States.

O'Leary's files were a treasure-trove of evidence for the police. Such was the extent it took a private plane to airlift it all back to Fort Lauderdale.

To their cost, O'Leary and Hennessey kept three files for each transaction: one for the client, another for auditors, a third for themselves. And it was the third file that was the key to unlocking the whole operation. It contained the code system, the handwritten notes, accounting for the wire transfers, cash transfers, the money orders, and the way they were all received.

O'Leary, faced with prison, had no choice but to cooperate fully with the US in return for immunity. Under interrogation, he admitted receiving in excess of $100 million dollars in proceeds. During one of his many interviews with police, the thirty-three-year-old British-born accountant felt the urge to implicate not just those who helped with his own activities but also those around him.

He identified ten or more large-scale, US-based trafficking organizations.

'If you think this is bad,' he told detectives, 'you should see what's going on next door in Anguilla.'

For his cooperation, criminal proceedings against him were dropped.

Although the revelation that there was a massive laundering scam going on in a neighbouring island was a nugget of gold, the US still had no jurisdiction over the British overseas territory. But Dean Roberts saw the significance of this report. If detectives from Scotland Yard could work with the DEA, there was the opportunity for a more official arrangement.

What if there was a joint taskforce between the FBI and UK police? Done correctly, it had the potential to circumvent the small matter of international law. By hooking up with their counterparts in the UK, the FBI could be armed with arrest warrants to investigate claims of money laundering in Anguilla.

With a spring in his step, Roberts strode to Lerner's office, clutching the dossier.

'When can we meet them?'

'Who?'

'The limeys.'

'Soon as you like. They're in town with the DEA.'

'Brush up on your colonial history, then, Rich. You'll need it when I set up a meeting.'

Heading the British arm of the investigation was fraud detective Trevor Davy. Similar in age to Roberts, he could have been cut from the same cloth. Although physically more imposing than his American counterpart, his desire to smash financiers and lawyers who bankrolled organized crime and drug gangs matched Roberts'. And his reputation for being cranky and downbeat when things weren't going his way also mirrored that of the FBI man.

At Roberts' insistence, Davy and his detective colleague Keith Black met with the FBI that week. From the moment they were introduced, both men knew they were going to work well together. The FBI could offer a reach into the US that Davy could only dream about, while, for Roberts, Scotland Yard could unlock the secrets of the tax havens.

It was to be the beginning of a joint taskforce to combat crime in these tiny enclaves of the British Commonwealth.

Agreeing to operate on an ad-hoc basis initially, the two agencies embarked upon a unique cooperative effort. Davy and Black made Miami their base and worked side by side with the FBI. The team was quick to formulate a list of targets, based on information supplied by O'Leary. One name on that list would hold particular significance to me.

'So, who's the main man in Anguilla?' Roberts asked Davy.

'Henry Jackson. Operates from St Kitts. He has the grand title of Her Majesty's Constitutional Adviser,' he said, in a tone that suggested the Englishman didn't much care for titles.

Roberts studied the debrief.

'Got his fingers in a lot of pies,' he mused.

'Let's pay him a visit.'

18. The More Things Change, the More They Stay the Same

Sometimes the most seismic changes in a person's life come from the slightest of tremors.

There should have been nothing exceptional about a house purchase I helped arrange for one of Andre's friends. I assisted people like this all the time. There was nothing out of the ordinary about the property – a smart, family home in Coral Gables, not far from where I used to live with Monique. And when it came to closing the deal there should have been nothing in the routine meeting to sign the necessary documents, deliver the cheque and receive the keys that could have suggested this would be anything other than a normal day.

So nothing prepared me for the moment when I walked into the meeting with Irene, Andre's friend, and for the first time met the realtor who'd arranged the sale.

'Hi,' she said. 'I'm Denise.'

Something sparked within me.

She had been sitting cross-legged and when she stood to greet me the first thing I noticed about her was her height. She was as tall as me and, dressed in a sharp black business suit, was striking and elegant. Plus she was a redhead. I was hooked.

From that moment, the formalities of the closing became a sideshow to the real purpose of the meeting – getting to know this woman better. The legal issues concluded, we exchanged contact details, all under the pretext of potential future business but I detected an interest from her too in the lingering smile she gave me as we parted.

I rang Denise almost immediately and asked her to dinner. I'd realized that if you sensed an opportunity you had to grab it.

After checking in with some clients on pressing business I needed to get finished before I thought about a social life, I raced back to my apartment. After a quick change, I paused and had a look around the home I'd created with Monique in the Brickell Bay Club.

Antique art deco furniture now filled every room, beautiful artefacts sourced from Europe and New York. Even the light switch I now flicked was a genuine piece from the 1920s.

Looking down into the bay I could still see the thin blue line of the Customs boats patrolling the harbour. There was talk that a new drug was on its way – more powerful than regular cocaine. More powerful meant more profitable. If this were the case it wouldn't be long before everyone tried to get in on the act.

I collected my things and was on my way out of the apartment when Monique came back.

'Where are you going?'

'Out. To see a client.'

'Again?'

'You know what it's like. They rely on me.'

Monique looked resigned. 'I thought you said you were stepping back. Sometimes I think your clients mean more to you than I do.'

'Don't be like that,' I said. 'It's these clients who have paid for this.'

'I don't want a fancy apartment. I want a relationship.'

'Monique . . .' I complained but it was devoid of any real emotion. I was itching to get out of the door. 'Come on, give me a break.'

I went to give her a reassuring kiss but she deftly moved her head and there was only air.

I could have stayed and calmed her down, but I was more interested in what the night with my new companion could bring. Without so much as a second glance, I walked out and shut the door.

As the elevator took me down to the car park I chastised myself for lying to her. The sad fact was that by now we were living such separate lives I didn't really have to make the effort. Neither of us had the heart.

I met Denise for dinner at a little seafood restaurant in Key Biscayne, the idyllic island community where she lived, just six miles from downtown Miami. We hit it off instantly. She told me she was twenty-nine and a former flight attendant, who worked for Pan American airlines flying on charters with the White House staff. I could well believe it given the care she obviously paid to her appearance. Her make-up was immaculate and her hair shone. Statuesque and leggy, she seemed to me everything that Monique was not.

It was the beginning of what you could call a whirlwind romance. I engineered slots in the day when I could see her and very soon gave up the pretence of trying to cover my movements. I'd been keeping secrets from Monique for so many years it had become second nature.

I'd tried to be the dutiful partner, even tried to play parent when her children came to live with us, but there was too much distance between us; too much had gone unsaid. She knew so little about the life I'd been living for the past six years that I couldn't even have turned to her if I'd tried.

I was starting to feel my age. I was in my forties, wasn't married, had no children and nothing that resembled a normal life. I probably would have struggled on with Monique; but Denise had changed all that. I was smitten.

Denise took me for who I was. She had an inherent understanding of the drug culture and the people who lived that life.

It was a good job – anyone who didn't wouldn't have accepted me. I even started introducing her to some of the clients. She wasn't scared off and was probably seduced by the ready cash. I didn't have to lie to her. She'd had a boyfriend in the drug business and so she knew what all the indicators were, could spot the red flags.

We were on the same wavelength. It was effortless.

It was no surprise when she suggested we move in together after only two months. I jumped at the opportunity.

Denise couldn't have been more different from Monique. Although undeniably pretty, being a child of the sixties and a cop to boot, Monique wasn't given to flaunting her sexuality and wouldn't dress provocatively. But Denise loved to show herself off. She appreciated the clothes and expensive jewellery I lavished on her. With Monique, the trinkets I brought back from the Caribbean lay in a box at the bottom of the closet.

Not that I had told Denise about Monique, of course. That kind of detail can ruin a fledgling relationship. She thought I was a single guy with a big disposable income who was between houses.

I tried to tell myself I was doing Monique a favour. By cutting her loose, I could save her from being innocently dragged into any investigation, which would almost certainly cost her the job she loved.

And so, for the second time in three years, I walked out on Monique. History repeated itself as I raced home, grabbed some clothes and some money and ran.

I figured the apartment, with all the art deco furniture I had painstakingly sourced and restored, she could keep. She'd earned it.

If that was impulsive, I don't know what you would call us getting married but that's what we were planning to do a month after I moved into Denise's house. And a month before we were due to tie the knot she gave me the news I thought I'd never hear.

I was going to be a father.

I was delighted. After suffering a bad experience with her first husband Denise had always worried that she would never be able to have children. It was a blessing.

Everything was falling into place. Could I really be settling down to having a normal life?

I was still laundering but, with Bernard and Charlie out of the picture, I started to dare to think I could take a step back from that life. I'm not sure whether it was jealousy that I was working so hard on the Frenchman's situation but ever since Bernard was arrested, my relationship with Ed was almost non-existent.

His restaurant with Kelly did launch, but I didn't make it to the opening night. That was just as well. Midnight Oasis, in Kendall, opened with a tremendous fanfare. Joining Ed and Kelly in the venture was Michael Lewis, the accountant, who had clearly been seduced by the money and had agreed to run the supper club on their behalf.

The opening night attracted several drugland figures – but also the DEA, who sat in the car park taking down licence plates. In its first year so much of their narco-profits were being pumped into the venture that the diner became the sixth highest grossing restaurant in the entire US.

Night after night, Ed held court, his gang of hangers-on around him, but from what I had been hearing his court was crumbling. Interestingly, his life had strange parallels to mine. He and Kelly had also moved from Coral Gables to Key Biscayne, not far from where Denise lived. I still ran errands for them but less so recently and when I did it was Kelly who came to me with the instructions.

And by the time I'd left Monique, I had heard from Andre that all was not well with Ed and his long-time partner.

He'd fallen so much out of my thoughts that it was a surprise when I popped into Tobacco Road – the oldest bar in Miami and a haunt of Al Capone's during Prohibition – and bumped straight into him. He looked terrible, so bloated and his skin, once so tanned and youthful, now looked greasy and blotchy.

'Ed?' I asked, because I genuinely wasn't sure if it was.

'Ken. Well, well,' he replied, lifting his head from his beer to study me.

'How have you been?' I asked.

'Wonderful,' he declared. 'Couldn't be better. Life is just swell.'

His response made me wonder how long he'd been in this den. But I'd gone there for a beer so I got my order in and sat next to him.

'How's business?' I tried to appear genuinely interested.

'Booming,' he retorted.

I was about to respond when he added: 'Now at last I have decent financial experts to advise me.'

I thought about challenging this but thought better of it. I'd seen Ed being obnoxious with plenty of other people. It was silly to think he wouldn't show me the same disdain eventually one day.

'I'm glad to hear that,' I smiled.

'Listen, Ken. I appreciate your help in getting us started and all that but the simple thing is you were out of your depth.'

Now his words stung. I said nothing.

'I mean, come on,' he went on. 'Did you know that those corporations you formed for me right back at the beginning dissolved after a year? What the hell was that about?'

I thought about fighting my corner, explaining exactly why I let the paperwork on those corporations expire so no one would trace who owned them, but I thought better of it. If he was too stupid to work out what I'd been doing I certainly wasn't going to explain it to him. That was my tradecraft, my secret.

I simply shrugged.

'There you go,' he said, as if justified. 'You haven't a clue.'

'I guess not,' I said. 'Still it sounds like you're doing well without me. Did you go down the Swiss route after all?'

'Best move I've ever made. Clever of you to make out what you did was so complicated. But it's not. I can do it myself and I don't have to pay the extortionate fees your cousin and his pal Jackson demanded.'

I had had enough of listening to his tirade so I sipped my beer and left him to it.

It saddened me that Ed could be so twisted in his logic that he couldn't see how much I'd helped him. The man who once announced we were like brothers was now happy to smear my reputation.

I drove to Denise's and tried to put him out of my mind. We had more important things to address. We had a wedding party to plan.

As we'd both been married before, we eschewed a church ceremony for something more in keeping with an episode of *Miami Vice*. It was 1986 after all.

I had hired a luxury yacht – that was going to be the location for the nuptials and the party. Denise looked sensational in salmon-coloured leather skin-tight slacks and a skimpy top. I showed up in white leather jeans and a shirt. The ceremony was timed to coincide with the setting sun and performing the honours was Trevor, the pilot who had occasionally helped deliver cocaine in from the Bahamas, but who also was, helpfully, a notary public.

We decided on a non-family affair. Instead, the guest list was an odd mix of twenty-five of our closest friends and clients, including Andre, who'd kicked the whole adventure off. Never one to judge, he'd chosen not to take sides in my split with Monique; his Christian live-and-let-live attitude always to the fore. Unsurprisingly Ed and Kelly were absent.

As the champagne flowed, we lounged on white leather cushions and partied into the small hours. Only my poor new wife couldn't have many sips of champagne on her wedding day as she spent the festivities gently stroking her tummy, protecting the growing life within.

Eyebrows were raised on my choice of honeymoon destination. Where else but Saint Martin – the French side for a change? And never being one to pass up on an opportunity to mix business with pleasure, I left Denise relaxing in the hotel while I paid a quick trip to Anguilla to register a few new corporations to replace ones that would soon expire.

Well, what did she expect? Vacations were a luxury I could ill afford.

After the wedding, it was time for some other changes. I moved offices, from the ex-prosecutors' law offices downtown to a little discreet place behind Tobacco Road.

Christine, my ever-faithful secretary, finally felt it was time to move on too. She'd been uncomfortable ever since the Jean-Luc escapade and wanted to move abroad. She had recovered some money in a civil settlement, and it was burning a hole in her pocket, so off to England she went.

I was sorry to lose her but completely understood her thinking. Plus, I had a reasonable solution. Denise became my secretary. I could keep things in-house. She still wasn't fully aware of everything I was up to but having her around me in the office helped legitimize everything.

It wasn't long after this when I was walking near my new office and bumped straight into Monique. I guess in a city of nearly 400,000 people it was bound to happen. It was the first time I had seen her since I'd disappeared with my things for the second time.

I hadn't told her I was leaving, hadn't left her a note, hadn't called. It might have been callous but my view was that there was nothing to say and it would only have been more painful for both of us. I'd convinced myself too that by walking out like that I might be helping her in the long run. She might spare her tears for me and feel more anger towards me than sorrow.

I was kidding myself.

'How's your life with your new girlfriend?' she asked sarcastically.

I didn't think it was a good time to update her with the news that I was now married with a child on the way. Instead I tried to placate her with noncommittal answers but made it clear I was now settled in a new relationship.

'Your life was in tatters when I met you,' she said, with the hint of a sneer.

I tried to reason: 'Come on now, we had fun but we wanted different things.'

'Like what?'

'Well, one day I wanted to get married, have kids of my own. You'd already been there.'

'I'd marry you now.' She was almost pleading, the beginnings of tears forming in her eyes.

I couldn't bear this. After everything we'd been through the last thing I wanted to do was hurt her.

'Monique, you don't understand. I. Am. Married. Now.' The words came out staccato.

For a moment I thought she would implode but she regained her composure. She stood there silent.

'I know this is hard but I still care about you, Monique. We obviously still have a lot of ties,' I said, shamefully mindful of the connections we shared and how damaging it would be if she chose to make things difficult.

'Is it too much to hope that we could still all get along?'

'What, like friends?' she scoffed. 'We'll all hang out and have barbecues?'

'Well, I . . .'

'Forget it. I'll never be friends with your new wife. She ruined my life,' she said bluntly.

I imagine if I'd run into her at any time in the first few weeks after I left our encounter would have been much different – more blood and thunder – but now the energy had drained out of her.

'If we'd gotten married it could have been different for us,' she said, almost dreamily.

'It might have. But then again, it would have been more complicated now if we'd split. This is the best for both of us.'

'Don't try to guess what's right for me.'

There was nothing more to say. I made some excuse that I was late for a meeting and we parted. I'm not sure if the chance encounter gave her the closure she needed but in a way I was relieved we'd been able to remain fairly civil.

Ours had been a relationship born out of drugs and, like a rush of coke, our love had reached incredible highs but the comedown had been long and drawn-out. I hoped I wouldn't repeat the same mistakes with Denise. The meeting with Monique made me determined to clean up my act. I went cold turkey. After several years of using cocaine, often daily, I resolved to give it up for good. I could no longer stand the hangovers, the dehydration, the headaches and the post-hangover depression that were the hallmarks of a long-standing habit.

It was tough at the start but as I started to feel better physically I rejected the urge to go back to my old ways and kicked it for good. Denise worried how I would be able to still move in the circles where cocaine was rife and sit quietly while clients got high in front on me, but I found that, once I had decided to quit, I lost interest in the whole cocaine thing. Only after I cut back on the coke did I appreciate how dependent I'd been. For years it had been a constant presence in my life. Having a new wife and the responsibilities of forthcoming fatherhood helped focus my mind.

Our son was born the following spring. We called him Anton and as I held him in my arms for the first time I wondered what life he would grow up in; whether his birth signalled a new start for me; whether I could ever become a normal lawyer again.

Introducing Anton to my father was a special moment. As Robert surveyed my new respectable life he said: 'Finally it looks like you're living a normal life.' I'd never given him or my mother the merest hint of my alternative lifestyle but maybe they knew well enough, or simply hoped, that this was a new period of calmness in my life

My focus now was to build up the real-estate side of my law practice. I wanted to turn my back on laundering, to slip out of the game with the same ease that I'd entered it. That was the dream.

19. Where Would You Like Your Twelve Million Dollars?

Dean Roberts never imagined it would be this easy.

His team of eight men stormed the Anguillan office of Henry Jackson, in a similar style to the Scotland Yard detectives raiding William O'Leary's premises.

At best he'd hoped Jackson would have been like a rabbit caught in the headlights, at worst a lawman who called for their badges for such an affront.

Instead he got compliance and no little charm. It was as if Jackson had been waiting on them to arrive. The politician hadn't got where he had in government and law-making to be fazed by the attentions of the police.

'We have reason to believe you have assisted in and facilitated laundering activities,' Agent Roberts had told him. 'We have a warrant to search the premises.'

Roberts loved this part of the job. When you could see the whites of their eyes. This was when you saw the real mark of a person.

Jackson was very calm. And he performed an impressive sidestep.

'Gentlemen, come in,' he said politely. 'Rather than pull my beautiful offices apart, why don't you make yourselves comfortable, take your time and examine my files at your leisure?

'You have a job to do and I'd like to assist you as much as possible. I obviously refute any suggestion of wrongdoing. But if you can find anything here that assists you in your inquiries, be my guest.'

Roberts exchanged quizzical looks with his English counter-part. Was this guy for real?

Jackson wasn't done.

'In fact, I don't think I really need to be here. Why don't I leave you gentlemen in peace? Let me take a vacation in the US for a week and you can look through my files.'

Roberts and Davy had a conflab. It was unusual but, frankly, they didn't need Jackson here looking over their shoulders, see-ing what files were spiking their interest.

He had too many ties with the two communities to do a run-ner and, besides, if there was evidence here implicating him in crimes they could arrest him later. What they wanted were the files and he was giving them – without fuss, or having to seek a court order.

They knew it would mean that Jackson would probably claim publicly that he was shocked by the police action, how he refused to cooperate and that such a search had been done while he wasn't present, but they could live with that.

As Jackson gathered his things and stepped out of the office, the taskforce moved in with their boxes and started examining the mountain of paperwork in front of them. This was going to take a while.

I checked myself out in the mirror as I left our house.

I was in the same type of garish shirt, shorts and shoes I'd worn for the trips to Anguilla. Since the first trip there for Ed and Kelly I'd made hundreds of cash runs to the tiny island. They'd become second nature to me. It had even got to the stage where I convinced myself I wasn't even doing anything wrong.

Maybe that's why I'd agreed to don the outfit – my money launderer's uniform – to make a deposit for David and Mary Vanderberg, the husband and wife organic farmers in North

Dakota. When they weren't employing Andre to market their
homegrown crystal meth they enlisted the help of the Hell's
Angels to do it for them. The bikers had obviously been busy.
David now had hundreds of thousands of dollars from the sale
of his home-cooked crystal meth to invest in an offshore account.

Today I was taking $150,000. It seemed small change – routine.
With some of the clients in prison or exile, my criminal activity
was dropping off. My life had flipped. In the beginning the
legitimate legal work was a sideshow to the main event. Now
though, I'd worked so hard to build up a bona fide business, it
took over the centre stage from the illicit stuff. I was kept busy
with real-estate closures and civil litigation. But I couldn't just
extricate myself from the scene completely. I still had clients
for whom I was the link to their accounts there. I still had my
own money in Anguilla. Despite spending tens of thousands
on the art deco furniture, some $75,000 was in my Jose Lopez
account. But, I told myself, as I checked myself out before
heading to the airport with my tatty hold-all, it was good to
keep your hand in.

As soon as I stepped off the boat in Anguilla I could feel
something was wrong. Coming towards me, heading in the
opposite direction, was a flustered-looking Henry Jackson.

'Ken?' he exclaimed. He looked like he'd seen a ghost. 'What
the hell are you doing here?'

'Business. What is the matter with you?'

'Can't stop, Ken. Got to catch a boat.'

His eyes were darting from side to side like a petrified animal,
as if he were terrified of being seen talking to me.

'Henry. What's going on?'

'Look Ken . . . I'm sorry. Can't stop just now.'

With that he was off, half-walking, half-running, towards the
boats.

Normally Henry was so jovial, so full of life. Convincing

myself it was nothing I continued to the bank. Gerald, the president, greeted me as usual but wore a grave expression.

He took me into his office.

'Listen, the police have been here. They want to look through the details of accounts held by Americans.'

That explained Henry Jackson's nervousness.

'Let them look,' I said confidently. 'I don't think we have anything to fear.'

Gerald looked at me, with a slight air of scepticism.

'It's okay,' I reassured him. 'I trust you. I'm not going to move my money out of there. Now's not the time to panic. Let's see what comes of it.'

I deposited the money for the farming couple and headed home.

I considered what he was saying. I could feel the panic rise but, when I thought about it, the accounts were secure. Thanks to the island's secrecy laws, no one had the right or the jurisdiction to go snooping around to find out the true identity of the account holders. There was no way this could be traced back to the clients. The only evidence of who the owners of the accounts were was in Henry's chambers. And no agency could get a court order in a foreign jurisdiction to go raking through confidential files. Could they?

It was a month or two later when the bomb dropped.

I was sitting in my office trying to organize some legitimate legal work when the phone rang. It was Gerald, from the bank in Anguilla.

'Ken,' he said, tersely. 'I don't know how to tell you this. Your bank accounts have been frozen.'

'What! Which?'

'All of them. I'm sorry.'

'Why are we being targeted?'

'It's not just you.' I could hear the stress in his voice. 'It's every account.'

'What do you mean, "every account"?'

'Every corporate American account.'

'What can I do?' I asked, more in hope than anything else.

'Nothing, for the time being,' he insisted. 'There's nothing you can do. There's nothing anyone can do. We just have to see what they want. They're still investigating.'

I hung up. This didn't make any sense. US police didn't have any jurisdiction in Anguilla. It was a British overseas territory. Even the FBI couldn't just walk in there and start demanding to see the files.

Had Henry been leaned on? Had he taken on one dodgy deal too many? I knew he was a crook but he was our crook. Unless he'd been bought.

I couldn't think what was now pushing our entire empire to the brink of collapse. All I knew was that having every account frozen had shaken everybody up. Although Bernard and Charlie had been arrested they had been caught in the act of smuggling. This was the first strike right to the heart of the organization, the first direct hit my original clients had taken. Some of the money seized was part of the original six million dollars I'd helped deposit with Ed and Kelly.

After my recent run-in with Ed, he was characteristically furious when I broke the latest piece of bad news.

He came on to me fuming: 'What does this mean? Why didn't you do something?'

I remained calm. 'The DEA are involved. They told the bank they wanted the money seized and forfeited to the US because they say it is drug money.'

'Fuck!' Ed screamed. He never took bad news well.

'It looks like they have specific information. They knew exactly where to look. Who don't you trust?'

'I don't trust anyone,' he snapped back. 'What can we do about it?'

That was rich. As if he'd be able to do anything.

'We just need to wait it out and see what happens.'

I tried to sound relaxed but the truth was I had no idea what was going to happen.

Then, just a week or so before Christmas, a little miracle. I was in my office when the phone rang. It was Gerald from the bank in Anguilla.

'You're not going to believe this but I have just heard from the magistrate in this case. The DEA were supposed to supply affidavits with proof of the criminal origins of the money by this week. They have failed. The money has been unfrozen.'

I sat in silence.

'Well?' Gerald asked.

'Well what?' I said.

'What do you want me to do with it?'

'Do with what? Our accounts?'

'Yeah, I can free the lot. There's some twelve million dollars in the name of American corporations. Where do you want me to send it?'

I thought for a second. Twelve million? My clients had only about two-thirds of that. He must be talking about everybody's money – mostly it belonged to their associates.

'Send it over to Harvey Smith. Send the lot to his trust account. I can work out what I'll do with it then.'

Where in the real world could you do that? Transfer that amount by word of mouth, over the phone, without authorizing documents? It was absolute trust. More importantly it was twelve million dollars. Only in the tax havens could such a thing be possible.

Even though it was nearing 5 p.m. in Anguilla the funds were immediately transferred to Harvey Smith, a criminal lawyer in St Kitts. He was a lawyer I'd used to mix up locations for a while so we weren't putting all our eggs into the Anguilla basket.

My Christmas changed instantly. Instead of having angry clients with frozen accounts and the fear of not knowing what had happened, we now had it all back again.

The next trick was to get it out of St Kitts. There were no cheques in that line of work and I couldn't transfer it to accounts in the US because we would have to prove the source of the funds.

There was only one thing for it. We'd have to do the opposite of what we did some seven years previously and bulk smuggle the cash back into the US. Only this time we would have to do it in stages.

There was another problem. Harvey demanded a 25 per cent contingency fee. He'd bailed us out and managed to facilitate the audacious transfer, and he wanted to be handsomely rewarded for it.

I don't know what was worse – breaking the news initially that all their money was frozen or telling them that they'd only be getting back 75 per cent. Two especially – Peter and Marcus from Ed's original crew – were aggrieved. They couldn't see I'd done them a favour.

I shrugged off their complaints at the time. They could moan all they want.

It might have been straightforward to hire another jet and repeat the original process in reverse but I couldn't take that risk. For all I knew, the DEA and Customs had all the details of the account holders and could be monitoring our travel arrangements. A private jet would create attention.

The only way it could be done was to smuggle it out in smaller cash lump sums. I arranged for some of the clients to meet me in Sint Maarten. I was comfortable there, knew the hotels and it was straightforward to ferry the cash from St Kitts. I literally was the bag man, meeting clients, handing them thousands of dollars in cash and waiting for the next man.

For my own seventy-five thousand I had to come up with a different plan. I called seven close friends, some in the business, some not.

'How would you like a holiday in the Caribbean?' I said. 'We're going away and we're coming back with nine thousand bucks each.'

Who would turn down a couple of days' fun and sun in St Kitts when all you had to do was bring some cash back into the country, perfectly legally? After all, anything under ten thousand dollars you don't have to declare.

We got the money back into the country without incident, completing a remarkable turnaround.

It had always been a source of mystery to me how the house of cards began to collapse. Years later, I was sitting at home watching TV when a British-made documentary came on detailing the money laundering trail that went all the way from the sunny island of Anguilla to the rainy Isle of Man. Among the informants on the programme was an accountant who, even blacked out and with his voice disguised, I recognized as William O'Leary. He was explaining how it was he who suggested to the FBI to start poking their noses around in little Anguilla. I had used O'Leary to form those British Virgin Island companies, taking them literally off his shelf, in several extremely fast visits. I was able to take a chartered aircraft from Anguilla and could get into and out of Road Town in less than two hours, with the plane barely having time to cool down between flights.

So that's how the taskforce found out all about my clients' money and about any Americans who had money next door in the bank.

Henry Jackson might have been calm and collected in front of Roberts and Davy but the moment he got out of that office his world must have collapsed. That must have been when I had run into him. No wonder he looked so frightened. I must have been the last man on earth he wanted to see.

The investigators had already been to the bank but, without the names of the accounts they were interested in, were easily batted away. Then they went through all the client lists and all the books and found the names of all the corporations. That enabled them to seize any cash for any firm owned by an American. Of course, that had been my insurance policy. We'd been so secure in the bank, but in Jackson's office I'd inserted the real name of the client with his file.

That safeguard I'd inserted all those years ago had nearly been the death of me. Yet somehow I'd got away with it.

Armed with those names, all accounts of companies identified as having American owners were frozen, regardless of whether there was any proof of illegal activity.

I wasn't the only one who would be starting to put the puzzle pieces together. The FBI and the DEA were furious when they realized what had happened at the bank. Believing Gerald had been bribed they forced him to quit his position.

They had the names of a lot of clients they now suspected of trafficking and laundering, but did they have the evidence?

20. Hellhounds on My Trail

It was an innocuous meeting. Part legitimate business, part criminal.

Roque Herrero was a low-level client, a retailer who sold the drugs down the supply chain. He certainly wasn't in the same league as his father. Ramon Herrero was what you could call a super-criminal. For a fee Roque could screw the electricity meter any way you wanted; wind it back, make it run slow, stop it. With a service like his he was very much in demand. He was a wanted man, not just by residents struggling on the poverty line in the ethnic-dominated suburbs but also by the power companies and the police.

Roque decided the drug trade was a less conspicuous profession. He'd done well for himself, selling on cocaine to places like New York and was looking to invest. But he shared his father's healthy paranoia. He always refused to meet me in my office downtown so on this occasion I suggested having lunch at a seafood restaurant in Key Biscayne, close to where we lived. So close in fact that I decided to take one of Denise's two little shaggy-haired Tibetan Lhasa Apso dogs.

With all the heat in Anguilla, my options were limited and I thought he'd be better investing in legitimate things like property. Roque was an amenable Cuban immigrant who listened to my advice.

We'd just finished lunch and were returning to our cars.

'What the hell,' Roque exclaimed.

He pointed to something across the street. I squinted in the sunlight, unsure at first what I was looking at. It was a man crouched down behind a small car. The sight in front of us was so incongruous it took a moment for it to dawn on us what he was actually doing. And then it registered – he was filming us.

The unwieldy block of metal he was holding at eye height obscured his face. But the methodical motion of his other hand made it clear he was recording us on what would today be described as an old-style camera. It was clear one of us was under surveillance.

Roque was shocked. 'Oh my God! Do you see that?'

Before I could answer, the man, seeing that he had been noticed, jumped in his car and with the impatience of a grand prix driver sped out of the car park, leaving dust trails.

Heart pounding, I glanced around, trying to determine if the man was alone. There was no sign of anyone else. Not taking any chances though, once I'd bade farewell to Roque, I took a circuitous route home, primarily to establish if anyone was following me and also to try and calm my rattling heart.

It felt like a bucket of ice had been poured over me. My senses were heightened. I'd frequently suspected we were under surveillance and, after the debacle in the tax havens pretty much took it for granted; but this confirmed my suspicions. The walls were definitely closing in now.

I drove down to the beach, where the Rickenbacker Causeway links the idyllic barrier islands to Miami, and stared out over the bay to where the downtown skyscrapers loomed in the distance.

What did I expect? I had to face the facts. There was every chance that for the past four years I had been under surveillance. All the times I had been thinking I had been covering my tracks, were the combined forces of Customs, DEA and police closing in behind?

What of the clients? They all seemed to come with personal

guarantees. But what if one was an agent, quietly compiling a dossier that one day hangs us all? Who was our Donnie Brasco? It could easily be done. I'm sure the Bonanno crime family – with whom Benny Hernandez's Italian cohorts had links – thought they were impenetrable before Joseph Pistone, the FBI agent, infiltrated and nearly destroyed their whole organization.

How far could I trust the clients to watch my back? When we'd been on the way up we were brothers in arms, but we would soon see how far loyalty went.

I'd been threatened once already. If the clients felt the squeeze, could my life be in danger? It's one thing to be looking over your shoulder, but how do you protect yourself if one of your closest allies decides to stab you through the heart?

Maybe I should have fled to Nicaragua when I had the chance. It seemed easier when the only person I needed to worry about was myself. Now I had Denise and Anton. What world of pain was I storing up for them to suffer?

Of course, it could have been that Roque was the target for this particular snout. But the fact that I'd been spotted with him implicated me further in this network. After Jean-Luc, Bernard and the swiping of the frozen twelve million dollars from under the noses of the FBI and Scotland Yard it would soon become apparent, if it wasn't already, that I had my fingers in a lot of pies.

In the days, weeks and months after that incident, I operated on autopilot. I went about my business, kept in touch with clients, worked on real estate, played the dutiful father and husband at home and tried to exist as normal. Yet all the time I wondered when the bomb would drop. When would this idyllic picture be smashed? We moved from Key Biscayne to The Falls, a quiet suburban area of south Miami, further out than Kendall.

Subconsciously it was a step further away from conspicuousness – deeper into lower profile territory, as if any watching agents might think: 'Well, look at him, he's a good guy now, living the quiet life, let's leave him alone.'

There wasn't a day when I could escape the creeping fear that this could be my last night of freedom. Would daybreak bring a dawn raid on my house? My head was filled with images of me being handcuffed and arrested, with Denise wailing hysterically and the baby screaming.

In the end there was no dawn raid, no screaming or wailing.

The knock happened very early one morning, when I was sitting in my office working on a real-estate division. Denise was at home with Anton. I was alone in the office when two people, a man and a woman, dressed smartly in suits entered without fanfare.

The man spoke first: 'Kenneth Rijock?'

'Yes,' I said.

'My name is Matthew Martin. This is my colleague Julie Richter. We are with the criminal investigation division of the Internal Revenue Service.'

This was it.

Martin was polite. He said they wanted to speak to me about forty corporations I had formed which they believed were fronts for criminal activity. They wanted to see all the documents I had that were relevant to these corporations. If I failed to cooperate they had a subpoena for me to appear before a grand jury.

I tried to remain calm but inside my nerves were shredding.

'I have no files here relating to anything like that.'

'Uh-huh,' the agent replied. 'You can explain that in front of a grand jury.'

They served me with the subpoena and – after dutifully explaining to me a procedure I was well aware of – bade me a good day.

I sat and tried to work out what the hell I was going to do.

Studying the paperwork I read that I was ordered to produce all documents in my possession regarding many offshore corporations that I had formed in the tax havens.

I had been telling the truth when I told the agents I didn't have any such documents on me. They were all held in Henry Jackson's chambers. But if they had raided those offices and been able to gather evidence, did they not have these files already? Did they want to establish that I had corresponding papers that would, beyond any doubt, show that I was responsible for the formation of the corporations and the accounts? Or did they just have the names of the corporations but none of the supporting documents and still needed the necessary evidence to build a case against me?

Or could it be that they were about to offer me immunity, hoping that I could give them the testimony that would enable them to arrest Ed Becker, Kelly and the rest?

In a week's time I would find out. My instructions were to appear in front of a grand jury in the northern state city of Gainesville, home of the University of Florida. Although the judge I would be appearing before presided in the state capital of Tallahassee, he was a circuit legislator and moved around the region. I had to go wherever he was sitting. A grand jury testimony, the procedure used to determine whether there is sufficient evidence to go to trial, is closed to the public, and is one of those rare places in the American legal system where your attorney cannot physically accompany you. I would have to go in alone, armed with nothing but my wits to protect me.

The very nature of it is intimidating, even for those who practise law. The grand jury is meant to be part of the system of checks and balances, preventing a case from going to trial based purely on the prosecutor's say-so. The prosecutor must convince the grand jury that there exists reasonable suspicion, probable cause, or a prima facie or legally sufficient case that a

crime has been committed. The grand jury, comprised of ordinary members of the public and selected in the same way as a
regular jury, can compel witnesses to testify before them.

At home that night I broke the news to Denise. I tried to
remain as calm as possible, as if this was all routine. She was
distraught.

'What does this mean?' she cried.

'I don't know,' I said, honestly. 'I'll just have to go there and
find out. They might only have half the picture and be trying to
put pressure on,' I added, more in hope than confidence.

'Prison?' She was getting hysterical. 'You can't leave me to be
a single mum.'

'I know. Look, it won't come to that,' I said, trying to reassure
her. 'They might think they know what's going on but it could
be they need me to fill in the blanks. It could be a bluff.'

As the day of the grand jury approached, Andre paid me a
visit. I still kept in touch with my old friend. He had been a
guest at our wedding and had grown fond of Denise. Wisely,
he'd stepped back from the scene when the heat started to build
and, as if it were possible, was even more low profile than he'd
been when I'd first met him all those years ago.

He got straight to the point.

'Hear you've been summoned.'

As I hadn't been under arrest, nor been under any instruction
that I couldn't practise law, I'd tried to continue as normal and
hadn't given any indication that anything untoward was happening. Word spreads, however, and I suspected Andre had
been sent on a fact-finding mission – an emissary dispatched to
establish if they had anything to worry about.

'Who's sent you, Andre?' I asked.

He laughed. 'No one. I came out of concern for an old
friend. But,' he added, 'since you ask, Ed and Kelly are also concerned that you are okay.'

'Is Ed concerned for my wellbeing? Or what I might say?'

'I'm sure it is wholeheartedly for your wellbeing,' he smiled.

In some ways I felt aggrieved that Ed would send Andre to check up on me, to make sure I held firm. But it was also slightly reassuring that the old network was holding together. If I stood firm it would set the benchmark for everyone else to do the same.

'You can tell them not to worry,' I said. 'I have no intention of testifying against anyone. I will protect my clients, current or former.'

'I didn't doubt you for a second, Ken. Let's just hope if the shoe is on the other foot they are equally loyal.'

We exchanged a look suggesting we both knew what the answer to that would be.

I hired a lawyer to represent me. A cousin was a partner in a Miami law firm and he recommended one of his associates, a very able lawyer called Stewart Coburn.

When the day came to travel to Gainesville, I comforted Denise by telling her it would all be fine. I would be back in a day or two and life would carry on.

How I so wanted that to be true.

For all I knew I might not be coming home. I could easily find myself in a Jean-Luc situation – ordered to testify and, if I refused, jailed indefinitely for contempt.

That night, Stewart and I left for Gainesville, anxious to be there in plenty of time for the following day's appearance.

Although having appeared in court hundreds of times as counsel meant I was familiar with the procedure, when the time came to make my way to the courthouse the next morning I was overcome with the same stress that must befall every witness who appears in front of a grand jury.

There was every chance I was facing jail today. The suspense in those final moments before I appeared was almost unbearable. It took all my strength of will to keep it together as I prepared to stake my freedom on the outcome of this short hearing.

As I walked in, leaving my lawyer to wait outside, I could see the twelve grand jurors to my right, preparing to watch and listen. I was sworn in, not a particularly pleasant thing for someone involved in criminal conduct, and who knows the penalty for perjury. I hardly had time to take in my surroundings and get my bearings before two US Attorneys bombarded me with questions. Any thoughts I had that they might soften me up with some exploratory openers were instantly dispelled.

The first prosecutor, the assistant attorney, got straight to the point.

'Mr Rijock, are you a money launderer for a criminal organization?'

'Absolutely not,' I replied firmly, trying to sound as convincing as possible.

I excused myself from proceedings to consult my lawyer. He objected to the question, sparking the usual argument between counsels over procedure. Once that was resolved the prosecutor moved on to the subject of the documents. Quite truthfully I stated that I wasn't in possession of any corporate documents. That of course was the reason I had kept them offshore but I neglected to volunteer this information to the court.

He then reeled off all the names of the clients and the companies. It was clear they knew a hell of a lot about the organization.

My response was to hide squarely behind attorney–client privilege. Of course, if the suggestion is that the attorney or the client has been committing crimes this doesn't apply, but I had to chance it.

As the allegations kept coming, I felt it was time to offer the bogus excuses, knowing full well there was no legal basis for them but hoping to bamboozle them on the key issues. I objected on the grounds that if I talked about these offshore companies I'd be committing an offence because it was illegal in those countries to talk about the owners without their permission. Perhaps unsurprisingly, this didn't convince the prosecutor.

I then argued that since the names of these companies and clients had been illegally obtained I was not required to divulge any information. Again I knew this wouldn't wash with him but I felt the defiance in me build. I had a reckless feeling of detachment. I felt fiercely protective of my clients. We were in this game together. It had made me feel more alive than anything I'd experienced as a run-of-the-mill litigator. I was so hardcore at that point, I was willing to go to jail for contempt of court. This was yet another new phase. I was going to have to take some chances.

I knew that if they wanted me to talk they had to give me immunity, in the same way that Jean-Luc was offered it. This was high risk because they might just offer me this but I felt I had no option. I would go to jail before I talked.

Clearly frustrated at my obfuscation, the attorneys were faced with one of two options. They could take me before the judge who could grant me immunity. Alternatively, they could excuse me from further testimony before the grand jury, in the hope that they could indict me later, providing they had managed to assemble sufficient evidence against me to be successful at trial.

Eventually the prosecutors instructed me rather tersely that I was to appear before a federal judge the following day. The trouble was the judge was moving on to Tallahassee so that's where we would have to be too. I feared that meant only one thing. I would be taken before the judge then and offered immunity. I'd therefore be jailed for contempt of court when I told them I wasn't prepared to testify. Just in case I was in any doubt that the judge would impose a stiff sanction for my non-cooperation, Stewart learned he was a staunchly conservative southern gentleman who was rumoured to have had a relative with a drug problem. The chances of him taking a soft line with someone connected to a narcotics case were slim.

After leaving court, there was just time for a quick call to Denise to give her an update before we had to make the drive to Tallahassee for the sitting tomorrow.

If she was uncertain as to what was going to happen she was even more so now. I did my best to reassure her but the facts were that I could be incarcerated that afternoon for contempt of court for refusing to testify against my clients.

Our first stop in Tallahassee was the law library at the Florida Supreme Court, where we spent several hours researching any tactics we could use to support the legal objections I intended to deploy if I was ordered to testify. Many of the excuses I'd already given were completely bogus. And if, as I expected, they would be thrown out, I needed a back-up plan. Our research produced some crumbs of comfort but we left knowing that the following day my fate would have to rely more on the disposition of the judge than any sound legal argument.

I must have been about the only case being heard because the courtroom was deserted, save for the prosecution and a few court officials.

Standing in the dock, I no longer felt bullet-proof. I was alone and scared at what lay ahead. In front of the judge, the prosecutors once again asked me outright if I was a money launderer and demanded I produce documents for all the off-shore accounts.

I stood firm, denied the allegations and asserted my claim that no documents existed.

I had to wait nervously while the prosecution team conferred.

Was I soon going to be led to custody?

Finally a decision. There was no offer of immunity. They wanted to charge me, that much was now certain.

I might have been spared the nightmare of being held in prison until I decided to testify, but the ruling meant the prosecutors were going to gamble on finding enough evidence to indict me at a later date. They excused me from any more grand jury sessions and said I was free to go.

I had my liberty, but as I shook hands with Stewart, the decision gave me a new sense of foreboding. In my experience only higher-ranking targets were not offered immunity. It was the lower level members of an organization who were offered the 'Get out of jail free' card because the US Attorney's office wants to roll over the smaller fish on the kingpins. I was no kingpin, but they must have thought my involvement was prominent enough.

Returning home, I wondered how anxious my clients were about the sum and substance of my grand jury appearance.

I had survived today's battle but there was still a war to win. I did not hold out much hope.

21. Call My Lawyer

Was the party over?

It certainly felt like Miami was facing a colossal collective comedown. The love affair with drugs that had grown since the sixties was starting to pall. As users tired of the cocaine buzz a new, more potent narcotic emerged. The spectre of crack cocaine was casting a shadow across the city.

From the moment in April 1986 when the *Miami Herald* first reported the existence of this new, more powerful substance, crack seemed to infect every pore of the city. Where cocaine had made people feel invincible, crack – so named because of the noise the rocks gave off when burned – offered intense highs but crippling lows. Users chasing a greater buzz binged for days on end, shutting out everything from their lives save for the pipes. This wasn't the drug of well-heeled professionals who partied hard and still made it to work the next day. Crack was a drug for the poor and within months its legacy of misery was felt across Miami.

As it spread from slum to slum, in its wake it left homeless addicts and crack babies. It was being blamed for drive-by shootings, the resurgence of gang culture, and a spike in burglaries, robberies, muggings and black-on-black youth violence. The response from Congress was to pass laws making penalties for *possessing* crack up to a hundred times greater than penalties for *trafficking* powder cocaine – which remained the recreational drug of choice for wealthy professionals. As the crime rate rocketed, so did the numbers in jail. Between

1980 and the end of the decade the US prison population tripled from 330,000 to over one million.

Now, two years after the emergence of crack, the nation's attitude shifted from pro-drugs and freedom of choice to a hard anti-drugs line and yet stiffer penalties.

Fortunately the national mood chimed with my own. After my appearance at the grand jury I felt at a crossroads. Surely I couldn't continue with laundering with this much heat around me. Yet what other life did I know?

Because the hearings took place out of town in northern Florida, word of the grand jury investigation hadn't yet filtered back to the streets of Miami. Certain prosecutors got wind of it and some of the clients had known in advance I was going up there, but the atmosphere in the day-to-day running of my practice was one of blissful ignorance.

I was torn between feeling I'd been given a second chance – an opportunity to sort my life out – and thinking I'd got away with it – so why quit?

In my more bullish moments I convinced myself that if the prosecutors had enough on me to charge me they would have done so by now. Their investigation had been based on information gleaned from files from Henry Jackson's office. Still no arrests had been made off the back of it, so were we off the hook?

I still lived in fear of the 'knock on the door' and after my appearance in front of the prosecutors I suffered sleepless nights, panic attacks and cold sweats. The FBI, the DEA, the police and Customs were all out there, potentially watching my every move, trying to come up with the crucial piece of evidence that could put me away for a long time. Sometimes I could sense the breath on the back of my neck.

Not for the first time it was as if I were back in the army, trying to detect how close the enemy fighters were, trying not to blow my composure. Now they were almost close enough to reach out and touch.

Some days it was impossible to think straight. Domestic life was a welcome distraction but simple tasks in the house were difficult to concentrate on.

The landscape had changed dramatically in the last few years but I still had clients out there who wanted to proceed as if it were business as usual. Career criminals don't just quit their vocation at the first sign of trouble. That way of life is in their blood. And, as much as part of me wanted to give it all up, a stronger driving force willed me to keep moving, keep trying to stay one step ahead.

I continued with my law practice in Miami but being back at work meant I had to exercise extreme care in my ongoing illegal operations. One false move could give the prosecutors all they needed to secure a case against me.

As if I didn't have enough to worry about, one of my biggest client's organization was embroiled in a major criminal case. Benny Hernandez had sold his stake in his empire to the brash gangster Rick Baker, the man who'd turned up unannounced on one of the cash runs to Anguilla. My instincts about him had been right. Baker had none of Benny's charm, expertise or intelligence. He cut corners and made mistakes. He was effectively caught red-handed and faced being prosecuted by a federal taskforce in northern Florida. That spelled bad news because juries there were known for being far more conservative than they were in urban Miami. The arrests of some forty people in Benny's old gang – including his brother Carlos Hernandez – had prompted him to flee the country for Spain with his American wife and seven children and he'd been smart enough to get his millions out of the banks before the accounts were frozen. In Spain Benny had been able to bribe enough of the right people to guarantee his immunity – at least in the short term – and he waited it out in Europe to see what would happen with Baker's case, where his millions ensured immunity from extradition, provided that certain government officials were adequately compensated.

Baker and Carlos chose to stay and fight the prosecution, believing that their hotshot lawyers would somehow get them off on a technicality. Unfortunately for them, such rare successes normally come in state courts, where prosecutors have huge caseloads and mistakes can be made, or defendants can take advantage of depositions where they can learn the strength of the government's case. In federal courts, however, there are effectively no advance warnings and rarely do prosecutors make errors. Carlos and Baker were in for a shock too because little did they know that presiding over their case was the same conservative judge who was on the verge of hearing my case at the grand jury.

From the weight of evidence against them – plus the testimonies of dozens of witnesses who gave evidence in return for reduced sentences – it was no surprise when both men were found guilty. What was a shock were the sentences: they were practically of biblical proportions. Baker was jailed for three life sentences plus two hundred years tacked on for good measure. He'd probably have got less if he'd tried to assassinate the President of the United States. Carlos got twenty years, lenient by comparison.

The swingeing sentences and the assertions from the court that the two men were part of a criminal conspiracy that extended to more than two hundred people and amassed a two-hundred-million-dollar fortune sent shockwaves through the other clients, forcing many of the other kingpins to take drastic action before the net closed on them.

From out of the blue Kelly got in touch and asked to meet me. I went round to her house in Key Biscayne. She and Ed had split up and she was more than capable of branching out on her own.

It had seemed a long time since I'd last seen her. Although years of hard living had aged her she still retained a certain allure. As I studied her I was reminded of Ed's callous comment in the early days when he'd dismissed her as 'just a little smuggler girl'. That was typically arrogant of the man but did Kelly a disservice. Beneath the archetypal blonde good looks was a feverish mind.

She got straight to the point.

'A lot of shit is coming down, Ken. I'm going to head out of town for a while until the heat dies down but it would be good to keep an ear to what's going on.'

'Okay,' I said, unsure where she was going.

'And should anything happen,' she went on, 'I'd like to retain your services . . . for a fee.'

She handed me a bundle of cash which looked about two thousand dollars.

'Like a retainer?' I asked.

'Kind of. I want you to represent me should the shit hit the fan.'

I took the cash and put it down to some twitchiness. Sure the heat was on but now was the time for a steady hand and clear thinking.

Just a month later she called me up again.

'Listen, Ken, about that arrangement. I'm not going to need you any more. I want my money back.'

'Kelly, that's not how it works. You paid me a fee to retain my services. It's non-refundable.'

'What? Who the fuck do you think you are, Rijock? Give me my fucking money.'

As she slammed the phone down I couldn't believe what had just happened. The arrogance was astounding. Like Ed, she'd been so used to her subordinates running around doing her bidding it had gone to her head.

A few weeks later I heard Kelly had fled to Mexico with fake ID. She wasn't the only one doing a runner. Ed slipped quietly out of the country to France and set up in business as a book publisher in Europe. Other mid-level operatives also fled the country or left the state until the heat died down.

Incredibly, as everyone else was leaving, and after seeing what punishment had been meted out to his brother, Benny returned to North America. When his property portfolio had been expanding he'd invested in a number of shopping malls in Canada and returned to recoup some money. Although he travelled on a fake passport, he made the mistake of carrying his real identity. He was arrested and added to the list of gang members awaiting trial.

Against the backdrop of this judicial crackdown I tried to live as normal a life as I could. With so many of my original clients out of the picture, among the few people I continued to do regular work for were the trigger-happy Martinez brothers. The Vanderberg organic farmers were bitter about the loss of money invested in offshore accounts that was reduced by the attorney Harvey Smith's fees in St Kitts. Such is the world of business.

Trips to the Caribbean now required nerves of steel and although I wasn't moving anything like the money I had previously, I always held my breath re-entering the US.

After they'd threatened my life over Charlie's boat, I'd tried to limit my involvement with the brothers, but Enrique, the eldest, approached me with a dilemma. He wanted to buy a light aircraft from a legitimate dealer in south Florida to smuggle some premium marijuana from Jamaica to Florida. He only had dirty cash to fund the deal but, with the agencies coming down heavy on any transactions that looked like they were funded by illegal means, he wanted it cleaned in lightning time. As it happened the Vanderbergs had cash in an offshore account they wanted my help in bringing back into the US. I saw a chance to execute a switch.

As I had access, or signature authority, over the offshore client funds, I saw no problem in organizing the arrangement. I figured both clients would be happy.

I travelled to the Caribbean and obtained a New York draft – a cheque drawn by the offshore bank on its correspondent account in Manhattan – payable to the aircraft seller, so that the first client could close on the purchase and the transaction would look like it was from a legitimate corporation.

Next, I took the profits from Enrique and delivered them to the Vanderbergs as if they had just been transferred from their offshore account. It was the same amount that had been drawn on their account.

The transaction appeared to go through without a hitch. Despite this Enrique called me in a rage, spitting through his grating Cuban Spanglish: 'What kind of stunt are you trying to pull, Rijock?'

'I did what you asked.'

'You sent me a banker's cheque. It took five bloody days to clear. Five bloody days.'

'Have you got your money? Is there a problem?'

'I have the money now but I had to wait five bloody days. I don't expect to have to wait for my own money.'

I let him vent his fury at me before he rang off. The plane appeared to make it to Jamaica so I didn't know what his problem was. When the time came to collect Enrique's fee I noticed it was considerably less than we'd agreed. He'd clearly exacted some sort of revenge for making him wait. Knowing how volatile the Cuban was I decided to let it pass.

The months after my grand jury appearance stretched into a

year and beyond and I continued like this, still laundering where I could help out clients while trying to give the impression that I was a run-of-the-mill small-time lawyer with his own practice.

We settled into a quiet routine. Denise worked in my office part-time, often bringing Anton in with her when there was no childcare available. The longer time went on the more I was able to convince myself that maybe I would escape.

The next associate to fall was Michael Lewis, the accountant who was behind the ingenious commission salesman laundering method and who'd been instrumental in setting up the Midnight Oasis restaurant for Ed and Kelly and some other clients.

Michael had been investigated after the IRS had grown suspicious of tax documents he'd filed on behalf of the clients in a bid to show they received regular income from legitimate enterprises. The IRS had the names of a whole host of clients, from Ed and Kelly through crewmembers and ship's captains on vessels they'd operated, down to transporters who'd moved their drugs when they came into the country to the wholesale dealers who'd sold it on. He'd pleaded guilty to a minor charge but was shocked when the judge decided to make an example of him and sentenced him to five years.

Not long after I took a call from David Matthews, a criminal defence lawyer I'd known since law school. He was representing Michael. I met David in his offices downtown. Michael was intending to testify against some other clients in a bid to reduce his sentence. David showed me a list of the people he had in mind. It was practically a who's who of the network. He asked my help to identify them. As I looked down the list of names I saw that it was a snapshot of the people I had been dealing with for the past eight years.

Michael had, perhaps understandably, been furious to be the subject of an investigation himself. He had always been in denial about his involvement. Anyone who actively assists known traffickers in defrauding the tax system and enjoys the perks of the life that narcotics funds by hanging out at their own restaurant has to expect they are going to come under the microscope at some stage.

David asked if I knew where some of these people were, whether they were evading justice or already in jail. In return he gave me some information about the case against Michael. I saw it as a mutually beneficial exchange of information but I failed to read between the lines.

There had only been one name missing from the indictment. Mine.

Six months after that meeting with David I got to my office early one morning to prepare for a real-estate closing. I was dressed casually in jeans and a polo shirt because I had a suit I was due to pick up from the dry cleaners. I'd only been in the office a matter of minutes when the door opened and two people walked in. I would have recognized them anywhere. They had haunted my dreams for two years.

'Remember us?' It was Matthew Martin and Julie Richter, the two IRS investigators who had summoned me to the grand jury.

This time they weren't as friendly.

'Kenneth Rijock, you are under arrest.'

Richter approached me with the handcuffs. Martin began to read me my rights.

'It's okay,' I said. 'Please can I leave a note for my wife?'

They agreed and watched while I scribbled a note for Denise who was due into the office at 9 a.m. with our son.

All it read was: 'I have been arrested. Call my lawyer.'

I didn't want to leave the name of my attorney for the officers to see so I wrote the number for my cousin who I knew would set me up with an able defence lawyer. They allowed me to lock up the office and then it was on with the cuffs and the march out of the back door to their waiting car.

The IRS had returned for me because they were the only agency that understands money laundering. The DEA focus is solely on the drugs, Customs focus on the smuggling, but the Internal Revenue goes on the paper trail. A multi-agency task-force had been collaborating for years to compile the evidence needed to secure convictions against an organization of our magnitude.

I might have been paranoid but Martin and Richter seemed pretty smug about the fact that this time they were getting to lead me away in cuffs. They must not have been very happy when I'd refused to testify last time around. They took me down to the federal courthouse where I would be processed.

That's the first time I found out I was getting charged under the Racketeer Influenced and Corrupt Organizations Act. Racketeering or RICO is the business of being a career criminal. Normally this is a charge reserved for organized crime and was designed to prosecute the Mafia. RICO carries a maximum sentence of twenty years. As if that wasn't bad enough I was also charged with conspiracy to defraud the IRS by interfering with the lawful collection of taxes, which carries a five-year sentence.

I was asked again if I wanted to cooperate. Although I knew they must have something on me to arrest me this time I felt bold enough to hold out until I could see the strength of their case. I was also still determined not to roll over and felt sure I would remain loyal to the clients. No matter what happens I can't betray them.

With that news to digest I was dumped in a holding cell to wait before I was brought before a magistrate that afternoon to determine if I qualified for bail. Sitting there in the cold, dark cell, with the moans and shouts of fellow inmates around me, I started to wonder how it had got to this.

I thought about holding my hands up to everything. They had caught me. I was guilty. But then I reminded myself that this was law and it was up to the court to prove a case against me. They might have some paperwork but did they really have the witnesses and the evidence to convict me of RICO?

My defence lawyer Allan Thomas arrived and our first priority was setting out the case as to why I would be eligible for bail. If I had been deemed a flight risk or if it was felt I hadn't had sufficient ties to the community they could have held me over until my trial. However, because I had a licence to practise law, I had a family and I had lived in Miami for twenty years, I felt sure I would be allowed to go.

When it was time for my arraignment, courthouse prison guards came round and I was unceremoniously chained to half a dozen inner city dealers who would be appearing at the same time. My career lows were coming thick and fast. Federal courts are the last place to expect favouritism for white-collar criminals.

Walking into the courtroom as a criminal defendant, in handcuffs and chained to a bunch of street-level dealers, was a rude awakening. Although I'd been in court countless times, I was used to sitting in the privileged position of the counsel table. Yet here I was the centre of attention as a newly arrested accused.

Allan was the perfect choice to defend me in a case like this. Unlike many defence lawyers in Miami who took on the drug cases, he was neither bold nor flashy but had a calm, southern manner.

He put the case for bail eloquently, adding that in no way was I a danger to the community, having no firearms on my person when arrested and there being no suggestion I was selling drugs.

The charges were read aloud. The magistrate listened to the details. There was one unusual aspect for him to consider, however. Because of initial arrests of witnesses in northern Florida, the case was being brought not in Miami but in Gainesville. Therefore, the court had to ascertain whether it was a risk to allow me to travel on my own to the site of the action.

After a fairly long deliberation on the matter, he approved my application for bail. I signed a promise to be present for all necessary court hearings in the case, and posted 10 per cent of the actual bail amount into the court registry.

As I walked out of the courthouse back into the light I was grateful for my liberty. I just didn't know how long I'd be able to savour it.

22. The Case for the Prosecution

Only on the way back home did it sink in.

There was the possibility of life imprisonment, should this go against me. The crimes I had been charged with might have carried twenty- and five-year terms but I could be certain that the Organized Crime Drug Enforcement Task Force would add up all the drugs and all the money and push for a life sentence. And under federal sentencing guidelines there was no time off for good behaviour. A life sentence would be exactly that.

I was staring into the abyss.

Going round and round in my head was the puzzling question of why. Why now?

I realized both counts were conspiracy felonies, meaning that they had enough to satisfy the basic elements of the crime. That meant two or more persons had conspired, or agreed, to commit certain crimes; that I knowingly and voluntarily joined the conspiracy; and that a member of the conspiracy later did one or more overt acts, for the purpose of advancing or helping the conspiracy.

I knew that the organization I had represented extended to some two hundred people if you added everyone who had played a part. I knew that several had been arrested in the Rick Baker/Hernandez brothers sting and I knew that several had testified to reduce their sentences. What this development meant was that a number must have now testified against me. But who?

While I agonized over who could have betrayed me, a more pressing matter was trying to convince Denise that this wasn't catastrophic.

Unsurprisingly she'd been hysterical. I tried to remain optimistic and pointed to the grand jury experience as evidence that this could yet turn in our favour but she wasn't a fool. She knew the stakes had got much higher.

'What is going to happen to us?' she wailed. 'What will I do when you're banged up?'

I had no answer.

'Just tell me where the money is,' she said.

'What?'

'Tell me where the stash is.'

'I don't know what you're talking about.'

'Come on, you must have put some away. You're the big-shot money launderer. Where's the stash?' Denise was hysterical now.

I wished I could tell her there was a pot of gold at the end of the rainbow, but the truth was I had made no contingency plans. I always feared that if I was ever arrested anything we had in our names would be seized as proceeds of crime. We would lose the cash, our cars, everything.

Since the grand jury I had never kept that much cash about because I thought they would seize all our cash, even that in Denise's name. There was a danger now she could even be questioned and implicated. The bottom line was that I didn't own a car, house or bank account and held no stocks or assets in my own name. There was no back-up plan.

'We'll work something out,' was the best I could offer. Her cries as she ran off to the bedroom, slamming the door behind her, told me that didn't convince.

Two weeks later, Allan called. He had the indictment. For the first time we would see the scale of the case against.

It made painful reading. Peter and Marcus, the two crew-members on Ed's boat who had been originally hired by Kelly and who had flown down to Anguilla with us on our first big bulk cash smuggling mission, had testified against me.

I'd helped make them wealthy beyond their dreams and they repaid me by telling the court I had laundered their money. When I thought back to the episode with the frozen millions in Henry Jackson's bank, I recalled that out of all the clients they were the two most aggrieved that Harvey Smith was taking a 25 per cent cut. This was their revenge.

I paused from reading to consider this. Although their testimony was clearly damaging and personally crushing, it wasn't the smoking gun the prosecutors might hope it was.

I read on cautiously but with renewed hope. Maybe this wouldn't be insurmountable. Maybe they had over-reached themselves.

But it was worse than I could have ever imagined. The words were like daggers through my heart.

Ed Becker.

The man who once called me his 'brother', who said we were cut from the same cloth, had given me up. There was no light at the end of the tunnel.

How? Why? Ed should have been out of the game. Retiring to the south of France, he should've seen out his days blissfully. But history is littered with stories of crooks who didn't know when to quit. Like Bernard Calderon and Benny Hernandez before him, he'd been lured back into the trade and from what it seemed had believed he could successfully launder his new profits himself. He was wrong.

He was arrested on charges completely unrelated to the investigations launched in Florida or the Caribbean. It seems Ed found out the hard way that the French penal system could be a lot tougher than even its American counterpart. He might have been over six feet and a former ship's captain and drug runner, but he found himself on the receiving end of some brutality at the hands of his cellmates and suffered broken ribs for his trouble. It seems the Arab inmates took exception to him being Jewish, something I was surprised to learn because he kept it well hidden and had such a German name.

Perhaps it was that experience that persuaded him to cut his losses and offer himself up. He believed I could be his 'Get out of jail free' card.

As I read the details of the evidence he had given I could hear Andre's words in my head all those years ago: 'I bet my bottom dollar, if the shit hits the fan he will be the first person to roll over on all of us.'

The irony was that if he'd only kept his nose clean he could have married the French fiancée he'd shacked up with and per- haps attained citizenship in his new homeland. From the experience of Bernard's case we knew how reluctant the French were to extradite its nationals.

There was no gloss I could put on it. Ed's testimony was the smoking gun. In order to limit his own punishment he had given them everything – the schemes, the clients, the money and the methods. I could see now that it had been his testimony that had done in Michael Lewis, the accountant.

I was stunned.

To think: two years earlier when I was in front of the grand jury I would have gone to jail to protect him. And now this?

That wasn't the end of the testimonies. A fourth witness, unnamed in the indictment, was willing to say I was on a private plane trip to smuggle drugs that he was a pilot on. I knew instantly who that was – Trevor, the notary who married Denise and me.

Trevor was a schoolteacher who bought his cocaine from Andre. He was happy to take the profits cocaine gave him but he was constantly jittery about the repercussions. Once, when he lived on the west coast of Florida, in a home with waterfront access, he panicked when he went to have his hair cut and the hairdresser said: 'You know, to look at you no one would ever guess what you really do for a living.'

That was enough for him to put the house on the market and move away. He had gone to flight school and got his pilot's licence. I utilized the twin prop he bought shortly after from time to time. He was a handy contact when you needed to make the short hop from the US Virgin Islands to the British territories across the water.

Trevor was impulsive. While in LA he rented a limo and fell in love with the blonde driver. With the same speed he sold his house in west Florida he divorced his wife, married the chauffeur and moved to Miami. His new front activity in Miami was a private post office. I helped out with the legalities when he bought it.

He was soon the dad to a young baby and I should have suspected that he'd do anything to save his skin should the DEA come calling.

His claims were nonsense, however. The only time I'd flown a plane was when Jimmy let me take over the controls on the first flight to Anguilla. Was there no end to the treachery?

Even after these sucker punches the US Attorney wasn't finished.

In the coming weeks the prosecution filed a motion that they intended to use Rule 404 of the Federal Rules of Evidence in relation to the charges against me. I knew instantly what that meant. If I decided to tough this out and proceed to trial, the prosecution would produce evidence of other, as yet uncharged, criminal conduct. That meant they'd lead evidence on Bernard and Charlie Nunez. They were going to smear me in front of the jury so I didn't have a prayer. The inference was clear. If I intended to stand up in court and try to claim that I was really a trustworthy lawyer – that this was just one transaction I was involved in – I wouldn't get away with it.

While I made up my mind whether I should plead guilty and limit the damage, I had to sit Denise down and prepare her for the worst. It wasn't pretty but speaking to her about it helped form a decision in my mind.

'Listen,' I said. 'There's no pretty way to say this. My situation is dire; there are at least three big clients who are going to be helping the US Attorney, and who would testify against me.'

If I went to trial, I told her, they will tell the court that I had opened companies in tax havens for them, bulk smuggled drug cash offshore with them and banked it, and advised them on a wide variety of criminal ventures involving narcotics smuggling and laundering the proceeds of crime.

Denise looked at me with pleading eyes.

'But can't you say you took on the work in good faith or something? Say you were innocent. Yes, you advised them but you had no idea where the money was coming from.'

'I could, but there's another factor. The trial would be heard in Gainesville. That means the jury is going to be full of small-town Floridians. They'll have made up their minds before they walk in. They'll take one look at me and think I'm a crooked lawyer. Then the US Attorney will throw the book at me, dredging up everything to do with Bernard and Benny and Rick Baker.'

'There must be something you can do. You've never been in trouble. You haven't had so much as a parking ticket. That's got to count.'

'It might. But only if I plead guilty. That type of record will be taken into account then. If I go to trial and they find me guilty I'll get the full punishment. They'll come down on me for trying to waste the court's time with a bogus defence.'

'What are you saying?' Denise asked, knowing what the answer was.

A good lawyer has to know when to be a zealous advocate, especially on his own behalf, but he also has to know when the case is hopeless – a lost cause. That's where I was.

'I don't think I have an option.'

Denise sat in silence, her head in her hands.

'This is my one chance to get a mild sentence,' I said, trying to sound reassuring. 'I think it is time to put my hands up. If I don't I might as well shoot myself in the head.'

Denise lifted her head and stared at me through tear-stained red eyes.

'And what about me? What about your son? How do you expect us to survive while you're rotting in prison and we have no money?'

'If I choose this way I might get five years. Anton will be eight when I come out. I'm not saying it will be easy but I can make it up. He's young enough to get over it. We can start off anew.'

'Don't talk like that,' Denise wailed. 'I don't know if I can handle this.'

Although the idea of pleading guilty to any offence seemed against everything I had been taught, I had no choice. Despite Denise's protestations, I notified my lawyer that I wanted to change my plea, and the Assistant US Attorney handling my case set up an appointment.

He requested me to make a Proffer. That meant I was to state all the incriminating facts surrounding my case, and the prosecutor would listen, and decide whether my statement was valuable enough for him to ask the sentencing judge to go easy on me.

First, I needed an immunity letter so that should he decide not to accept my admissions in regard to sentencing he could not use the material and testimony against me when the case went to trial.

And so it was that in a crowded room in the courthouse, in front of prosecutors and the IRS, I laid bare ten years of criminal activity. The significance of what I was doing was not lost upon me. I was admitting violating the very laws that as a lawyer I had sworn to follow. I had to bare my soul to strangers who would have thought I was on the same side as they were.

I told them as much as I could – about Ed Becker and Kelly, the formation of the corporations and the offshore accounts, the other ruses to hide the money and the schemes to dodge tax. After all, the clients I had zealously protected for a decade had just rolled over on me big time.

'What happened to your plane?' one heavy-set officer asked.

'Excuse me? What plane?' I was incredulous. 'I can fly but I've never owned a plane before.'

'The one that was set on fire on the runway in Jamaica, killing the pilot.'

I stared in disbelief and looked to Allan who sat there equally horrified.

The Customs agent went on: 'You were registered as the owner.'

I racked my brains. It couldn't be the Martinez brothers, could it? Enrique had been furious about the banker's cheque taking five days to clear. Could he really have been that vindictive to have put my name as the owner on a plane they knew would be forever linked to a drug smuggling operation?

I passed this on to the assembled prosecutors.

The Customs agent said: 'That might explain it. A plane had come into Jamaica. They hadn't paid off the police. Some mob rushed the plane, set it on fire, killed the pilot. Your name was down as the owner of the plane.'

I was stunned. With each passing minute I was finding out

the lengths my so-called clients would go to protect their own interests and to destroy anyone else.

It didn't end there. A DEA representative spoke up.

'And what can you tell us about the UPS truck?'

'You've lost me,' I said, shaking my head.

'The boat owned by the Nunez brothers that was dumped in Anguilla. It made so many deliveries into the US we called it the UPS truck. That one.'

How could I forget that boat? It was the same one the Martinez brothers – them again – threatened to kill me over if I moved it from the harbour, even though I knew it had long been a target for the law.

The DEA agent said: 'We know you were involved with that. The mechanic you warned to stay away from it?'

I thought about arguing the case that I had nothing to do with any clients' boats. As I did so he opened a file and passed it to me. Sitting on the top of the paperwork was a handwritten note scribbled on some paper. It read: 'Get out of here, there are law enforcement looking at the boat. Don't go near the boat.'

It was my own handwriting.

I should have known there would have been something wrong with that boat. Once again my actions incurred the wrath of trigger-happy Enrique Martinez.

'And another thing,' the prosecutor added: 'Where was the house you owned in Anguilla?'

'I didn't own a house in Anguilla,' I said. 'I don't think in all the times I've been there I've even spent the night on the island let alone bought a home there. What makes you say that?'

'You were there for seven months solid in 1982. We got you going in there but it was months later before there was a record of you leaving. You must have had a base there.'

I smiled. While I marvelled at the attention to detail my

pursuers had been paying to my movements during all the years they had been on my trail, I also took some satisfaction that my unorthodox modus operandi for getting in and out of the tiny tax haven had stumped them.

I explained the beauty of the island territories and their lax security that meant you could enter and leave simply by showing a birth certificate for identification, thereby hardly ever denting your passport with stamps of entry.

I tried to be as open as possible during the hearing, hoping I would give off the impression of being repentant and willing to cooperate for the greater good – and for the reduction in my sentence.

I continued to be amazed by how wide the investigation had spread. Transporters, smugglers and crew – they got all sorts of people to cooperate. The further they went down the pipeline the more people they found to prosecute. They were all in the same situation I was in. And, like me, they probably realized the only chance of a lighter sentence was to roll over.

When my hearing was over, I was allowed to go home. My next court appearance would be in Gainesville where I would learn my fate. In the weeks following my decision to plead guilty, Denise retreated into the depths of depression, rarely speaking to me. I wondered how well our marriage would cope with an enforced separation.

The only good news was that the prosecutor's office contacted Allan's office to advise us that they would agree to file a motion requesting a lesser sentence than that which would normally be commuted. It was settled, then. Only my sentence was left to be decided. I would be entirely at the mercy of the trial judge, who could still stun me with a long term.

The next communication confirmed the date of the sentencing hearing. Not long now.

23. Trips You Have to Make Alone

I can't think of many more humbling experiences for a lawyer than attending your own sentencing.

It is one thing to represent a client in a case: while you can feel for their plight, you are somewhat detached from proceedings.

I travelled to Gainesville with Allan Thomas, my defence attorney, full of fear and loathing. I was learning how lonely it was to be a criminal defendant. Just before the hearing was due to start I was overcome with panic. I felt my life slipping away and I was powerless to prevent it. I needed no more reminders of Vietnam but the siren was blaring – I was just waiting for the bomb to drop.

Allan submitted copies of the awards and decorations I had received while serving in Vietnam and Cambodia, but the judge could not have looked less impressed. My attorney then gave a summary of my career, focusing on the positive points.

When the time came I decided to say nothing save for a humble comment that I was ready to receive my sentence.

After a deliberation, the judge was finally ready to deliver my sentence – four years in a federal prison. Given I had calculated five, you might think the news might have come as something of a relief, but there is nothing pleasing about being told you are to be incarcerated.

My immediate thoughts turned to Anton. He would be seven when I got out, if I had to serve the entire four years. It seemed like a lifetime.

The only other instruction I received that day was that I would have to report in thirty days' time to begin my sentence; exactly where was still to be determined.

The hearing over, I returned to Miami. Denise was distraught. It was a longer sentence than she could handle. What made it harder for her to accept was that we still had no idea where I would serve my time. There was every chance I could be sent to a federal institution outside of the state. That would mean no family visits. That unsettled detail kept me on edge during my final days before becoming an inmate. With a wife and young son, I needed them to be as close as possible. I worried about my parents too. I had shielded them from every detail about my dark money laundering life, and when I was arrested it was a major shock to them. They were elderly, but not infirm, and would be able to travel, so long as it was not a great distance. While they were very supportive, as was my sister, I know that it was hard on them.

Bizarrely, for a couple of weeks before I had to make final preparations to leave, life went on as normal. Since my case was filed outside of Miami, and did not make the newspapers, few people, apart from some close friends and some lawyers involved in the case, were even aware that I had been arrested. I then had to go about the depressing business of winding down my legal practice. Ten years previously the practice had dwindled to nothing when my life was in chaos. Now, history was repeating itself yet in wildly differing circumstances.

I concentrated on closing out my pending files, putting my affairs in order and spending as much time as possible with my now three-year-old son. The beautiful Florida weather was just beginning, but I could see only dark clouds. From Denise's disposition I could tell that my marriage was not going to survive my prison term. I could not count on having a home to come back to.

As the day loomed I started to panic about prison. I still didn't know where I was going, who I would be thrown in with. Would the other prisoners resent me because I was a lawyer? I had heard that the correctional officers in the prison system had made it difficult for some lawyers who had represented drug defendants. What was in store for me?

With two weeks to go, the word came that I was to report to the federal prison camp at Eglin Air Force Base to begin my sentence. Eglin was in north Florida, not handy for Miami but at least it was still within the state.

I counted down the days.

In another throwback to my time in the armed forces, I got my hair cut short in preparation for my incarceration. And, in a scarily familiar episode, I had the painful act to perform of putting the dogs to sleep. Denise had been sure the two pets would be too much of a burden for her to look after with our son as well. As I took them to the vet, memories of doing the same thing with my parents' cat and dog before I left to go to Vietnam came flooding back.

At work, I closed down the files, put the client details into storage and referred any active business out to other lawyers. With a clean slate, work-wise, it was time to close up the office, move the last of the files to an attorney friend, and make the travel plans to Eglin.

In the days before I was due to leave I had a farewell dinner with close friends. The mood was sombre and there was a finality to it that seemed to suggest would last longer than my time in prison. I really had no idea what kind of life I would be coming back to.

The night before I felt feverish. The most difficult thing was leaving Anton, because I knew things would be different when I came back. Life moves on, whether you are there or not.

Denise came with me to Miami airport with Anton for my

one-way journey north. It was more painful than I could have possibly imagined. My son had no idea what was going on but he picked up from his distraught mother that some seismic change was happening.

In no time they called the flight.

Andre had offered to come with me to Eglin but I had declined his generous offer, telling him I didn't want him to have to make the return journey alone.

There are some journeys that a person should endure alone.

24. Withering on the Vine

It was dark as the plane flew north up the east coast of Florida. I was slumped in my seat.

Suddenly the sky lit up with a brilliance that aroused me from my depression. The Space Shuttle Atlantis was taking off from the Kennedy Space Center. Although the launch pad, on Merritt Island, north of Cape Canaveral, was many miles away, the dazzling light from those massive rocket boosters illuminated the sky for as far as my eyes could see.

Night had become day. I had a ringside seat and as I watched the rocket soar skywards I couldn't help but feel that this was some sort of omen. I was heading to a place where I would be denied even the most basic of luxuries. And, although I had no concept of how bad prison life was going to be, I couldn't help but wonder if I was being shown one last glimpse of how awe-inspiring the world could be before the light was snuffed out.

I wasn't due to report at the prison until the following morning so I checked myself into a basic motel not far from the air force base. Like soldiers who have one last night of freedom before embarking on their army careers, I found a small bar nearby and savoured what would be my last beer for four years.

As I did not have to report at the base until midday, I had a quick breakfast and killed time before I was due to leave. I made sure I drank plenty of water to wash any last traces of alcohol from my system, as I knew they would test me for drink and drugs. With my clipped hair and military-style kit bag, I fooled even the taxi driver who collected me from the motel. He was surprised when I assured him it was the prison camp I was headed to, not the military base.

Nothing happens swiftly inside the correctional system and, on my arrival, a surly guard told me to sit in the administrative offices for twenty minutes before I entered the facility itself through R&D – receiving and discharge – the place where convicts enter and leave prison life. I was sitting contemplating my fate when the time came to begin prison life for real.

'Kenneth Rijock,' came the shout from the guard and it was time to walk into what, for the foreseeable future, would be my home. My belongings were examined, and those few items that I could not bring into the prison were boxed up and sent home. The only thing I wanted in that they wouldn't let me have were some olive drab T-shirts, a personal link to my military past, and the civilian clothes I was wearing. I stripped from those and donned the navy blue air force-type utility uniform I would have to get used to. I was now inside a United States Air Force facility but for me there was no nametag, no stripes to denote rank, no patches or other identification. It was an anonymous identity, and, carrying my issued bedding, like a new recruit in any military, I went into the next room to be interviewed by one of the staff.

The questions were short and to the point and seemed designed to establish whether I was going to be a troublemaker.

'Have you, or are you about to, testify against other individuals?'

'No.'

'Is there any reason why you should fear for your safety?'

'No.'

The brief interview over, I was escorted on to the grounds of the prison and towards my housing block, which, at first sight, was the same barracks-style accommodation that I knew well from my military service. But any illusion that I was back in the army was shattered when, from nothing, a fight suddenly broke out in the yard between two inmates. In a flash several officers were on hand to defuse the violence. As they handcuffed and led away those responsible, my heart sank even lower when I considered what I'd let myself in for.

As it happened, the housing unit was actually much better than those I remembered from the army, and especially my primitive quarters in the jungle in Vietnam. I was to be on the top of a two-man bunk bed, and my blanket was a reassuring olive drab. As one might expect, there was no privacy whatsoever, just an open room for sixty or so inmates.

Since this was a minimum-security institution, there were no bars, no locks, and no barbed-wire fence, just a line painted around the outer limits of the prison camp. Crossing that line was forbidden, and to do so would be considered an attempt to escape, a nice little federal crime that would add five years to your sentence.

Inside the dormitory block, the officer pointed me to my sleeping quarters and advised me all new inmates must take a top bunk. He showed me the tiny locker in which to store my meagre personal effects and explained I had to share a desk with my 'suite mate'. As I smiled at the inappropriate terminology, he advised me not to stray too far from my bunk, as there would shortly be a head-count. Another feature of minimum-security facilities is that they count the population several times a day.

How I felt at that moment – as I stood dutifully by my bed – is hard to describe. The closest I can come is lost. My only consolation was that I felt reasonably confident that I would be safe.

I'd been in tough places before, I told myself. And my predicament could be so much worse. I could have been starting a twenty-five-year stretch for the crimes I'd committed had I chosen to defend myself in court. The storm clouds of the first Gulf War were just beginning to gather, and I consoled myself that at least I wasn't in the Middle East, wearing a sand-coloured uniform.

There was a commotion as the sound of people returning to the block broke the silence. The inmate workday was over and the prisoners were flooding back to their quarters. Most were dirty and looked weary. They spent their days cutting grass or performing some other repetitive chore at the air force base itself, which – being the largest of its kind in the world and taking up the best part of three counties – surrounded the prison camp.

Amid the grubby and disconsolate faces I saw one I recognized. It was our old accountant Michael Lewis, who'd set up the commission salesman method scam we'd pulled off for Ed and Kelly.

'Michael?'

'Ken Rijock. Welcome to the neighbourhood.'

I had heard Mike was bearing a grudge after he'd perceived that he'd been led into the murky criminal world. But it was such a surprise to see each other – and in such inauspicious surroundings – we both set aside opinions, temporarily at least.

'They finally caught up with you too.'

I nodded. 'Ed gave me up. I was warned that he would be the one to fold.'

'Happens to the best of us,' Mike said, referring to the testimony from one of his old clients that had led to his arrest.

'What did they eventually get you on?' he asked.

'RICO,' I said.

He let out a whistle.

'The big one. How come you're here though? You cooperating with the DEA? How long did you get?'

'Four years.'

He let out a scoffing laugh.

'Four years? You set the whole thing up and you get four years. I get duped into it and I get five.'

'That's not quite how I remember it, Mike. We were all willing partners. I put my hands up to it the minute I saw the case they had against me.'

'So did I,' Mike protested.

I considered bringing up his attempts to evade justice but I thought better of it. What was the point? Those facts were immaterial now. We were both in prison.

Seeing him standing before me in dirty standard prison uniform it struck me how ridiculous the situation was. There was a time when we'd thought we were both above the law – thumbing our nose at the establishment.

'It's good to see a friendly face,' I said, trying my best to be conciliatory.

Mike nodded.

After he cleaned up he told me his fiancée Trudy was actually living in an apartment not far from the prison camp, which meant she was able to visit him most weekends and holidays. That, he'd said, had helped keep him sane.

Our catch-up was interrupted by the signal for dinner and I joined my fellow inmates as we trudged across the grounds to the mess hall. My first trip to the dining facility once again took me back to my army days. The food could best be described as adequate: part of the punishment.

Lights out on the first night was yet another depressing milestone to get past. Despite my earlier resolve to be optimistic, as I lay there in the darkness with the moans and noises of my fellow convicts, I couldn't help but sink once again into the depths.

I thought of Denise and our tearful parting at Miami airport. Would she remain loyal like Mike's Trudy had? What would happen if she wanted a divorce? Would I still see my son? I tossed and turned on the flat, hard mattress and endured a long and fitful night.

Wide awake before dawn I got up while my fellow inmates were still in their slumbers and showered, shaved and dressed. I was due to begin my 'Admissions and Orientation' programme: basically being lectured on the dos and don'ts of prison life and to be reminded of why I was in there.

It was here I was going to be assigned my job while inside Eglin. After speaking to Mike and some other prisoners over dinner I had feared I'd be started off with some sort of degrading menial task, like picking up cigarette butts from the yard, as I was warned federal jails liked to initiate newcomers with hard labour.

I was automatically put into a drug treatment programme. Ironically, given my former near-addiction to cocaine, I'd been clean for two years and nothing in my file even hinted at substance abuse. The prison authorities figured that, since I'd advised traffickers for years, I must need to be re-educated. I had no option but to enrol.

The class was taught by a pleasant, bored, former air force captain who read from a well-worn script. Figuring it was a better detail than being outside as the temperature would soon dip in northern Florida, I tried to be as enthusiastic as possible and soon volunteered to help take the group. We split the syllabus between us.

As the days went by I started to recognize more people from the Miami scene. Low-level offenders, or people from the fringes of the organization that I'd met at parties when the champagne was flowing. Here they were, cleaning the visiting rooms and working in the kitchen.

Most of my fellow prisoners were drug offenders with little time left on their sentences, plus a few white-collar crooks and those that had cooperated with the government. There were doctors who had defrauded Medicare insurance payments; corrupt police officers who had turned snitches; accountants who'd committed financial fraud; even the odd judge and politician who committed felonies; and other lawyers. Lots of lawyers.

Some of the inmates were nursing a grudge against lawyers because their legal counsel might have promised them a successful outcome. The prisoners weren't the only ones with a downer on my profession. From my knowledge of the penal system and my experience of visiting clients inside prisons, I knew that the federal system didn't much like lawyers in jails because of the advice they can give to other inmates.

Giving advice to fellow inmates was generally forbidden. I had only been in there for a week or so when one approached me and asked me for advice on his appeal. Word had obviously spread that I was a legal expert.

When the young man – jailed for drug trafficking – outlined the evidence I realized his chances of bringing a successful appeal were next to zero. I did my best to give him a reality check. Then another inmate wanted help understanding a point of law in his case. Gradually more and more came to me. Mostly their stories were the same; they refused to accept their fate and were determined to persevere with some bogus appeal.

Another thing I was amazed to find out was that a quarter of the inmates didn't have any form of high-school diploma. The lure of easy money through drug trafficking had led them to quit school without finishing their education.

I had a chance to help rectify this when, following my stint as a teacher on the drug programme, the authorities assigned me to the education centre to assist the inmates on their mathematics exam. Given how much I detested math in school I couldn't help but think that this was yet further punishment, but I relished the opportunity to give something back.

There was an inmate working there with me, very young, with a horrible attitude. I later found out that his girlfriend had bothered him for several months to get her a large amount of cocaine, and when he did so, he was arrested. Apparently she had been busted many months before for drugs, and the DEA had set her up to entrap him into criminal activity, because his father had a history of trafficking. His tale reminded me there were a lot of casualties in the war on drugs, with many bystanders caught up in the moment. Bad decisions that carried terrible consequences.

Inmates had continued to approach me for advice so I hatched an idea, which amazingly was supported by the education centre. Possibly I'd won some leeway after volunteering to help with the teaching but they agreed when I suggested running a weekly class on legal research and writing, similar to the type attended by first-year law students.

First, I had to sort out the law library. The federal system intentionally didn't have enough of the tools there to do serious research but I knew a couple of the short cuts. I remembered that when we were in law school we acquired a lot of free books from the legal publishers, because they wanted the students as clients later, so they were happy to hand out a lot of sample information and 'How to' books.

I asked the education department to order a range of material and have it sent to the prison. I had a ball with the course. I taught prisoners what the appeal process was, how motions work and how to go about doing their own legal research. And I found the course deeply satisfying. After all, how much TV can you watch? How many times can you walk around an athletics field?

Some weeks into my four-year stretch I was glad to have found a routine and some purpose to my days. And I would need it too. For it was around this time that Denise broke the news that she wanted a divorce.

Inside prison you cling to any sliver of hope. I should have known the writing was on the wall when my parents visited with my son.

The end came in a collect call I made from prison one night after dinner. Denise broke down in tears. She wanted out. She couldn't handle the stress. She needed to get on with her life. Four years was too long.

I sat there on the other end of the phone, speechless. If that was how she felt I was powerless to change her mind.

I came off the phone and went for a walk to the athletics field. Fall had turned into winter and the wind was bitingly cold. For the first time in nearly twenty years I was experiencing winter weather. Even the sensation of wearing a coat was alien to me. I pulled up the collar against the elements and trudged around in the darkness. I wasn't sure if it was the fact that I was losing Denise or the reality that I was in my forties, with a young son, and facing being divorced for the second time. I prepared the divorce pleadings myself and sent them off.

At that moment four years seemed an eternity.

As Christmas approached and the mercury dropped even lower, many of the inmates sought solace in the chapel, looking for some sort of salvation because, despite my best efforts, they realized there would be no miracle solution from the courts.

The only relief was that the nature of the minimum security and the claustrophobic weather meant there was little in the way of violent behaviour. There might not have been walls and barbed wire but supervision was strict and the inmates went about their business without feeling the need to pick fights.

Occasionally you would hear that someone had made a run for it. With the base located near a bayou leading to the Gulf of Mexico, the favourite option was to flee by boat to a new state or country, but given the penalties were a high-security prison for the remainder of your sentence, with five years on top, the risks were too high for many inmates.

For six months I forged an existence for myself. My legal class had become so popular I extended it several weeks beyond what I had originally intended. I had never seen such attentive students.

All good things must come to an end. Some of the correctional staff found out about the class and were unhappy about it. Realizing that a little knowledge was a dangerous thing, they pulled the plug and stopped me working in the education centre. They moved me to the tractor shop, administering spare parts to the men who cut the grass.

Then, from almost out of the blue, a phone call.

My younger sister Michele, still working in real estate, had made it her duty to examine my case and see if there was any way she could find for me to reduce my sentence by what the law calls 'substantial assistance' – in other words snitching on others to get out early.

She got in touch.

'Ken, you're not going to believe this. Someone in the US Marshals Service wants to talk to you about a big European case. Do you want to do it?'

I didn't need long to think about it. I was in prison precisely because I did not cooperate in years past, when my stubbornness and misplaced sense of loyalty to clients resulted in my eventual incarceration. Could I switch sides? The clients had abandoned me, so I was no longer bound by my perverse interpretation of the attorney–client privilege.

'Let's do it.'

25. Payback

Deputy Marshal Don Carter was blunt.

'Mr Rijock, you've made a lot of bad choices in your life. You started out a Vietnam veteran, you were a young bank lawyer and look at what's become of you. You need to come back to the right side of life.'

Carter and his partner had come to Eglin to discuss with me the possibility of testifying against Ed and Kelly. It was an opportunity for some instant revenge.

The marshals said the US Attorney was involved in the first American–Swiss joint investigation into lawyers and bankers in Switzerland who had aided and abetted traffickers in the States. They had identified the money Ed and Kelly had moved to Switzerland, ironically against my advice, but still needed to link it to criminal conduct. They wanted me to provide the missing parts of the puzzle.

There was me telling my budding prison law students not to expect a miracle when it came to overturning a conviction or getting a reduction in their sentences, yet here might be one for me.

That was the good news. The bad news was that they needed to transfer me to Wakulla county jail, twenty miles south of Tallahassee, to be near to the attorney's office where a Swiss magistrate would come to take my testimony. That was the same county jail where Ed and some of the other clients were currently serving out their time.

I suggested it might not be such a good idea to have me

where I might encounter the very person I would be testifying against. The deputy agreed and it was decided they would send me to a federal prison in the county instead.

In July, almost eight months into my sentence, I was picked up from Eglin, manacled at the hands and feet like I was a mass murderer, and transported to the Federal Correctional Institution (FCI) Tallahassee.

An old, forbidding place, it reminded me of a prisoner of war camp I saw once while serving in Vietnam, or of a Hollywood version of a jail. The difference was that it wasn't on the big screen and I wasn't free to go home at the end of the picture. I was going into this dark place.

The military-style barracks of Eglin were like the Waldorf-Astoria compared to this place. From the moment I arrived I was placed into a cell in the Special Housing Unit, or SHU, which was basically solitary confinement.

I was shown to my cell and informed bluntly that this was where I would remain for twenty-three hours a day. My one-hour respite would be to hit some hoops on a basketball court, alone. Three times a week if I was lucky.

The cell was a bleak, lime-green room, with a combination stainless-steel toilet and sink, and a bunk bed, each of which were bolted to the floor, I assumed, to prevent it from being used as a weapon against the guards or as an aid in escape. The windows were small vertical slits placed in the thick wall just in case anyone was thinking of trying to break out.

The only interior window was a small square security opening into the hallway, which allowed the guards to check on the prisoners, but, for the inmate, provided only a small view of the cell door opposite. Three times a week they would let me out to have a shower and a shave. Meals would be served on a tray and pushed through a slot in the door. And once a day a telephone would be delivered in the same way for a ten-minute collect call.

I swapped my blue Eglin uniform for new khaki and olive garb, which made me smile at its military connotations. Left alone for the first time in my cell I began to wonder whether I might have been better taking my chances with Ed in the county jail.

From the cells around me I heard screaming and yelling, the wailing so unearthly it sounded like the building was haunted. Obviously, some of my fellow inmates had trouble coping. Inmates with discipline problems, those that required segregation for their own protection, and violent ones, they were all in there.

In the morning, the hall window was thrust open and a mental health professional checked me from the corridor, as if I was an exhibit in a zoo, asking me what my condition was. I didn't know it then but that would be my sole human contact for the day, short of the meals being pushed through the latch and the hour I was led out to the deserted basketball court. Every movement through the prison was carefully regimented to avoid contact with other inmates.

I had no option but to wait for the unknown event that might shorten my sentence. Each day I marked time by watching the sun slowly cross the sky.

I felt myself disconnecting from the world.

For three weeks I existed like this but it felt like six months. Then, finally, I got word that the Swiss magistrate would soon be ready to take my testimony. In preparation for this they were transferring me to Wakulla county jail after all – the prison I had been so keen to avoid.

There was always the prospect I could bump into Ed or some other clients I knew to be in there, like Benny's brother Carlos and Rick Baker, the lieutenant to whom Benny passed the running of his organization. When I considered the risk, however, I realized I had nothing to be concerned about. After all, it was his testimony that had put me in here.

Besides, the very fact they were in such a county facility

indicated they were further trying to reduce their own sentences by continuing to cooperate with the government.

The relative comforts of Wakulla were a godsend after the misery of Tallahassee. The cell was typically spartan but at least I had human company, the rooms being arranged around a common area. I could shower every day and there was a phone to make collect calls from.

I was even permitted to wear my own clothes for my meetings with the Swiss magistrate. I called Michele to send me a business suit, plus some shirts and ties for my meetings at the US Attorney's office. I felt I was getting some of my identity back.

On the morning the officers from the DEA picked me up to take me to my first meeting with the magistrate I felt like I was getting a taste of freedom. I once again looked every inch the respectable lawyer, aside, of course, from the handcuffs I had to wear for my journey downtown.

Before the testimony began one of the agents explained he would act as translator for me and the magistrate. He had lived in France and was bilingual. He warned me that the magistrate might be blunt and impatient, but if I concentrated on giving my first-hand knowledge of Ed and Kelly's financial history I could prove helpful.

When finally introduced to the magistrate he was quite pleasant. Thrown by my appearance he said through the translator: 'You are not in custody just now, no?'

'No,' I replied. 'I'm still there.'

He got serious and turned to the business at hand – finding out how my former clients got started, how they moved their money and where it ended up so they could tie it up with transfers from Anguilla to Switzerland. He had surmised some of the methods generally but didn't know any of the detail and he certainly wasn't versed in the tradecraft.

I gave my testimony in private and as I spoke – freely by then as I had nothing to lose – I could tell this was an eye-opener for him. It was clear this meeting would be the first of many.

I returned to the prison feeling upbeat about my chances. If my testimony was successful it would enable the US and Swiss authorities to recover six million dollars of illicit funds that could be shared between the two nations. At the time it would have been the largest amount of drug money ever seized.

Over the next two months I had more meetings with the magistrate. On one occasion I was in the lock-up inside the US Attorney's office waiting to testify further when a whole bunch of marshals came in. There were six of them with one prisoner. It was Danny Rolling, the Gainesville Ripper. He had murdered five students on a grisly killing spree the year before. He'd pleaded guilty but was being charged with additional felonies. The marshals put him in the cell next to me. Chanting began. When the marshals removed him to be processed they put me into the newly vacant room. Scattered about the floor were writings and scribbled drawings. I started to have a glance but the marshals spotted them and hurriedly tidied them up.

Rolling was later executed by lethal injection for his crimes, but shortly before his death he confessed to three more brutal murders.

When my testimony eventually concluded with the Swiss magistrate I learned the government had yet more plans for me. More members of the client organization had been arrested so I was required to be on standby should I be needed to testify against them in a subsequent trial.

For this they wanted to move me once again – this time my destination was a county jail in Gilchrist, near Gainesville in northern Florida. When I mentioned to one inmate where I was heading, he smiled and vowed: 'You won't want to leave!'

I looked at the old timer as if he was mad.

'I think you've been behind bars too long, my friend.'

When I got to Gilchrist I realized he might have had a point. It was a very small jail, in a rural Florida county where the tiny town of Trenton was surrounded by wetlands and lowland swamp. The county itself was the newest in the state, having been carved out of a larger municipality in the 1920s.

The first sign that this place wasn't your usual prison came from the moment the marshal presented me before the desk sergeant. She was a small woman who was dressed in civilian clothes because, she cheerfully told us, they couldn't find a guard's uniform in her size.

The orientation meeting was the strangest I had encountered since I'd entered the penal system. One of the first things the lieutenant in charge of new admissions said to me was: 'You don't have to wear the uniform in here at all, you know. You can wear civilian clothes.' He added: 'You're permitted to have as much as forty dollars on you at any one time.'

That's strange, I thought. Why would you need money inside a prison?

There were only sixteen beds in the entire facility, neatly divided with eight for the local prisoners and eight for federal prisoners.

Night brought with it another surprise. I was waiting for the food to be brought to my cell when I was shocked to see the person delivering the trays was Benny. A former kingpin who masterminded his own trafficking empire was now handing out burgers in a county jail.

He got as big a shock as I did.

'Ken! I don't believe it.'

'It's good to see you, Benny. You're looking in good shape.'

Benny explained to me the set-up in Gilchrist.

'I'm a trusty. Means I'm in charge of food. Every week I get to drive downtown and fill up with burgers, steaks, fish, everything to sell to people like you.'

'Sell? So that's why we're allowed cash. We buy our food?'

'Uh-huh.'

'You need any drugs – I mean over-the-counter remedies? Someone will go get you what you need. You like working out? There's state-of-the-art exercise gear.'

It was like he was giving me a sales pitch for a private club.

'This is insane. It sounds like a private jail.'

He laughed. 'Not far off, brother. Not far off.'

It was good to see Benny again. He seemed as easy-going and good-natured as he had been on the outside. Later we caught up properly. He filled me in on the fate of some other members of the organization and we played cards and swapped stories.

I started to marvel at the scam the prison was running. I realized the sole purpose of the federal prisoners being there was to generate some cash for the county facility and the local economy. By sourcing their own food, they could buy it from downtown, add 25 per cent and sell it on to the inmates.

That wasn't the only scam. When I got to the communal room there were piles of blank videotapes. There was a satellite dish on the roof of the jail showing premium movies on the home box office channel HBO. The inmates were watching the movies, taping them and sending them back home to their kids.

After a couple of weeks in Gilchrist I felt bold enough to approach the lieutenant with a suggestion on how he could improve his establishment.

'Forty dollars is not enough,' I said. 'We need more cash.'

'Fine,' he shrugged. 'You can have more sent in if you wish.'

Only in small-town America, I thought as I thanked him and returned to the common room.

Although I was grateful for the relaxed surroundings, I was

living on tenterhooks, waiting to find out if my testimony to the Swiss magistrate was worthy of a sentence reduction. It was up to the judge in my case to decide. Only the government can ask for a sentence to be reduced and even then the judge was under no obligation to accept it. The rule of thumb on a reduction was that it was usually 50 per cent of the original sentence and even that wasn't written in stone. In federal courts the judges really do rule the roost.

I sat on pins and needles.

Several weeks went by until one day a jailer came round and handed me a letter. I could see by the markings it meant they had finally ruled on my sentence. Like all legal mail, it remained sealed. I paused, took a deep breath and slowly opened the envelope. The rush was greater than any cocaine high.

I just got back two years of my life.

I had to read and re-read the letter to make sure I was seeing right. My sentence had been halved. I only had about eight months to go. I was euphoric.

I had to get organized. The letter also detailed my coopera-tion so the last thing I wanted was to leave it lying around. I mailed it to the correctional staff at Eglin with a letter request-ing them to reduce my sentence computation.

I called Michele. She was overjoyed that I was coming home earlier than expected. She liaised with the marshal to see about getting me back to the federal prison in Eglin, but in the first instance I had to go back to the county jail in Wakulla. That presented the same problem as before – the prospect of bump-ing into Ed or Rick, clients of mine who had testified against me.

Since I was successful in reducing four years to two would it be possible to cut my two years to one?

According to my research a second reduction was possible if an inmate overheard someone admit guilt to a crime or learned the location of someone's hidden proceeds of crime. My idea was to acquire information that might persuade the US Attorney's office to file a second sentence reduction motion on my behalf. I was certainly pushing my luck but the last thing I wanted to do was sit around accepting my fate. Nothing ventured in the legal system, nothing gained. Besides, what else was I going to do?

I planned to give up the name of a fugitive I knew had been on the run to escape a trafficking warrant. He was a lower-level operative in the network and wasn't someone I'd met in the flesh – I was just aware of his role. He was attempting to live quietly and had his own shop.

Armed with this information I secured another trip to the US Attorney's office to find out if they were interested in my testimony. Dressed once again in the standard prison utilitarian shirt and pants and handcuffed, I was shepherded into the back of a bus with half a dozen other inmates for the journey to the courthouse.

Everyone stared at the floor as the last of the prisoners climbed into the back and shuffled to their seat. Instantly I recognized Rick Baker. I caught his eye and was sure he had recognized me but he averted his gaze. He would know that I was aware that it was his testimony that had helped convict me. I said nothing.

I scanned the other prisoners. At first I didn't think I recognized anyone else but then, wait, I looked again at a man staring at his feet. At first his appearance threw me – the sight of him in such humble circumstances, in worn and degrading prison clothes. But then I was certain who it was.

Sitting across from me, as the bus shuddered towards the prison exit, was Ed – the man who put me behind bars.

26. My Life Back

What threw me at first about Ed's appearance was that he had dark brown hair. I'd always known him as fair-haired and now the revelation that for all those years he had been a bottle blond was almost as shocking as the reality that he was sitting here in front of me.

Seeing him stripped of all the trappings of his wealth and influence with no one to impress, no one to bark orders to, was startling. At first I almost pitied him. He looked pathetic. Then I remembered why I was here. He'd ratted on me at the first opportunity, just like Andre warned he would.

Anger started to build inside me. Part of me wanted to rip his head from his shoulders but, as quickly as the rage built, it dissipated. In the outside world Ed Becker had liked to think he was a cut above everyone else. But now, seeing him in shackles, I realized he was just the same. Just trying to cut a deal to save his own skin.

We looked at each other. It was the first time we'd met in two years. I stared for some sign of remorse behind those eyes but there was nothing. Not even a flicker of recognition. His eyes were dead.

He would not have known that I had recently testified against him and could have possibly cost him six million dollars. That gave me a sense of satisfaction. It also might sound strange but I actually began to understand his actions. It took me to see him in prison, see he was suffering the same miserable fate as me, to understand that Becker had done me a favour. True, without his testimony I probably wouldn't have been here, but at the same time he'd removed me from that life. They were all queuing up to give me up so it would only have been a matter of time before I'd be arrested – and perhaps I'd have been looking at a much longer stretch.

Seeing him there in the prison van also removed any last traces of guilt I might have been harbouring for testifying against him and Kelly over the Swiss money. This was just part of the game. For these Miami traffickers, *omertà*, the Mafia code of silence, didn't come into it. It was every man for himself. He'd ultimately been undone by his original crewmembers.

Back in the prison several days passed before I encountered him again in one of the recreation areas. This time I did speak.

'Ed, fancy seeing you here.'

'Hello, Ken.'

Although the spark had gone from his eyes the same arrogance remained. If he had remorse he certainly didn't show it.

We exchanged pleasantries but it was strained. He hated me seeing him in this situation.

'I'm getting out on bond,' he said, which I took to mean only one thing. He was cooperating with the DEA to build cases against other members of the organization. I didn't give any indication of my own deal with the authorities. Our reunion ended with the call that recreation was over.

After everything we'd been through, it was a strange way to meet, but it reminded me what a self-centred individual he always was. If you weren't useful to him he didn't want to know. There, in a county jail, each of us trying to find a way out, there was nothing we could do for each other.

Meanwhile there had been a development in the information I supplied to the US Attorney. State police had raided the shop my former client now ran with his son. Yet, while it looked as though the authorities were about to secure another conviction, they did not feel what I'd done was deserving of a further cut in my sentence.

I can't deny this was disappointing but I had to look on the bright side. I now only had six months left to serve and would soon be going back to Eglin to see out my time.

US marshals made arrangements to transport me back to the Florida panhandle on a weekend. That proved to be problematic because Eglin wouldn't accept a transfer on a Saturday or Sunday so alternative arrangements had to be made to put me into Escambia county jail in Pensacola, an hour's drive west along the Gulf Coast, near the Alabama border.

It would prove to be yet another lesson in US prison colonies. The place was bursting at the seams with crack cocaine dealers who had been rounded up in a federal clampdown. To make matters worse, I arrived in the middle of the Mardi Gras celebrations. New Orleans might get all the attention at this time of year but I was now detained just a few miles from the oldest carnival in America, held in Mobile, Alabama. And for the inmates, the idea that there was a massive party happening on their doorstep and they were stuck in jail seemed to be driving them even crazier.

Once more, even though it was a county facility, I was assigned to a section composed solely of federal inmates. When I was shown to my cell I couldn't help noticing it had two bunks. Given the numbers inside the prison I knew I'd soon be getting a room-mate.

The first night was fitful, given the noise from the other inmates who seemed incapable of settling down. They were hanging out the window shouting to people I assumed were their girlfriends on the street below. Initially the marshals assured me I would only be here for the weekend before continuing my journey back to Eglin. But as the days wore on I started to fear I was being forgotten about.

After a couple of days my cellmate duly arrived. He was very young and so scared it was obvious it was his first time inside a prison. He seemed convinced he'd be attacked. I tried to allay his fears then showed him how, by removing the blade from his disposal razor and taking off the bristles from his toothbrush, he could fashion a makeshift knife.

His eyes widened and he immediately requested a transfer to another cell.

Not a day went by without some sort of incident. One day a suspected arsonist slashed his wrists in the shower block and had to be carted out while blood gushed everywhere.

I tried to take solace in the meagre law library but whenever I saw a marshal come into the jail I prayed for a ticket out. Eventually Michele – who else – made contact with the US Marshals Service and the day came when my transfer along the coast was arranged.

If I thought the grass was greener back at Eglin I was in for a bit of a shock. As I had testified I was now deemed a security risk and wasn't allowed off the camp to the air force base. That meant I was assigned landscape gardening duties on site. My last six months would be spent raking and cleaning.

Two months before the end of my time I was offered a release to a halfway house in downtown Miami. There, I would be able to go to work every day but then would have to come back to sleep in the facility. I knew the place they had in mind. It was slap in the middle of a rough neighbourhood – indeed bullet holes peppered the exterior. As nice as all that sounded, I turned down the offer; I felt it was worth sticking out the last eight weeks so that when finally I was home I was there to stay and could enjoy what my fellow inmates termed 'to the door' release.

By now I was itching to get out so my parents helped by bringing Anton to see me. He was still young – only five – so it didn't really affect him but it made a big difference to me.

Mike, the accountant, was still at Eglin. He didn't take the news that I had a sentence reduction well. After I left he would still have six months to serve on his term. To his credit he remained civil and was a companion for the remainder of my time.

I was counting the days. Those last few seemed to take an eternity. At last – after nineteen months and several days in custody – I prepared to leave. I gave away my army watch and law books. I said my goodbyes to Mike and other people I had befriended in Eglin, plus those I had already known from the scene in Miami.

Michele, my rock, came to pick me up. Leaving the camp for good was a lot like being permanently transferred out of the army, but tasted even sweeter. Not only was I rejoining society, I was getting my life back.

As our plane soared into the skies heading for Miami I realized that, once more, I was embarking on a new chapter. In the same way I had to readjust after coming back to America after Vietnam, once again I would have to reinvent myself.

We touched down back in Miami and, as we drove around the city, I noticed how much taller the trees seemed. I'd lost all sense of perspective. The sight of so many new developments in southern Miami Beach – which now seemed to be called South Beach – amazed me too, although it saddened me to see that so little consideration now seemed to be given to the original concept of art deco.

After a quick reacquaintance with some of my old haunts, it was back to my parents' house. Now that I was divorced – I had drafted the papers and completed the formalities myself inside prison – their spare bedroom would once again be my home until I was able to stand on my own feet; just like when I'd returned from service twenty-two years earlier. I had to start my finances again from scratch. Even in my heyday of laundering – when I could easily earn over ten thousand dollars a week – I had never planned for a day when I might lose the lot. I had no savings, no funds stashed away, nothing.

Michele threw me a welcome home party at a local restaurant, which I was grateful for. It was such a relief to be reunited with my parents and old friends, yet I was already aware that as a convicted felon I would be stigmatized as an outcast. Then just as I was thinking about what I was going to do with my life, one of the partners in my cousin's law firm, the one who had represented me during my refusal to talk to the grand jury five years before, offered me a paralegal assistant job. I accepted it instantly. The next working day I was back in a suit and tie.

Working in a law firm again, doing research in civil matters did keep me busy. But I was left wondering what I would do for a future career. I knew that I could do something with my skills and my experience, I just didn't know what. Feasibly I could practise law again but only if I was allowed back into the profession by the Bar, meaning I had to sit the Bar exam again, followed in all likelihood by years of futile applications.

I had other matters to contend with. Although I was home and working, I was still on supervised release – a development of the parole system, and a hangover from my original sentence of four years in prison, three years' supervision. It meant the authorities would be keeping tabs on me. I had to report regularly for tests to make sure I was drug free, and any time I changed address, wanted to take a flight or even left south Florida I had to notify them.

This was but a mere inconvenience compared to incarceration. If I did anything to break the supervision order or offended again I'd be returned to custody instantly. The only way to secure a reduction in the supervised release order was to become not simply a model citizen, but actively show the parole board that I was worthy of leniency.

I set about living to a new agenda. Since my clients, whom I had zealously represented and protected for years, had turned on me as their version of gratitude, I wanted to return the favour. I applied to have myself transferred to the High Risk Section of probation, which is mainly composed of individuals who are testifying against others.

The scene had changed so much. The *Miami Vice* image of the city had gone. After the devastation wreaked by the crack cocaine epidemic, policing had become so tenacious and the penalties so severe that most trafficking had moved to the Mexican border – the place of least resistance. Many of my former clients were either dead or in prison though some were still out there, eluding justice.

My new mission, frankly, was payback. Since the clients had put me in jail, I figured I owed their organization a similar good deed. There is nothing like a desire for absolute freedom, mixed with a healthy dose of vengeance, to focus the mind. I was now firmly on the side of the law, and ready to make amends in whatever way possible.

The first opportunity I had to show what a good citizen I was presented itself almost immediately. I was working away as a legal researcher and one Friday, when paying a visit to the post office near the firm's office in Coconut Grove to deliver a letter, I heard a scream. I looked across the road and saw a woman come out of a dry cleaner's, and then a man running down the street. I'm no detective but I was pretty sure he was the culprit – as well as her bag and purse, he'd also grabbed a pile of garments. He was trying to make his escape with a pile of cellophane-wrapped clothes.

Without thinking I took off after him. He ran into one of the roughest neighbourhoods but I kept on his heels. It turned slightly farcical, as I had to stop every few hundred yards to pick up a dress or skirt he'd dropped, but on I chased into the ghetto. Eventually the man – a typical hoodlum, possibly funding a habit – tried to take refuge by scrambling under a house. In no time at all the police were on the scene, while I stood watch on the building to make sure he did not wriggle free. A standoff ensued before more police showed up, this time with dog handlers. He was duly arrested.

I had made it known to the marshals that I would do anything I could to assist them in bringing cases against my former clients. One day I got a call to say some items had been recovered from a house once used by Kelly, who was still on the run in Mexico.

I took delivery of a box of papers, random documents and letters she'd clearly left in a hurry. Among the items was a manila envelope, with a handwritten note on the front. It read: 'Last letter sent from his cell in Cuba, before he was executed.'

Accompanying the note were details of where his sister could collect half a million dollars of drug money before he was executed. Although no name was on the envelope I narrowed it down to two or three people it could be, most likely a Cuban refugee who had been caught smuggling drugs into American waters. The penalties in Cuba were severe: many perpetrators were executed. It was a timely reminder of the life I had left behind.

After a year working as a paralegal I finally had enough money to move out of my parents' house and into an apartment. It was good to be self-sufficient again and I had the added bonus of my son coming to live with me. Denise had returned to her old job as a flight attendant and, with her erratic work schedule, we agreed this arrangement was better for Anton.

It finally gave me a chance to bond properly with him. Being with Anton and seeing the world through his innocent eyes helped put things into perspective. I still met some disapproval within my own community. Anyone who knew about my background wasn't interested in spending time with me. I had been here before of course. I was *persona non grata*, particularly with lawyers or bankers. I continued to work as a paralegal but was struggling to get a regular job.

I was home one night and the phone rang. It was John McLintock, a sergeant in the intelligence division of a police department in Florida.

What now?

Although I knew this officer from my time with Monique, I automatically assumed it could only be bad news.

John got right to the point.

'Ken, I wondered if you can help me. We were set to have someone give a speech tomorrow in front of a host of different agencies but he has been called away. I was wondering, could you do the lecture?'

I was stunned.

He wanted me to speak for half an hour about what it was like being a money launderer, in front of a state-wide organization of agents and financial investigators. I could talk about my experiences for the last fifteen years and reveal some tradecraft.

'A lecture?' I said. 'In front of cops?'

'Well, yes. Not just cops. Other agencies too.'

'I suppose so,' I faltered. 'When is it?'

'Um, tomorrow morning. You're the only person I could think of. You'd be brilliant. What do you say?'

'I don't know. Can I think about it?'

'Not really,' John replied. 'I need a fast answer. It's tomorrow.'

How could I possibly stand up before a room full of officers who knew full well that I had been convicted of, and did prison time for, the serious crime of racketeering? For years these people had been my adversaries, sworn to bring me to justice.

'I'll do it.'

27. Changing Sides

Escorted into the room I felt hundreds of eyes on me, all of them hostile.

I was the enemy. Police and other officers don't differentiate between traffickers, their attorneys and the bankers who fund them. I was just another crooked lawyer – a once honourable professional whose head had been turned by greed and a lust for notoriety.

It wasn't unlike my first appearance in court, that feeling I was on the other side of the line. But if I'd learned anything over the last few years it was that sometimes you have to face your fears. That's why I said yes to John. Some fifteen years previously I had taken a leap into the dark when I felt my life was going nowhere. Now my career was in a similarly bleak position and here was an opportunity to step back into the light.

I travelled to the conference knowing it was an important step, not just in my rehabilitation but also as a personal choice. If I was truly back on the right side of the law, then I needed to be proactive by obeying the law – taking action to assist those who were charged with enforcing it.

I told the packed but hushed assembly how I first became involved with narco-criminals, detailing the characters of the various kingpins I represented – how I was the middleman between the Medellín cartel and the Mafia – and what my role was in bankrolling their little empires. I told them how I smuggled millions of dollars out of the country more than a hundred times and was never caught. I told them about the placement of the funds into offshore accounts, about layering the money into a number of offshore financial centres, and then integrating the funds into the global financial system through investments.

I told them how my clients used to launder dirty money through legitimate businesses and explained ingenious schemes like the commission salesman method. Finally, I explained why I had targeted some of the Caribbean tax havens and steered clear of others.

After I'd finished there was a spontaneous round of applause, which was most unexpected. It was an uplifting – even cleansing – experience. For the first time in years I felt good.

I was no longer part of the problem. I was part of the solution.

I must have been shedding light on a previously shadowy world because I received other offers to talk at other events. One of the more unusual ones was from the Royal Canadian Mounted Police. They asked if I would assist in a training programme to assess their agents who were going undercover to expose illicit practices. They were attending a two-week training course and wanted me to help with the credibility of their cover stories. My job was to cover the techniques and strategies they would employ, to discuss some of the more esoteric tactics, and to cover the advantages and disadvantages of each Caribbean tax haven.

The programme ran covertly at one of the country's leading universities, and they put me up anonymously at a local bed and breakfast. Effectively I was now teaching money laundering to agents to help them catch people like me. The experience was mentally challenging but, frankly, fun. At the end of the week, I was presented with a plaque of appreciation, and left with a real feeling that my rehabilitation was gathering pace.

At another lecture I was part of a panel with other speakers. One introduced himself as Dean Roberts, a retired FBI agent.

During his speech he revealed he'd been part of a unique federal agency taskforce that had joined up with Scotland Yard from the UK to investigate laundering in the tax havens.

I was amazed. Only then did I realize Agent Roberts had been on my tail when he'd walked into Henry Jackson's office in Anguilla and demanded to see who were the owners of the American corporate accounts in the bank next door.

When it was my turn to speak I could see the FBI agent listening attentively as I went on to discuss my favourite destination for secreting drug profits – Anguilla.

After the talk was over, I approached him.

'I feel like we've met before,' I said.

'Yes, Mr Rijock,' he replied, smiling. 'I know all about you.'

We shared stories about our work in the Caribbean, me in my efforts to stay one step ahead of the law, he on his attempts to reel us in. The communities of crime and law enforcement are so closely linked at times it is astonishing.

Over the next few months I met Dean again at other events and conferences. He filled me in on how the net had closed in on Jackson's little operation and how an arrest in the UK had sparked a trail of information that eventually led the Anguillan bank offshore accounts scheme to come crashing down.

Yet just as I was amazed by the attentions of the agencies trying to catch us, so too was he by the methods we employed to evade their clutches. There was mutual appreciation.

Aside from the excitement of the lectures and talks, I continued to work as a paralegal. Career-wise it felt like I was wasting away in the badlands but the job had allowed me to regain some self-respect in the community. Whenever I could I tried to do more and more lectures, but I could only find an audience with law enforcement agencies.

I made approaches to the banking community, offering my services as someone who could point out the tradecraft to their compliance officers. I don't know if it was because I was a convicted money launderer, or whether a combination of ignorance and arrogance led financial institutions to think they were impervious to crime, but the reception was frosty.

Undeterred, I looked at ways of improving my lectures and tailoring them to suit my audiences. Soon I was offering a range of classes, from looking at how to uncover money laundering schemes, to exploring how Russian organized crime had been moving their operations to the US and also discussing the tricks used by traffickers to smuggle their shipments into the country by plane or boat.

Another invitation was to teach a class at a coastguard academy in St Petersburg, on Florida's Gulf Coast. For this lecture I focused on maritime smuggling and explained Ed's inspired idea to smuggle drugs inside a safety device he had called Stayfloat. As I was talking a number of hands went up at the back of the room.

I paused and asked one of the men whose hand was in the air to make his point.

'I once boarded a boat,' he said. 'I'm sure I remember seeing those Stayfloat tubes. It never occurred to me they were anything other than safety devices. I can't believe it.'

Other officers whose hands had been raised nodded their heads.

It was astonishing. Here were coastguards who had boarded some of Ed's boats and had failed to find any drugs. His scheme had worked, even more brilliantly than I had at first given him credit for.

After each lecture – which I gave for free – I was invariably approached and asked my advice on a problem. It was my policy never to refuse requests from law enforcement. I might have spent the best part of ten years trying to outwit them but, strange as it may seem, I felt I owed these people. I never forgot that I could have been looking at twenty-five years in prison had it not been the fairness shown to me by the investigators and prosecutors. I aimed to repay that favour in as many ways as I could.

While the lectures offered me a sense of purpose in my business life I could have done with the same in my personal life. Since coming out of prison I'd felt like a pariah. With the exception of a few dates with the woman I rescued from the dry-cleaner thief, I'd hardly had any opportunity to meet anyone.

However, just as the opportunity to deliver that first lecture sprang out of nowhere, so it was that I unexpectedly found myself chatting to a woman I'd never met before at a party held by mutual friends.

Her name was Jane, she was a teacher and, like me, had a child from a previous relationship. Although I was used to keeping aspects of my life from my previous partners, with Jane it was a relief not to have a hidden agenda. I could simply be myself.

We came along at the right time for each other. Thankfully Jane was from the 99.9 per cent of humanity not caught up in the world of traffickers so I didn't have to go into the full gory details of my former life. She understood I had a past and didn't judge me for it.

As our relationship developed it got to the stage where I was ready to meet her family. I must admit I wasn't looking forward to the point when I would have to reveal the shame of my time in prison. The news didn't go down well but they accepted me, which was all I could ask for.

28. 'If anything goes wrong, kill him'

Just as I was settling into a domestic setting, a couple of opportunities arose that — if only for a short time — would see me once again play the role of a launderer.

I was approached by a television network to set up and manage an undercover operation targeting lawyers working in Caribbean tax havens, for broadcast on a popular prime-time programme that specialized in investigative journalism. The purpose was to demonstrate that offshore financial centres were still accepting illicit cash.

My task was to show that recent 'reforms' amounted to little more than window dressing, and that, if offered dirty money, local lawyers would still eagerly accept it with few questions asked.

I met up with one of the producers in Miami over dinner at a quiet location at the airport, and we spent a couple of hours discussing alternative ways in which to conduct the operation. When he was satisfied that I could plan and successfully supervise the project, he flew back to New York to organize the production crew, and I set to work composing the lines of dialogue that our 'criminals' would be speaking to our lawyer-targets as they tried to convince them that they had money to hide in the tax havens. The network was going to supply the cash, which we would launder and send back to ourselves, to show how things had really not changed in the Caribbean since I ran riot in the eighties.

My next job was to find a suitable volunteer to pose as a

money launderer to approach the lawyers. At once I thought of Nico Nunez, Charlie's brother. He was perfect because he was a survivor of the Miami scene and, although he had gone straight, knew the lingo and was bold enough to pull it off.

The producer provided an undercover camerawoman to pose as Nico's girlfriend. To secretly film our targets, she wore sunglasses with a camera in the bridge and another in her handbag, which also contained secret microphones and transmitters.

I chose St Kitts as the perfect place to test the theory because not only was I familiar with the methods of placing illicit cash there, I also had personally worked with some of the lawyers from my money laundering days. I even had one in mind. The lawyer, then a prominent advocate, commanded high fees, and travelled widely in the region. The idea was that we would sting him on camera, and show the evidence to the American television audience. I was confident that the lawyer would not risk a lawsuit in the US, because he was in danger of being arrested for his past activities.

Nico and I met the production crew at Miami international airport and we flew down into Sint Maarten. Our original plans were to photograph our cast of two taking a catamaran into St Kitts, but the inclement weather caused us to scrub that for a light plane into neighbouring Nevis. The island, which is actually federated with St Kitts, is a former British possession that was a huge sugar plantation during the colonial era. It was perfect for our base: only a couple of short miles to St Kitts via boat, but away from prying eyes.

We got to Nevis but no sooner had we made our first call than we hit a snag. Our prominent lawyer had been called away from the island on some big criminal defence case. Not to be deterred, I pulled out our list of available local attorneys, and we proceeded to call most of them up. By the end of the day, we had made firm appointments with a number of them.

Landing in Basseterre the next morning, we hired a driver with a van, which allowed us to transport the cast, crew, producer and support staff, and started keeping those appointments. The second cameraman worked the sound and video recording equipment remotely, and monitored the meetings on a small screen. We had cash available, should an opportunity arise to make a deposit under the right circumstances.

Our cover story was that Nico was a prominent married American businessman contemplating a divorce, so that he could marry the 'girlfriend' who accompanied him. They wanted to transfer a large amount of his wealth, in cash, to an offshore account, lest it be seized or awarded to the wife during the upcoming divorce proceedings. The story was crafted to appear to be so transparent that any lawyer worth his salt would easily see that it was a fiction, poorly covering up the proceeds of some crime needing to be moved offshore.

We got a few who declined, but by the end of the day, we netted three lawyers and a sitting part-time magistrate, all of whom offered to assist in the placement of what was obviously illicit cash into their banking system. The cameraman shot location film in the capital, to supplement our dynamite undercover footage. I also literally stumbled into the country's financial intelligence unit, unstaffed and much smaller than you would think a government agency should be. It was anything but functional.

Unfortunately, after all our hard work, the network's legal team feared they might be exposed to lawsuits from the lawyers if they aired the footage and the programme was canned. The project never saw the light of day.

Although we were unsuccessful on that occasion, I had enjoyed using my old tricks to expose wrongdoing rather than exploit loopholes in the system.

A short while later it was Nico's turn to ask me for a favour.

A mid-level Cuban marijuana grower called Jorge Lopez had used him to help warn off bandits who threatened to raid his farm and seize his drugs, but then reneged on paying Nico the money he owed him.

Nico was enraged.

'Did he think I put my life on the line out of the kindness of my heart? He owes me – big.'

Despite being given a second chance, Lopez had continued to flaunt his business and it was little surprise when he was arrested by the DEA for cultivating his dope farm.

Nico thought he'd lost his opportunity to remind Lopez what happens to suppliers who don't pay their debts.

But fortune had smiled on him.

'He's out on bond,' he told me. 'And he's asking me to help him flee the country. It's too good an opportunity.'

Lopez wanted Nico to help him launder some money to pay for his escape before the trial. He had a yacht that had been seized and impounded by the government. Brazenly though, he wanted to try and sell the boat to a third party, under the noses of Customs, to free up some more cash.

'I need your help.'

'How?' I asked, not following.

'I want to get him before he disappears.'

'Take him out?' I started to feel concerned.

'No, no. Set the fucker up.'

Now I followed.

He wanted to expose Lopez before he escaped. I was to be the bag man to help him release the funds from the yacht.

The old juices started flowing.

It takes a thief to catch a thief.

Convincing Jane that the risks were low and that this was a good opportunity for me to further ingratiate myself with the law, I went to the DEA and offered to pose as a launderer to get the necessary evidence to help put Lopez in custody. The DEA agents I met agreed that it was an operation worth undertaking and a plan was set.

I rang Lopez.

'I hear you got a problem.'

'Not here. Let's meet.'

He agreed to meet me in downtown Miami believing I was going to offer him my expertise in setting up his escape route to the Caribbean.

I met the DEA agents beforehand and they briefed me on the evidence needed to bring charges. Fitting me with a hidden microphone, they asked me to get on tape exactly what he was planning to do. They also wanted me to set up another meeting where he could hand over the money for my services.

My emotions as I prepared to meet Lopez were not unlike those I'd felt nearly fifteen years before when I'd prepared to conduct my first bulk cash smuggling operation. Then the stakes were high because one false move could have led to our arrests. This time one mistake could have Lopez after my blood.

The drug farmer was understandably edgy when we met in a downtown restaurant, but greed and a desire to flee overrode any self-defence mechanism. He wanted his cash moved to the tax havens and he eagerly agreed to meet the following week in Fort Lauderdale with fifty thousand dollars to get the whole thing moving with some offshore companies and bank accounts.

Just days before the drop Nico called me.

'Thought you should know. Lopez sent me a message.'

'What's that?'

'If anything should happen to my money, kill that money launderer.'

'Really? I'm honoured.'

'Just be careful, eh?'

I was long enough in the tooth to know some threats are idle. But it was a reminder of what was at stake.

A week later my associate was standing at Fort Lauderdale airport awaiting the drop. The weird symmetry of the situation struck me. Here he was, in casual clothes, with a bag, at an airport, awaiting the cash from a client. Yet instead of fearing the DEA were watching my every move, I was now hoping they were keeping a very close eye.

Again wired for sound, they waited for Lopez to show up. This time I wasn't required to meet him. With the evidence I'd already gathered it was enough that Lopez kept to our rendezvous for the DEA to pounce.

Right on cue he emerged among a group of passengers. In his hand was a battered suitcase.

He'd brought the cash.

We were on.

It happened in an instant. The agents sprang from nowhere and hustled him away from the crowd.

He didn't know what hit him.

It was deeply satisfying. He was charged with additional crimes, his bail was refused and he was jailed for a lengthy stretch.

A new career beckoned. I could catch criminals at their own game, be a force for good.

But a part of me would forever be the laundry man.

Epilogue

'My name is Kenneth Rijock. I am a veteran of over one hundred domestic and international bulk cash smuggling operations, all of them successfully completed.'

So began my testimony in front of the US Congress in 1999 – the only civilian to do so in favour of cash smuggling laws.

After my sting on Jorge Lopez I took it upon myself to try and educate the banks on the damage money laundering was doing to our economy and security.

I testified two further times, but attempts to tighten laws were met with fierce resistance from the banking lobby – whose supporters, interestingly enough, included a prominent financier who would later face fraud charges for setting up one of the biggest ever Ponzi pyramid investment schemes, left millions of investors out of pocket.

It took the World Trade Center attacks on September 11, 2001 for the banks to step up their levels of compliance.

That gave me an opportunity to put my skills to good use and I landed a job as a compliance officer for a large Florida investment company. It was a lot of fun pitting my wits against people I could see using the same tricks I had.

The role only lasted a year, but I went on to work on many other projects for law enforcement and the financial community. I believe I am now the only former banking attorney turned career money launderer who works as a financial crime consultant, providing risk intelligence to banks and other institutions.

Money launderers are only limited by their own imaginations.

I know that the most effective ones are constantly updating their methods because the moment somebody observes a pattern they can get caught. My job now is to explain to clients how to detect money launderers and how to identify emerging trends.

I travel the world giving talks and lectures on tradecraft. The most common question I am asked is how I managed to evade capture for so long. And it is a source of amazement – and frustration – for the officials that I was never caught in the act.

Of course, I explain that I was only convicted because three clients, convicted and looking at serious prison time, turned upon me and our accountant in order to get their sentences reduced.

At the time my attitude was so hardcore that I believed I would never give up my clients. When they did I felt betrayed and angry. Yet, looking back, perhaps Ed and the rest did me a favour.

By testifying against me, they forced me to face up to my crimes. If they hadn't, who knows what would have happened? Although I was always careful to cover my tracks, I was still continuing on a destructive path, and the incident in Anguilla when the accounts were frozen indicated that several different agencies were closing in. If I'd been arrested under different circumstances perhaps the US Attorney might not have been so willing to look favourably on my sentence. I should have cooperated when initially called before the grand jury.

Society's attitudes to drugs have changed beyond all recognition since the time I started laundering. From being a recreational pastime they are now a deadly killer that wrecks people's lives and puts immense strain on the fabric of our economy.

I needed prison to rehabilitate myself and pay my debt. Only after that could I be truly reformed and, although the process was painful at the time, it has allowed me to embark on my new career with greater integrity.

Although I have been talking about my exploits to select audiences, it is only because of the years that have passed that I feel comfortable about putting it all down on paper. There's enough distance between the events of my past and now to give it some perspective.

I make no apologies for being a money launderer and for committing the crimes I did. If I hadn't done it I couldn't now advise people on how to catch people like me. It is that experience which gives me a unique perspective on the tradecraft of money laundering.

To this day, though, I still feel a twinge whenever I approach the immigration counter at Miami international, and they run my name through the Customs computer. I guess that it will never go away.

And what of the other main players in the remarkable drama that was my life in the 1980s?

Ed managed to convince the DEA to let him out of jail before the end of his sentence in a bid to sting other people in the organization. Brazen to the last, he even contacted me during his extended release. He again needed help with his taxes so I recommended a competent and legitimate accountant. He didn't say anything about informing on me while in jail in France, nor did he make any comment about the six million bucks I had cost him. And his partner's lawyer also happened to know friends of Denise, my ex-wife. He told her: 'Ken cost my clients a lot of money.'

So he knew eventually what I'd done.

US marshals shut down his restaurant, Midnight Oasis, just three years after it opened as they rightly suspected it was a front for trafficking. However, in an unusual twist the federal

government decided to reopen it and, subcontracting the cater-
ing out to private firms, put the marshals in charge of running
the restaurant where it stayed a popular haunt. The truth is
always stranger than fiction.

Ed didn't manage to execute any stings so he was returned to
jail to complete the rest of his sentence. He served his three
years and came back to Miami but by then he had cut himself
adrift from all his former friends. He never got over the shame
of being caught.

He still lives in the Magic City but in obscurity as a manu-
script editor. It's still not bad for a high-school dropout, but the
years have not been good to him.

His ex-lover Kelly was arrested last year, after eighteen years
on the run. What her sentence will be I can only speculate, but
the court will not look favourably upon the fact that she chose
not to face the music. Will she get twenty or twenty-five years?
Only time will tell.

Henry Jackson survived the scandal of the frozen bank
accounts and the stigma of money laundering but then mysteri-
ously disappeared with members of his family during a routine
fishing trip. His body has never been found.

I once shared the podium at a conference with a former
senior agent, who told me that Jackson stole money from an
Irish terrorist group and his remains were buried at the bottom
of a swimming pool in St Kitts together with a dozen people he
had invited along on the trip.

The accountant Mike Lewis served his sentence at Eglin. On
his release he resumed his practice and continued working as an
accountant as he was only charged with a minor crime, and his
professional licence was not affected. He eventually relocated
to another city in Florida but whether he has licked his gambling problem I do not know.

Charlie Nunez served his sentence and after coming out of

prison reinvented himself as a Hispanic media executive. That's a tribute to his intelligence and ability to make a fresh start.

Benny got out of jail eventually and moved to Georgia with his wife, who also served some time for her involvement. The Feds gave her a couple of years for picking up some money; apparently they were not happy with the fact that she enjoyed an affluent lifestyle for many years, with her husband's drug profits. I don't know if that's real justice, or just revenge on the part of the officers. It seemed excessive at the time.

Rick Baker has disappeared off the face of the earth after serving a reduced sentence from the one originally handed down. But after his testimony brought down Benny and his gang that is maybe a good thing for his own safety.

Despite managing to escape justice when all about them were falling like stones, all three Martinez brothers were finally jailed for trafficking offences. They served eight years and are now back living somewhere in Florida.

Trevor the pilot was one of the few not to be prosecuted. After cooperating fully in return for immunity he sold his business and moved to Ohio where he works as a flight instructor.

Bernard Calderon served twenty years in a French prison but since his release date I haven't heard from him. It is hard to believe he is retiring quietly. Did he die in prison? I cannot say. Tao, his dutiful wife up until his conviction, embarked on an affair with her bodyguard before the law caught up with her too.

My first wife Sarah got her life back on track. She now lives in Hollywood, California. Police paid her a visit when they were investigating me; what they expected to learn I don't know, for that was my old life, the one I left behind when I became a money launderer.

Monique quit the police force after we split but continued counselling. Police had questioned her after I was arrested but were satisfied she knew nothing about my operations. My decision to keep from her much of what I was up to at least spared her the shame of fighting criminal charges. She became a marriage and family counsellor and left Florida for another state where she still lives. I wish her well.

Years later, her son Luke admitted to me he once found a bag containing a strange substance under our bed. Thankfully, he left the 500 grams of cocaine in place.

My second wife Denise went back to work as a flight attendant after I went to prison and later ran a modelling agency. She still lives in Miami and has never remarried.

And as for my old friend Andre? His dedication to living a low-profile life served him well. Never arrested in any criminal case, he finally got married and moved to small-town Florida with his bride, and today works as a youth counsellor at a local church. He has a son, to whom he has given a biblical name, maybe in recognition that God looked after him over all those years.

Like Andre, I was a lucky winner in a game where many of the losers, including several of my own clients and close associates, suffered an early death.

I hope I've shown just what would make a young but very unhappy lawyer risk everything, become self-destructive, and experience the inevitable hand of blind justice.

I also hope I have shed new light on a business that has always thrived in chaos, and that is increasingly important in the wake of the financial crisis. Money laundering bankrolls the underground economy, corrupts markets, finances warfare and fuels crime.

I should know. I was there.